Frontier Markets

FOR

DUMMIES®

A Wiley Brand

by Gavin Graham and Al Emid

FOR

DUMMIES®

A Wiley Brand

Frontier Markets For Dummies®

Published by: **John Wiley & Sons, Inc.,** 111 River St., Hoboken, NJ 07030-5774, www.wiley.com

Copyright © 2014 by John Wiley & Sons, Inc., Hoboken, New Jersey

Published simultaneously in Canada

No part of this publication may be reproduced, stored in a retrieval system or transmitted in any form or by any means, electronic, mechanical, photocopying, recording, scanning or otherwise, except as permitted under Sections 107 or 108 of the 1976 United States Copyright Act, without the prior written permission of the Publisher. Requests to the Publisher for permission should be addressed to the Permissions Department, John Wiley & Sons, Inc., 111 River Street, Hoboken, NJ 07030, (201) 748-6011, fax (201) 748-6008, or online at http://www.wiley.com/go/permissions.

Trademarks: Wiley, For Dummies, the Dummies Man logo, Dummies.com, Making Everything Easier, and related trade dress are trademarks or registered trademarks of John Wiley & Sons, Inc., and may not be used without written permission. All other trademarks are the property of their respective owners. John Wiley & Sons, Inc., is not associated with any product or vendor mentioned in this book.

LIMIT OF LIABILITY/DISCLAIMER OF WARRANTY: WHILE THE PUBLISHER AND AUTHOR HAVE USED THEIR BEST EFFORTS IN PREPARING THIS BOOK, THEY MAKE NO REPRESENTATIONS OR WARRAN-TIES WITH RESPECT TO THE ACCURACY OR COMPLETENESS OF THE CONTENTS OF THIS BOOK AND SPECIFICALLY DISCLAIM ANY IMPLIED WARRANTIES OF MERCHANTABILITY OR FITNESS FOR A PAR-TICULAR PURPOSE. NO WARRANTY MAY BE CREATED OR EXTENDED BY SALES REPRESENTATIVES OR WRITTEN SALES MATERIALS. THE ADVISE AND STRATEGIES CONTAINED HEREIN MAY NOT BE SUITABLE FOR YOUR SITUATION. YOU SHOULD CONSULT WITH A PROFESSIONAL WHERE APPRO-PRIATE. NEITHER THE PUBLISHER NOR THE AUTHOR SHALL BE LIABLE FOR DAMAGES ARISING HEREFROM.

For general information on our other products and services, please contact our Customer Care Department within the U.S. at 877-762-2974, outside the U.S. at 317-572-3993, or fax 317-572-4002. For technical support, please visit www.wiley.com/techsupport.

Wiley publishes in a variety of print and electronic formats and by print-on-demand. Some material included with standard print versions of this book may not be included in e-books or in print-on-demand. If this book refers to media such as a CD or DVD that is not included in the version you purchased, you may download this material at http://booksupport.wiley.com. For more information about Wiley products, visit www.wiley.com.

Library of Congress Control Number is available from the publisher.

ISBN 978-1-118-61589-8 (pbk); ISBN 978-1-118-61563-8 (ebk); ISBN 978-1-118-61592-8 (ebk); ISBN 978-1-118-61605-5 (ebk)

Manufactured in the United States of America

10 9 8 7 6 5 4 3 2 1

Contents at a Glance

Table of Contents

Introduction

*W*ithin the past five years, we've heard more and more about Frontier Markets: what they are, how they compare with other markets, the potential rewards they offer, and the risks they hold.

For the big picture, think of the world as having four major types of stock markets:

- ✔ **Developed Markets,** such as the United States, Canada, and many but not all European countries.

- ✔ **Emerging Markets,** including the much-discussed BRICs – which refers to Brazil, Russia, India, and China. This category also includes countries such as Mexico, Turkey, and Chile.

- ✔ **Frontier Markets,** such as Colombia, Panama, many of the African countries, but not including South Africa, some of the Middle East countries, including the United Arab Emirates, and many of the former Soviet Bloc countries, including Slovenia.

- ✔ **Exotic Frontier Markets,** such as Sierra Leone and Yemen.

We have designed this book to provide you with a comprehensive map to navigate all the dimensions that you need to know in order to understand the concept of Frontier Market investing, the types of frontier investments, and the choices that you will face with these investments. By the time you finish this book, you will have learned what advantages Frontier Markets have to offer you and the reasons we believe they exist. We also show you how you can reap the rewards of frontier investing, the types of investments available to you, the advantages and disadvantages of each type, how you can get started, and how you can measure your success with frontier investments. We even suggest circumstances under which you should *not* put additional dollars into frontier investments.

About This Book

Throughout this book, we discuss issues that are common in all types of investments along with some situations that specifically apply to frontier investing.

We emphasize the importance of having a successful relationship with your financial advisor in all areas of your financial life, including your frontier investments. We aren't financial advisors but have worked with members of this profession for over four decades between us. We view their role as important for the successful investor at any time and even more important for the investor navigating through the new territory of Frontier Markets investing. Be patient with us on this: We really believe in the importance of good professional advice at all times, but it becomes even more important when dealing with Frontier Markets.

There's nothing fundamentally wrong with handling some of your investments independently, but we believe that becomes even more complicated than usual when you're dealing with these markets.

In several chapters, we talk about the importance of a well-defined asset allocation. This refers to a large focus in your overall investment plan.

Financial advisors and others set up the asset allocation as a structure within which to divide your total available investment dollars into the various types of investments.

Drawing up an asset allocation plan precedes the Frontier Markets decision and provides a framework for deciding how much of your portfolio to allocate to Frontier Markets as well as other types of investments.

An asset allocation plan needs regular review because some of the preceding factors, such as your own view of your risk tolerance, your employment status, or your marital status, will change over time. Ideally, you and your advisor will agree on the circumstances under which a review takes place. Some advisors prefer reviews on a calendar basis, such as once annually or once every six months or once every three months. Other advisors believe in doing reviews when a specific threshold occurs, such as when the weighting of a specific category changes by more than a stated percentage amount.

In other chapters, we explore in detail the various ways in which you can invest in frontier funds. A basic list includes:

- Global Frontier Market funds
- Exchange-traded funds (ETFs)
- Sector funds
- Country funds
- Closed-end funds
- American Depositary Receipts, often referred to as ADRs
- Global Depositary Receipts, often referred to as GDRs
- Individual shares, whether in companies domiciled in Frontier Markets or in developed nations but having large involvement in Frontier Markets

Although we explore all these types of investments in detail, including their advantages and disadvantages, we strongly recommend that you do most or all of your Frontier Markets investing through an actively managed global Frontier Markets mutual fund. That allows for the greatest possible diversification between countries, industries, and types of markets. A skilled fund manager knows when to shift your dollars between countries and industries to take advantage of buying opportunities or to escape from negative developments. Because Frontier Markets are still illiquid and inefficient, a good fund manager can add substantial value against passively investing in an index fund or ETF. The largest companies aren't always the best investments.

Foolish Assumptions

Several foolish assumptions might lead to inaccurate conclusions about Frontier Markets and frontier investing. These include:

- ✔ **Believing all Frontier Markets are the same.** That's not true, any more than all developed markets are the same. The Middle East provides the best single example since parts of the region, such as Egypt and Syria, continue in tumult at time of writing while the United Arab Emirates continues its role as a "safe haven." Similarly, each African country needs separate consideration and in Latin America, Brazil and Mexico rank as Emerging Markets while Argentina and Panama rank as Frontier Markets. Even the former Soviet bloc countries are not the same; the Czech Republic's stability and the relative liquidity of its markets qualify it as an Emerging Market, but former Soviet bloc republics such as Kazakhstan, Slovakia, and Slovenia are Frontier Markets.

  Even individual countries do not remain the same; Egypt was relatively stable until the overthrow of then-President Hosni Mubarak in 2011, but hasn't achieved a reasonable level of stability since that time.

- ✔ **Believing that Frontier Markets are for the short-term, which definitely isn't the case.** We suggest that the dollars you invest in Frontier Markets be money that you can set aside for five years or more. Cash, near-cash, balanced funds, and domestic funds are all better suited to short- and medium-term investments than Frontier Markets.

- ✔ **Believing that you can easily go from investing in only domestic equities and funds to Frontier Market investments.** You should have at least some experience in Emerging Markets investments and become familiar with their risk and volatility before moving on to Frontier Markets. Think of Emerging Markets investments as the last step before Frontier Markets investments; get comfortable there and then go onto the frontier!

Icons Used in This Book

We include several icons to help you spot ideas and information you may find particularly useful. Here's what each one means:

This icon draws your attention to a piece of advice that's worthy of special attention.

This icon flags important information to keep in mind as you develop your understanding of Frontier Markets.

This icon helps you avoid mistakes that may negatively affect your portfolio.

This icon flags highly technical mumbo-jumbo. You can read this stuff if you like, or you can skip it if you're not interested.

Beyond the Book

You got more than you bargained for when you bought this book. You can access bonus material online at www.dummies.com:

- ✔ You can download the book's Cheat Sheet at www.dummies.com/cheatsheet/frontiermarkets. It's a handy resource to keep on your computer, tablet, or smartphone.

- ✔ You can read interesting companion articles that supplement the book's content at www.dummies.com/extras/frontiermarkets. There's even an extra top-ten list for your amusement.

Where to Go from Here

Like all *For Dummies* books, you don't have to read this tome from cover to cover. If you're an absolute beginner when it comes to investing, then we definitely recommend that you start from the beginning and read through to the end. But if you're a seasoned investor, it's totally okay for you to jump around and read the chapters or sections that interest you most.

Part I

Getting Started with Frontier Markets

In this part. . .

- ✔ Get acquainted with the concept of Frontier Markets.

- ✔ Learn what qualifies as a Frontier Market.

- ✔ Get to know the nations and regions considered as Frontier Markets.

- ✔ Decide whether Frontier Markets have a role in your portfolio.

- ✔ Developing an understanding of Emerging, Frontier, and Exotic Frontier Markets.

- ✔ Understand the concept of the Next 11, MIST, and CIVETS.

- ✔ Learn why indices are important.

- ✔ Discover the risks of Frontier Markets.

Chapter 1

Forging into New Investment Frontiers

*L*et's lay some groundwork here!

We consider Frontier Markets a subset of Emerging Markets that offers you, the investor, the opportunity to make returns similar to those delivered by the major Emerging Markets over the decade ending December 31, 2012. At that time, the MSCI Emerging Markets Index returned 13.7 percent per annum, more than doubling an investor's initial investment, depending on date of deposit.

Comprised of countries ranging from the large, young, and fast-growing nations of South Asia and sub-Saharan Africa to the middle-income and middle-aged group of South American and Eastern European states to the small, wealthy emirates and nations of the Persian Gulf, the 41 frontier economies in the MSCI and S&P Frontier Markets Indices make up 14 percent of global population and 7 percent of global gross domestic product (GDP) on a purchasing power parity (PPP) basis.

Including those Frontier Markets with barriers to entry due to lack of liquidity or restrictions on foreign investment brings these totals to 25 percent of global population and 11 percent of global GDP.

Acquainting Yourself with Frontier Markets

Frontier Markets are less-developed economies not included in either the MSCI World Index of developed countries or the MSCI Emerging Markets Index. That index includes 21 emerging economies, including the largest and best known, the BRICs, comprised of Brazil, Russia, India, and China.

While the established Emerging Markets comprise almost two-thirds of the global population and one-third of global stock market capitalization, Frontier Markets make up less than 2 percent of global stock market capitalization. With those basic definitions in mind, the rest of what we suggest may make more sense to you.

As another quick definition, *market capitalization* refers to the total value of equities available for public trading, whether referring to the total for a specific corporation or country's stock market.

With Frontier Markets, this means that their capitalization-to-GDP ratio is extremely low (2 percent against 11 percent). Because they include some of the world's fastest-growing economies, including six sub-Saharan Africa countries, their stock market capitalization should grow just to reflect their growing GDPs.

Moreover, we believe that, in a fashion similar to what occurred with Emerging Markets over the last 15 years, the valuations that investors will pay for the growth in Frontier Markets will rise as well. That would give early investors putting money into these markets in the next couple of years the strong probability of excellent returns. Still, those same investors will need strong nerves to absorb the volatility of Frontier Markets and to adjust to their lack of familiarity. However, we suggest to you that by investing in an actively managed global Frontier Markets fund, investors give themselves the best chance of succeeding.

What qualifies as a "Frontier" Market

There are no firm guidelines as to what constitutes a Frontier Market. On July 1 of each year, the World Bank divides countries into four categories, based on annual gross national income (GNI) per capita on a purchasing power parity (PPP) basis. The four categories on July 1, 2012, were:

- Low income: Below US$1,025
- Lower-middle income: US$1,026–$4,035

✔ Upper-middle income: US$4,036–$12,475

✔ High income: Above US$12,476

The World Bank notes that low- and middle-income countries are often referred to as "developing economies," but goes on to note that although the term is convenient, it does not imply that all countries in the categories have reached a similar stage of development.

While Emerging Markets are essentially all countries whose GNI is below US$12,476, Emerging Market indices also include some countries with higher GNIs or GDPs per capita, such as Chile, South Korea, and Turkey. These countries are also members of the Organization of Economic Development (OECD), which is regarded as peopled by developed economies.

Frontier Markets, a term first used by the head of the International Finance Corporation's Emerging Markets database in 1992, are Emerging Markets that have lower market capitalization and liquidity than the established Emerging Markets or more restrictions on investment, or both limitations. While most Frontier Markets' GNI figures per capita rank in the low or lower-middle income categories, they include a number of wealthy countries that lack sufficient liquidity or have restrictions on investment that exclude them from the major emerging indices. These traits make Frontier Markets in general unsuitable for inclusion in the larger market indices, but they share many of the same attractive characteristics as the longer-established developing markets.

The nations and regions populating this sector

The MSCI and S&P Frontier Market indices, which are the most widely followed among investors, include the following 41 countries:

Africa

✔ Benin

✔ Botswana

✔ Burkina Faso

✔ Ghana

✔ Kenya

✔ Ivory Coast

✔ Mauritius

✔ Namibia

✔ Nigeria

✔ Senegal

✔ Zambia

Asia

✔ Bangladesh

✔ Kazakhstan

✔ Pakistan

- Sri Lanka
- Vietnam

Europe

- Bulgaria
- Croatia
- Estonia
- Latvia
- Lithuania
- Romania
- Serbia
- Slovakia
- Slovenia
- Ukraine

Latin America

- Argentina
- Colombia

- Ecuador
- Jamaica
- Panama
- Trinidad and Tobago

Middle East and North Africa (MENA)

- Bahrain
- Jordan
- Kuwait
- Lebanon
- Morocco
- Oman
- Qatar
- Tunisia
- United Arab Emirates (UAE)

Morocco was added to the Frontier Markets index by MSCI in November 2013. Qatar and the United Arab Emirates will be upgraded from Frontier to Emerging Market status by MSCI in May 2014.

Although this list appears fairly extensive, a number of quite large countries — either by population or by market capitalization — are excluded from these indices and are regarded as "Exotic Frontier Markets." These include Saudi Arabia, Iran, and Iraq in the Middle East, Cambodia, Laos, and Myanmar (Burma) in Asia, and numerous African economies, some with large populations, such as Ethiopia and the Democratic Republic of the Congo (DRC).

As the examples of Morocco and Qatar and the UAE demonstrate, the index providers change classifications with changing conditions. Indeed it is reasonable to assume that they may upgrade a number of Frontier Markets to Emerging Market status as their market capitalizations and liquidity grow. Similarly, Exotic Frontier Markets may graduate to full Frontier Market status. Countries with severe economic problems may find themselves going the other way, as happened to Argentina when it was downgraded to Frontier Market status in 2009 and Greece when it fell from developed to Emerging Market status in November 2013.

The risks in these markets

A number of Frontier Market companies have American Depositary Receipts (ADRs) trading on American exchanges and Global Depositary Receipts (GDRs) listed in London or Luxembourg, and therefore have to conform to the high standards of reporting and accounting in those countries. This reassurance does not alter the fact that these are highly volatile markets with a higher level of political and economic risk attached.

In the Financial Crisis of 2008–2009, the MSCI Frontier Markets Index fell 55 percent, even more than the MSCI Emerging Markets Index or S&P 500 indices. While the MSCI Frontier Markets Index was less volatile than the MSCI Emerging Markets Index over the five years including the financial crisis ending August 2012, it was much more volatile than the S&P 500 or the MSCI World Index of developed markets.

Furthermore, the Frontier Markets did not rebound as rapidly as the Emerging Markets, only regaining their 2008 high point in late 2013, compared with 2012 for the Emerging Markets. This provided investors with a benefit since it meant that Frontier Markets' valuations fell to low levels, making them good values compared to developed and Emerging Market valuations.

Why the average investor is stepping into these markets

First, it may be a mistake to refer to "the average investor," but you know what we mean!

Despite the high volatility and perceived level of risk in Frontier Markets, investors in North America and Europe are showing increasing interest. The Templeton Frontier Markets Fund, the oldest American retail frontier mutual fund, was launched in the United States and Europe in 2008 and Canada in 2011. It closed to new investors at the end of June 2013, as assets under management had exceeded US$3 billion, with over US$500 million being invested in the first half of 2013. The closing meant that the assets would not grow too rapidly, which meant that managers could continue investing in the same style as long as the inflows did not continue at the same rate.

Several new global and regional Frontier Market funds were launched in the United Kingdom and Europe during the year before we wrote this book, and institutions are beginning to allocate small percentages of their Emerging Markets portfolios to these countries.

This display of interest resulted from several factors, starting with appreciation in Frontier Markets. They have risen 20 percent in the last year while Emerging Markets indices have been flat or down.

Moreover, there is increasing recognition of the higher level of GDP growth Frontier Markets are enjoying compared to the maturing Emerging Markets, with Brazil's GDP growth in 2012 falling to only 1 percent and India's GDP growth for 2012–2013 forecast to fall to 4 percent, its lowest for a decade. Even China's GDP growth fell to 7.6 percent in 2012, well down on the 11.5 percent average rate it had attained between 2006 and 2011.

Investors have become more informed about the lack of correlation between the Frontier Markets and developed and Emerging Markets. Because of their small size and lack of liquidity, Frontier Markets do not move in line with the more liquid and larger developed or Emerging Markets. They have a correlation of less than 0.3 over the last decade with the MSCI World Index and 0.4 with the MSCI Emerging Markets Index.

A correlation of 1.0 means that two indices move perfectly in line with each other.

As a result, investors are becoming increasingly aware that adding a small percentage of Frontier Markets to portfolios reduces volatility. Even though they are volatile individually, they are not correlated with each other particularly. What happens in Estonia has little effect in Nigeria or in Bangladesh.

Identifying Special Issues Affecting Frontier Market Volatility

There are several issues that, while not peculiar to Frontier Markets, tend to have a greater effect on them due to their lower liquidity and less transparent reporting and accounting. While many Frontier Markets companies are well run and have good corporate standards of corporate governance, especially the locally listed subsidiaries of multinational corporations, the less-developed nature of institutions in developing countries results in non-financial factors playing a major role in how markets behave.

The influence of political systems

While most readers of this book live in a prosperous developed world democracy, many Frontier Markets have not yet moved to allowing their citizens to choose their government. You need to consider the different types of political systems when deciding where to invest your hard-earned dollars.

Monarchies

A number of kingdoms and emirates still exist in the Middle East and North Africa, ruled by third- or fourth-generation rulers. Among the monarchies in the MSCI Frontier Markets Index are:

- ✔ Bahrain
- ✔ Jordan
- ✔ Kuwait
- ✔ Morocco
- ✔ Oman
- ✔ Qatar
- ✔ Saudi Arabia
- ✔ United Arab Emirates (UAE)

These countries are generally wealthy due to oil and other natural resources. With the exception of Morocco and Saudi Arabia, they are small in population and size. Their wealth and competent governments have kept them relatively secure during the unrest that swept the Middle East and North Africa after the Arab Spring began in 2011. However, there were riots in Bahrain, suppressed by the authorities. Historically, Middle East monarchies have proved vulnerable, with the overthrow of rulers in Egypt, Iraq, Libya, and Iran between 1952 and 1979.

Communist and autocratic regimes

The following Frontier Market countries have Communist or autocratic governments:

- ✔ Kazakhstan
- ✔ Laos
- ✔ Myanmar
- ✔ Vietnam

Although officially Communist, Vietnam, like China, has adopted capitalism under state oversight. That means that its economy has expanded substantially over the two decades since its opening, or *Doi Moi.* Laos has begun the same process in a limited fashion, with its stock market only having two listed companies at the time of writing.

Myanmar, formerly known as Burma, has been isolated under its military junta for most of the last 50 years and has become one of the poorest countries in the world. Its recent relaxation of controls, including the release of Nobel Prize winner Aung Sang Suu Kyi from house arrest and permitting opposition parties to win seats in parliament, may indirectly signal a willingness to permit economic reforms.

Kazakhstan, despite being a former Communist state, has developed a vibrant stock market and listed a number of its major companies on the London Stock Exchange. An autocratic regime, Communist or not, is not necessarily a negative when considering it as an investment destination.

Democracies

In numbers too numerous to list, Frontier Market democracies range from the very large poorer countries of Africa and South Asia, such as Nigeria, Kenya, Pakistan, and Bangladesh, to some very small European states. They also include middle income Latin American countries like Colombia and Peru and small, relatively wealthy African states such as Namibia and Botswana. Additionally, the list includes East European former satellites of the Soviet Union, like Estonia, Slovakia, and Croatia, as well as middle-income countries like Bulgaria, Romania, and Ukraine.

East European countries that want to join the European Union tend to be more vigorous about protecting democratic rights, as this is a condition of membership. Nonetheless, the rise of democratic governments in Latin America and Africa over the last two decades has been one of the more exciting Frontier Markets developments. There tends to be a correlation between higher GDPs per capita and democracy, if only because removing a corrupt or incompetent government is much easier and less painful.

The scope of corruption and income disparity

Among the information that we include in this book is a chapter on corruption and income disparity, or the difference between the wealthiest and poorest sections of society. The perception by most foreign investors is that poorer countries are more corrupt, and we clarify this by using the Corruptions Perceptions Index produced by Transparency International. It asks international businesses how difficult or easy it is to do business in different countries.

While Scandinavian countries, Australia and New Zealand head the list, many Frontier Market countries rank near the bottom. However, the fact that poorer countries experience higher levels of corruption is not a surprise, and one of the interesting features of the survey is that some of the larger Frontier Markets are gradually improving their scores from very bad to less bad. In one example, Bangladesh has moved up from dead last to three quarters of the way down the table.

Similarly, income disparity as measured by the Gini Index (named for its inventor Corrado Gini) shows how far away a country is from a perfectly equal distribution of income. While Scandinavian social welfare states are the most equal, many Frontier Markets are among the most unequal, with southern Africa and Latin America scoring particularly poorly.

When corruption and income equality scores are both high, the combination produces a higher-than-normal risk of social unrest. That can spill over into outbreaks of popular protest, such as the Arab Spring of 2011.

Market restrictions

Some Frontier Markets such as Saudi Arabia prevent foreign investment in their stock markets. In other cases, countries like the Philippines and Thailand limit the percentage of local companies that can be purchased. When the foreign limit is reached due to the country becoming a popular investment, share prices for *foreign shares,* as they are known, can trade at a premium to local shares. That means that they become a more expensive way to own a stake in the company. If the market then falls, not only will foreign investors suffer losses, but the premium they have paid can disappear, hitting them with a double whammy.

It is important to understand issues, such as ones with using participation certificates to access markets unavailable to direct investment, like Saudi Arabia.

P-certs, as they are known, are issued by investment banks and the investor has counterparty risk in the event of trouble, as happened with Bear Stearns and Lehman Brothers in 2008.

The influence of currencies, exchange rates, and accounting differences

As with other overseas markets like the United Kingdom, Japan, and Brazil, when investing in Frontier Markets investors get exposure to a foreign currency which will fluctuate against the American dollar. Even when buying frontier company ADRs listed in New York, or GDRs in London, the underlying security is still denominated in local currency.

Frontier Markets tend to run weak currency regimes, allowing their currency to fall against major global currencies.

In this way, they can help their export industries compete and remain competitive, while discouraging too many expensive imports, such as autos and luxury goods. Investors in Frontier Markets should be aware of the fact that they will experience a headwind in terms of a depreciating currency, which should be more than compensated for by the strong performance of the underlying stock markets.

Likewise, accounting standards in emerging and frontier economies are often different from GAAP (Generally Accepted Accounting Principles) standards, usually using some version of the International Financial Reporting Standards (IFRS) accounting. If the accounts are those of a subsidiary of an international or multinational company then there will be a higher degree of confidence. Confidence is also high with accounts audited by one of the big international auditing forms.

However, that is by no means a guarantee that the accounts will provide an accurate picture, and it's important to use common sense when looking at companies in these markets. If the business is relatively straightforward, such as manufacturing or retailing, then fund managers will have greater confidence in their analysis, regardless of what accounting standards are being used. When an economy is growing between 5 percent and 10 percent a year, revenue growth can make up for many issues in management and controls.

Getting Real about the Role of Frontier Markets in Your Portfolio

We're not suggesting that you take your hard-earned life savings and plunge them all into a global Frontier Markets fund, although it would probably be a rewarding investment if you were able to sleep at night. Realistically, most investors cannot afford to be so concentrated in their portfolios, which is why we stress the importance of finding a financial advisor that you can work with, and making Frontier Markets part of your overall financial plan.

Working within your larger investment plan

Why do we suggest finding a financial advisor with whom you feel comfortable? Among our most important reasons is that a good advisor will establish a financial plan for you and fit Frontier Markets into that plan. Having a plan means telling the advisor about your financial circumstances — all of them.

In the same way as you wouldn't keep vital details about your health from your doctor, you shouldn't keep vital details about your wealth from your advisor. This includes the number of credit cards you have and how much you owe, any mortgage payments, and projected pension plans.

The latter is especially important if you are one of the lucky people who still have a defined benefit (DB) pension plan through your employer. If so, you have a guaranteed income in retirement, and that means that you can have a larger percentage of your non-pension investments in more volatile but higher return assets like Frontier Markets.

If, like most of us, you have a Defined Contribution (DC) pension like a 401(k) in the United States or a Registered Retirement Savings Plan in Canada, then your pension income depends on returns generated by your investments and you may need to have a lower percentage allocated to volatile assets. That still means that Frontier Markets can help your overall portfolio's performance, as their lack of correlation with other equity markets means that adding even a small amount reduces the overall volatility of your portfolio.

Respecting your risk tolerance or aversion

One of the other valuable functions your advisor performs is to work out your risk tolerance. Most people will say that they have a reasonable tolerance for volatility, which is what financial experts mean when they talk about risk. In other words, the average investor feels that he or she can handle a period when investments drop by 15 percent over a relatively short time.

The problem arises when this actually happens, as occurred during the Financial Crisis of 2008–2009. What many investors discovered was that their risk tolerance was lower than they had believed.

While they were perfectly happy when stocks rose by 15 percent over the course of three or six months, the opposite was not true. In many cases, investors panicked and ended up selling their shares at the worst possible time, when prices had fallen sharply.

An advisor can help you be realistic about your ability to endure sharp falls in your portfolio, and what you need to do to prevent them from making you deviate from your financial plan. One of the simplest but most effective strategies is to construct a balanced portfolio, comprising cash, government and corporate bonds, domestic and international equities in developed markets, and Emerging and Frontier Markets.

The percentages that an investor has in each category depends on several factors, including age, salary, liquid and non-liquid assets (house, car, antiques, etc.), and risk tolerance. A younger investor with a good salary who has a house with a partially paid 30-year fixed mortgage might seem like an obvious candidate for investing in higher return assets like Emerging and Frontier Markets equities. However, if that investor has a low risk tolerance, he or she will worry too much about the volatility that comes with these assets. The first rule of investing successfully is that you should be able to sleep easy!

Nonetheless, an advisor can still perform a valuable role in overcoming the inbuilt psychological biases that make people ineffective investors. One of these is the familiarity bias, which makes most investors more comfortable with companies they know from their daily lives.

Analysis of pension funds, corporate as well as individual, finds that most investors generally have a higher percentage in their domestic market than would be expected if they were investing for the best risk-adjusted performance.

Just like individuals, pension committees tend to be comfortable with the stocks they know or have heard of, even if there may be Swiss, Japanese, or British listed companies that are just as effective operators and cheaper.

Allocating a small slice of your portfolio to Frontier Markets

If you have decided that Frontier Markets make sense as an investment, you then need to decide on an appropriate percentage of your portfolio. As we said earlier, we're not suggesting that you invest all or most of your equity portfolio in Frontier Markets.

But you should have a small percentage of your international equity portfolio invested in these markets. Somewhere between 5 percent and 10 percent of the international equity section of your portfolio would be appropriate. Within that scenario, if you have 30 percent of your equity portfolio invested outside of the U.S. or Canada, then 1.5 percent to 3 percent of your total equity exposure would be in Frontier Markets.

Even that small percentage will help reduce the overall volatility of your portfolio, given the non-correlation between Frontier Markets as well as between Frontier and Emerging and developed markets.

If the these markets perform as well as the Emerging Markets have done over the last decade then within a few years, this percentage could easily have doubled or increased by 50 percent or more. Usually, it makes sense to rebalance your portfolio periodically in order to prevent one asset class becoming too dominant in the portfolio.

However, that may be the exception that proves the rule.

If our projection works out, the Frontier Markets will have grown because of their faster GDP growth and their cheap valuations will become less cheap. Until investors become wildly enthusiastic about these markets in the same way that they had embraced Emerging Markets before the Financial Crisis, and as fund companies launch new Frontier Market funds regularly, it probably makes sense to let these markets become a bigger percentage of your portfolio. After all, even if they double, that will only mean they reach 5 percent to 6 percent of your equity exposure — not a massive amount.

Investing with Caution

As we mentioned, we don't recommend putting a large amount of your investment dollars into Frontier Markets investments immediately. For a start, you should check how much exposure to these markets you already may have through your own pension fund at work and through the domestic companies that you own. Some well-known and recognized companies derive a lot of their revenues and earnings from non-US or Canadian sources. Companies such as KFC, Taco Bell, and Pizza Hut operator Yum! Brands (NYSE:YUM) had over 75 percent of their revenues coming from outside the U.S. in 2012 and 44 percent from China. There are many other consumer, auto, pharmaceutical, media, and technology companies in the U.S., Japan, and Europe that also derive more than one-third of their revenues from Emerging and Frontier Markets. If you hold any of these companies either directly or through mutual funds, you already have at least some exposure to Emerging and Frontier Markets.

You should also be comfortable that Frontier Markets are the right investment for someone with your tolerance of volatility and uncertainty. They're not called "frontier" for nothing! Your investment dollars will be outside the boundaries of well-known and familiar territory.

It's extremely unlikely, for instance, that you would have bought a product made by a company domiciled in a Frontier Market, although it's very likely that you own a garment or decoration made in a Frontier Market for an American or European company. With labor costs rising rapidly in China, many suppliers of clothing, footwear, and cheaper electronics are now sourcing manufactured goods from such frontier countries as Vietnam and Bangladesh.

Sizing up your current investments

The first step to finding out your current exposure is to contact your pension plan administrator and see what percentage of your pension is invested in Emerging or Frontier funds. Frontier Market funds will almost certainly not be included, unless your pension fund is managed by a progressive pension management company such as Russell Investments, which introduced a Frontier Market portion into its Emerging Market pooled funds in 2011. Some major public sector pension funds, such as the California State Teachers' Retirement System (CalSTRS), do break out countries where their international investments are listed, and therefore you can discover that 1 percent of its international holdings are in Frontier Markets.

Then you should look at your own self-directed investments, either in your 401(k) or RRSP or in a nonregistered brokerage account. Do you have an Emerging Market mutual fund, such as the Templeton Emerging Markets Fund? How much of that fund is in the Frontier Markets that we list earlier in this chapter, such as Colombia? How much of the revenues of individual stocks that you own comes from Emerging and Frontier Markets? Well-established multinationals such as Guinness and Johnnie Walker maker Diageo (NYSE:DEO; LSE:DGE), or Dove and, Ben & Jerry's ice-cream maker Unilever (NYSE:UL), get 45 percent and 57 percent, respectively, of their sales from Emerging and Frontier Markets.

Deciding whether to invest directly or indirectly

You may discover that you already have some exposure and the question then becomes whether you want a dedicated exposure through a global regional or single-country Frontier Market fund or whether you feel comfortable with the diluted exposure that you receive through your existing pension fund and domestic stock investments. This is really a question you should answer only after discussing the matter with your financial advisor. If you manage your own investments, you need an unemotional and realistic assessment of your own investment character and risk tolerance.

If you decide that these markets are suitable, and we hope that you will after reading this book, then you need to determine whether to use indirect methods of gaining access, such as a global multinational company that has a high percentage of its revenues and earnings coming from these markets, or an Emerging Markets fund that has some Frontier exposure or even a frontier fund. These are perfectly sensible ways to invest, and we list ten of the most promising developed market companies with frontier exposure in Chapter 18. However, both methods share a common disadvantage.

One of the great benefits of a dedicated global Frontier Markets fund is that it is not correlated with either developed markets or Emerging Markets, thereby reducing the overall volatility of a portfolio. By comparison, developed markets global multinationals are most influenced by their own stock market's performance, regardless of the fact that their emerging and frontier exposure may help them grow faster and make more money. Similarly, Emerging Markets funds with some frontier exposure will have their performance driven by the economies of the BRIC countries, not the excellent growth provided by African developing economies.

Considering global frontier funds

Investors should make their investment in these markets through a dedicated global Frontier Market fund with an active manager. Our study of the performance of existing actively managed global frontier funds showed that almost all of them beat the MSCI Frontier Markets Index despite paying over 2 percent per annum in management fees and expenses. That occurred because these are illiquid and inefficient — ideal conditions for active managers to add value against the market capitalization weighted index since these conditions require expert judgment and decision-making. The two Frontier Markets exchange-traded funds (ETFs) available in North America, the iShares MSCI Frontier Markets ETF (NYSE:FM) and the Guggenheim Frontier ETF NYSWE:FRN) have 65 percent and 85 percent in the Middle East and South America, respectively, making them unsuitable vehicles for gaining exposure to the markets of Africa and Asia, which are the most attractive Frontier Markets in terms of valuations and demographics.

The largest and longest established global Frontier Markets fund, the Templeton Frontier Markets Fund, run by Dr. Mark Mobius and his team from Hong Kong, is unfortunately closed to new investors since June 30, 2013. This leaves three funds available to US retail investors: the HSBC Frontier Markets Fund, the Wasatch Frontier Emerging Small Countries Fund, and the Harding Loevner Frontier Emerging Markets Fund, all of which had operated for at least two years at the end of January 2014. All had outperformed their benchmarks despite their 2 percent plus management fees and expenses. There are another seven European registered global Frontier Markets mutual funds and a couple of global closed-end funds from BlackRock and Advance also investing in these markets.

Investors can also buy regional Frontier Market funds. There are US-registered mutual funds investing in Eastern Europe (US Global Emerging Europe Fund), the Middle East and North Africa (T. Rowe Price Africa and Middle East Fund), and Africa (Nile Pan African Fund and Commonwealth Africa Fund), as well as several regional ETFs. However, we don't recommend using regional Frontier Market funds unless you have a strong conviction that one region is going to be the best performer. All too often, events do not work out as you hope, and leaving the manager the flexibility to allocate money to where things are working well is a great strength of a global fund. Single country funds are even more exposed to this problem, and we don't recommend them as a route for frontier investing.

Monitoring your investments diligently

Finally, you've made the decision and invested a small percentage of your international equity allocation in an actively managed global Frontier Markets fund. Now you can sit back and relax while the attractive valuations and rapid economic progress of these countries carry your investment higher. Well, don't forget about things quite so fast. As with any investment, you should monitor it carefully and at least look at your quarterly statements to check your returns.

While we expect that Frontier Markets will produce excellent long-term returns similar to those from Emerging Markets over the last decade, please expect some bumps along the road. Remember, these are small, volatile, and illiquid markets with political systems still prone to rapid change.

You may wake up one morning and find that the TV and Internet are filled with stories about riots, uprisings, floods, famines, disputed elections, and terrorist attacks. Some of those crises may occur in countries in which you have some holdings.

Don't be discouraged. The mainstream media's attention span is short and easily diverted, but it also doesn't appreciate or try to get across the fact that what's happening in one part of the Middle East, for example, may have no relation to another market several hundred miles away. In fact, the Gulf kingdoms of Qatar and the United Arab Emirates have benefited over the last 18 months from flows of money looking for a stable safe haven out of Egypt, Syria, and other parts of the region. Their stock markets have soared while the nightly news was filled with the horrors happening in Syria and protesting civilians on the streets of Cairo, and now, the two countries have been upgraded to Emerging Market status effective May 2014.

All of this points to the importance of keeping an eye on what's happening in the Frontier Markets fund that you have chosen, but it's also important not to become discouraged by negative news coverage. Frontier Markets, just like Emerging Markets 15 years ago, will experience periods of economic and political turbulence, but as long as the investor owns a well-diversified global fund with a good active manager, the long-term return should be very satisfactory. Moreover, having even a small percentage of them in your portfolio reduces its overall volatility because these markets aren't correlated with other markets.

Chapter 2

Examining the Appeal of Emerging Markets Investment

*W*e're focusing on Frontier Investments in this book and don't want to go too far off in any other direction, but we do believe we need some discussion about Emerging Markets. We include it here because we see Frontier Markets as a subset of Emerging Markets.

Various index providers such as MSCI Inc., Standard & Poor's, the Financial Times Stock Exchange (FTSE), Dow Jones, and the International Monetary Fund (IMF) all produce definitions of the countries that they rank as developed, Emerging, or Frontier.

Getting to Know the Market Segments

In order to better understand the differences between these categories, take a look at all the categories of stock markets in the world today:

✔ Developed

✔ Emerging

✔ Frontier

✔ Exotic Frontier

Don't view the groupings here as carved in stone, but you can view them as changeable when economic conditions warrant rethinking of a classification.

Think of the four types of markets (developed, Emerging, Frontier, and Exotic Frontier) as having greater or lesser levels of gross domestic product (GDP), average annual income, market capitalization, sophistication of equity markets, and investment restrictions. Generally, Emerging Markets have lower gross domestic product (GDP) and market capitalization and may have greater investment restrictions than developed markets.

These divisions, while commonly held and reflected in indices such as the MSCI Emerging Markets Index and the MSCI Frontier Markets Index, are subject to change, especially those between Emerging and Frontier Markets as evidenced by Argentina's and Morocco's downgrades, which we explain in other chapters.

The groupings change over time. Barring a last-minute reversal, Qatar and the United Arab Emirates will move from the MSCI Frontier Markets Index to the MSCI Emerging Markets Index in May 2014. By comparison, in November 2013, Greece lost its developed market status and moved to Emerging status, while Morocco lost its Emerging Market status and became a Frontier Market.

Developed markets

In the MSCI World Index, MSCI classifies the 23 developed markets as follows:

- ✔ **North America:** Canada and the U.S.
- ✔ **Asia:** Australia, Hong Kong, Japan, New Zealand, and Singapore
- ✔ **Europe:** Austria, Belgium, Denmark, Finland, France, Germany, Ireland, Israel, Italy, Netherlands, Norway, Portugal, Spain, Sweden, Switzerland, and the United Kingdom

MSCI had formerly classified Greece as a developed market but downgraded it to Emerging Market status, effective in November 2013. MSCI took the action in light of the severe recession Greece had endured over the previous five years and the effect on its stock market capitalization and liquidity.

Emerging Markets

An official at the International Finance Corporation (IFC), the equity arm of the World Bank, first coined the term *Emerging Markets* in the early 1980s, in part due to a desire to replace the negative phrase "less-developed countries."

In the MSCI Emerging Markets Index, MSCI classifies the following 20 countries as Emerging Markets, which includes such large and well-known countries as those in the often-cited BRIC nations — Brazil, Russia, India, and China:

- ✔ **The Americas:** Brazil, Chile, Colombia, Mexico, and Peru

- ✔ **Asia:** China, India, Indonesia, (South) Korea, Malaysia, Philippines, Taiwan, and Thailand

- ✔ **Europe, Middle East, and Africa (EMEA):** Czech Republic, Egypt, Hungary, Poland, Russia, South Africa, and Turkey

MSCI had formerly classified Morocco as an Emerging Market but downgraded it to Frontier Market status, effective November 2013, as it had done with Argentina in 2009, while it upgraded Qatar and the United Arab Emirates (UAE) from Frontier Market to Emerging Market status starting in May 2014.

As we write this book, the acronym BRIC (Brazil, Russia, India, China) has started becoming less relevant than when first coined in 2001 by Goldman Sachs Asset Management's Chief Investment Officer Jim O'Neill. The economies of Brazil, Russia, India, and China have diverged in their progress over the decade since he coined it, with Russia and Brazil having large resource sectors that have driven their economic growth, as opposed to China's focus on capital investment and the export of manufactured goods, or the growth of India's large domestic consumer market.

China's economy has grown to become the second largest in the world behind the U.S.'s over the last 15 years, while both India and Russia have huge financial issues to reconcile. Brazil's economic growth has recently slowed sharply to only 1 percent in 2012, but could recover with the upcoming soccer World Cup competition in summer 2014 and the 2016 Summer Olympics.

Frontier Markets

An IFC official coined the term "Frontier Markets" in 1992. Frontier Markets are a subset of Emerging Markets that are investable but have lower market capitalization and liquidity and sometimes more investment restrictions than the Emerging Markets. These limitations make them unsuitable for inclusion in the larger Emerging Market index, but nonetheless they display some openness to outside investment, a lower GDP that may be gradually increasing, lower income levels, and evolving equity markets.

Some of the former Soviet bloc countries, such as Kazakhstan and Slovenia, fit this description as they metamorphose from tightly controlled Soviet economies to more flexible market economies. Question marks overhanging these definitions include whether Greece and Morocco will eventually regain their lost classifications.

Although we describe Frontier Markets as a subset of Emerging Markets, these two categories of countries differ in economic outlook, liquidity, and sophistication of their stock markets, political stability, and most other economic factors.

MSCI classifies the following 26 countries as Frontier Markets. These countries are regarded as a subset of those considered to be developing by the World Bank, the United Nations, or those whose stock market capitalization is less than 3 percent of the MSCI World Index.

Their criteria for including a country in the MSCI Frontier Markets Index is that it must have at least two stocks with a market capitalization (number of shares freely available multiplied by the share price) of at least US$500 million. This compares with a minimum market capitalization of at least US$2 billion necessary for inclusion in the Emerging or developed market indices.

- ✔ **Africa:** Kenya, Mauritius, Morocco (from November 2013), Nigeria, Tunisia

- ✔ **The Americas:** Argentina

- ✔ **Asia:** Bangladesh, Pakistan, Sri Lanka, Vietnam

- ✔ **Europe and the Commonwealth of Independent States (CIS):** Bulgaria, Croatia, Estonia, Kazakhstan, Lithuania, Romania, Serbia, Slovenia, Ukraine

- ✔ **The Middle East:** Bahrain, Jordan, Kuwait, Lebanon, Oman, Qatar, and the United Arab Emirates (the last two moving up to Emerging Market status in May 2014)

Generally, there are fewer indices and index-linked investment funds in the Frontier Markets category than in the Emerging Markets category. Over the coming years, that could change as Frontier Markets become better known and as fund companies look for ways to capitalize on the trend.

Exotic Frontier Markets

Finally, there are what is known as Exotic Frontier Markets, which are those which do not meet the index compilers' standards. These may be countries that do not permit direct foreign ownership of listed stocks, such as Saudi Arabia, even though its stock market had a market capitalization of over US$300 billion in 2012. They may be countries under foreign sanctions, like Iran, whose stock market had total capitalization of over US$100 billion in 2012, or countries that do not have a stock market at all, like Myanmar (Burma) and Cambodia. Finally, they may be countries whose political or economic management has been extremely volatile and uncertain, such as Zimbabwe and Iraq, dissuading foreign investors from considering them.

TECHNICAL STUFF

Who or what is the index?

Throughout this book, other financial books, radio and television broadcasts, newspapers, and magazines, you will read and hear references to "the index" or "the indices." We promise that, in this book at least, we'll always identify the index to which we are referring. Indices may seem complicated and blurry, but try to understand them as the basis for classifying companies, countries, or types of investments. The more familiar Dow Jones Industrial Average and the S&P 500 contain well-known American companies. The less familiar MSCI Emerging Markets Index and the MSCI Frontier Markets Index contain stocks listed in Emerging and Frontier Markets respectively.

Exotic Frontier Markets such as Azerbaijan, Belarus, and Macedonia, Iran, Iraq, and Sierra Leone in general have lower GDPs, lower annual income, and relatively unsophisticated and illiquid stock markets. However, in some cases, such as Iran, these are countries with an external barrier for foreign investors, in this case, economic sanctions.

However, even given those *current* limitations, the Exotic Frontier Markets have future potential. Depending on their governments' ability to monetize their resources, Exotic Frontier Markets may become Frontier Markets over time and Frontier Markets could rise to Emerging status over time. Iraq and Iran have huge oil resources that could finance their future growth in GDP and therefore change their category.

Recognizing the Importance of Emerging Markets

Recognizing the importance of Emerging Markets means recognizing their accomplishments and seeing them as a precursor for what we suggest the future holds in the long-term for Frontier Markets and for Exotic Frontier Markets.

Economic performance

As noted previously, the MSCI Emerging Markets Index has more than doubled over the last decade. Through the ten years ending August 31, 2013, the MSCI has returned 9.5 percent per annum. This is despite the perceived "riskiness" of investing in markets and economies that can be very volatile, where political risks are high and the quality of information available is low.

The reasons for their outperformance compared with developed markets, which have returned only 5.2 percent per annum over the same period, are perfectly straightforward. At the beginning of the last decade, Emerging Markets were cheap: Their valuations were at low levels after the Asian Crisis of 1997–98, the Russian default of 1998, the devaluation of the Brazilian real in 1999, and the Argentinean default of 2001. However, their underlying fundamentals, the principal reason for investing, remained attractive.

These countries had young populations, low social costs in the form of low or no government expenditures on unemployment payments and pensions, as well as high levels of domestic savings. Those savings were due to the absence of a government safety net in the form of unemployment payments or pensions, rising living standards as they industrialized, and improved competitive positions through currency positioning and devaluation.

As a result, they have enjoyed a decade of improving GDP and rising incomes, while running trade surpluses and keeping government spending under control. Their stock markets have reflected these improvements and delivered excellent returns to shareholders, although fast growth in an economy is not always reflected in stock prices, an economic principle demonstrated by China.

China's growth

China itself proves the importance of Emerging Market countries. At time of writing, the economic and financial news regularly features stories and analyses about whether China is or is not going to have a recession and whether this will affect Western economies. We constantly hear reports about rising and falling growth in the Chinese GDP, the outlook for the next few years, the impact of policy changes by the new Communist leadership under Premier Li Keqiang, over-investment in domestic infrastructure including the glut of unoccupied residences, and what all this means.

In one example, after reports suggested that China's potash requirements would decrease, the share price of Potash Corporation fell dramatically. That shock will eventually subside and the growth of the middle class in the Emerging Markets will also benefit commodity producers in developed countries such as Australia and Canada.

China, the largest and most powerful of the world's Emerging Markets, has always been important, even in medieval times, but started down the road to its present importance in the early 1990s. When China began developing its stock markets at that time, it reserved what were known as *A shares* listed on the Shanghai and Shenzhen exchanges for local residents, while only allowing foreign investors to purchase *B shares*.

The liquidity of the B shares has always been low, while the A shares, as one of the only three avenues for Chinese domestic savings (along with bank deposits and property) remained extremely liquid and traded at much higher valuations than the equivalent B shares.

When the Chinese government began privatizing its state-owned enterprises (SOEs) in the mid-1990s, listing them both as A shares on the Shanghai stock exchange and as H shares also on the Hong Kong stock market (hence the "H"), foreign investors found themselves in the unusual position of being able to purchase shares in some of the leading blue chip companies in a major Emerging Market at substantial discounts to the domestically listed shares. With only domestic Chinese investors officially permitted to own A shares, their valuations soon became much higher than the H shares available to all investors, even though both classes provided exposure to the same underlying company.

Usually, the situation is reversed; when foreign investors are restricted in the percentage of a domestic company they are permitted to own, foreign shares tend to move to a premium to local shares, as demand from foreigners drives up the price of shares they can own. This has happened in such markets as Thailand, the Philippines, and India, as we discuss in Chapter 6, and has led to the creation of mechanisms to permit foreign investors to own a higher percentage of such restricted companies through participation certificates.

The certificates allow foreign investors to enjoy the price performance of the underlying equity without actually becoming shareholders in the company. In countries such as Saudi Arabia, where foreigners cannot own locally listed shares on the Tadawul (the Saudi stock exchange), these certificates or notes issued by investment banks are the only means available for non-Saudi residents to own local companies.

The improvement in the financial situation of the Emerging Markets is reflected in their credit ratings by the major agencies, where by the end of 2010, 57 percent of the JP Morgan Emerging Market Bond index was investment grade (rated BBB or above) compared to 34 percent in 2002, and only 5 percent in the late 1990s.

Russia's reemergence

Meanwhile, at time of writing, Russia appears to be trying to shake off the bad-boy image created by accounts of corruption and economic difficulties within the country. It appears determined to reacquire a place on the world economic and political stages. In late summer of 2013, Russian President Vladimir Putin cast himself as peace broker between the United States and Syria over accusations of the latter's use of chemical weapons, taking the hitherto unheard-of step of publishing an opinion piece in *The New York Times* urging American President Barack Obama not to launch military strikes against Syria.

Within the opinion piece, Putin stated his desire to speak directly to the American people, a daring strategic ploy that earlier Russian presidents would not have contemplated. The significance of those few inches of narrative goes well beyond the crisis playing out at the time and can be read as another step in Russia's plan to stake its claim as a leading member of the G-8 group of nations.

Brazil's growing pains

Meanwhile, Brazil has staked at least part of its economic future on the Football (soccer) World Cup to be played there from June 12 to July13, 2014, the first time since 1950 that it has hosted the competition. Just over two years later, it hosts the Summer Olympics from August 5–21, 2016. These developments may lead to a recovery in Brazilian equities, after their decline in 2012–2013, which reflected slowing economic growth and popular unrest at the cost of staging these expensive sporting contests. It should also lead to more interest in investing in Brazil by multinational companies based in developed countries such as Europe and the U.S. with a presence in Brazil, to take advantage of the anticipated rise in consumer demand.

Currency considerations

The improving fundamentals of Emerging Markets are reflected in their currencies, which have tended to hold their own if not appreciate gradually against developed market currencies over the last decade. This reflects their improving economic fundamentals and superior demographic profile compared to the aging and debt-encumbered Euro-zone, Japanese, and U.S. economies. Over the past decade, the Chinese Renminbi has appreciated against the American dollar, the Japanese yen, and the Euro, as well as against such rival Emerging Market currencies as the Mexican peso and the Brazilian real.

Having said all this, some historic realities illustrate the limitations of China's ascendancy. Perhaps surprisingly, analysts have speculated that the American dollar could lose its status as the world's reserve currency, a role held by the British pound sterling until after World War II. (Foreign governments hold huge quantities of a reserve currency as an integral component of their foreign exchange strategies. Moreover, they use it as the means of quoting prices for products traded globally and for commodities such as gold.) Meanwhile in June

2010, the United Nations issued a report calling for dropping the greenback as the main global reserve currency, a recommendation endorsed by Russia and China.

Seeking a Lack of Correlation

Within an investment context, *seeking a lack of correlation* means selecting investments that do not move together because of economic or political events. In a familiar example, rising oil prices might drive up oil company stocks but depress consumer stocks, on the belief that consumers will cut back on discretionary purchases in order to pay for higher gas at the pump or higher oil prices for home heating.

In Emerging Markets, as discussed earlier, the BRICs do not correlate with each other since at time of writing, China has the fastest growing economy. Brazil, looking to restore GDP growth with the World Cup and Summer Olympics, remains dependent upon resource prices set by Russia. Meanwhile, India is struggling with high inflation and inadequate infrastructure, which has led to the Indian rupee sinking to record lows in late 2013 against developed market currencies.

This leads to the need to treat each country separately and avoid generalizations about the Emerging Markets (or for that matter, any other category of markets).

The principle operates similarly in the Frontier Markets category. Much of Kazakhstan's economic future rests on oil prices and on its ability to monetize its resources. Rising world demand for oil would likely benefit Kazakhstan's economy. By comparison, rising oil prices would threaten the economic viability of energy importer Bangladesh if it led to a decrease in global consumer demand for the low-end consumer products such as garments and footwear manufactured there.

We saw another demonstration of the noncorrelation principle in the Frontier Markets category during the Middle East crisis of summer and fall 2013. While parts of the Middle East, including Syria and Egypt, suffered grievously due to civil war in the former and political uncertainty in the latter, other areas such as the United Arab Emirates and Qatar retained their well-known status as safe havens. In fact, cash from other Middle Eastern areas flowed in large amounts into the UAE.

Noncorrelation sounds confusing but it boils down to a simple statement: What happens in one country in a region does not necessarily affect all countries in the region, an equation demonstrated by the UAE's safe haven status in spite of turmoil elsewhere in the Middle East. As Mark Mobius, manager of the Templeton Emerging Markets Fund since 1987 and one of the longer established Frontier Market Fund managers, has noted, "If you take Estonia and compare it to Lebanon . . . you find there is zero correlation. They don't move together at all."

The significance of the principle of noncorrelation in terms of your investments remains equally simple: Do not judge the potential of one country in a region by your knowledge of the potential of other countries in the same region. In another example, among the former Soviet bloc countries, now known as the Commonwealth of Independent States (CIS), Kazakhstan is further along the road to becoming a viable market economy than other former bloc countries. In Chapter 6, we look at measures of corruption and income disparity, and our conclusion is that there are enormous differences even between countries in the same region.

Eyeing the Effects of U.S. Policy on Emerging Economies

The effect of U.S. economic policy on emerging economies was most strongly demonstrated in 2013 when world markets feared that the American Federal Reserve would embark on a policy of *tapering,* a phrase that referred to the possibility that the Federal Reserve would cut back on its efforts to stimulate the economy by Quantitative Easing (known as QE for short). It involved increasing the supply of greenbacks in the economy by purchasing US$85 billion of Treasury bonds and mortgage-backed bonds each month. The possibility that the Federal Reserve would reduce the total stimulus from over $1 trillion a year saw the yield on long term Treasury bonds and other investment grade bonds shoot up by over 1 percent from 1.75 percent on the benchmark US 10-year Treasury bond in less than 3 months.

That fear, combined with the increase in American interest rates, caused outflows of funds from both Emerging and Frontier Markets which were regarded as vulnerable to a slowdown in global growth in the event of a tightening. There was also a belief by investors that less liquid and developed markets such as the emerging and frontier nations might have to increase the yields on their bonds in order to staunch the outflows. The same factors and fears of further unfavorable developments in the government bond markets led to a rush to borrow and lock in record low interest rates on foreign debt by these countries.

While there have been short-term negative effects on Emerging Markets due to interest rate and monetary policy in the developed markets, particularly the U.S., the growth of China over the last decade and the importance of its purchases of commodities to build its economy now have just as great an influence on many Emerging Markets. In the three years to the end of August 2013, the MSCI Emerging Markets Index has declined by 1.4 percent per annum, against an increase of 9.3 percent per annum over the same period for the MSCI World Index of developed markets. This disparity is largely due to concerns over the slowdown in Chinese GDP growth to 7.5 percent per annum in 2012 and 2013 from the 11.5 percent it had previously achieved over five years between 2006 and 2011.

With commodity producers Brazil, South Africa, and Russia comprising over 20 percent of the MSCI Emerging Markets Index, their stock markets have reacted to lower Chinese purchases of commodities and lower prices for their raw materials. While United States and European economic policies will continue to have a major effect on the outlook for Emerging Markets, especially American interest rate expectations, investors need to be aware that the demand from other Emerging Market economies (particularly China) has as much or more of an effect on their progress.

The Bottom Lines for U.S. and Developed Market Investors

We see two conclusions for investors in the United States and in fact for most other countries.

A common theme between both bottom lines requires recognition of some investment realities in the developed markets.

We see these factors as very changeable and hope that you view them in the same way.

Those realities include:

- ✔ Although at the time of writing, the American markets continue a rally (in part artificially induced by the United States Federal Reserve's monetary policies), it simply cannot continue indefinitely. At some point in the future this rally must slow.

- ✔ Economists generally believe that sustained recovery in the United States would require 250,000 new jobs for several consecutive months — that appears an unlikely development within the foreseeable future.

✔ As we are writing this book, the United States has over $17 trillion in national debt, Social Security liabilities approaching $17 trillion, a prescription drug liability of over $22 trillion, and Medicare liabilities approaching $85.5 trillion.

These figures don't include state and city debts, nor do they include personal debts, such as mortgages and credit card balances. We can reasonably suggest that at some point in the future these figures will lead to some sort of economic backlash. We aren't presumptuous enough to try to predict the impact on the American economy and American investments at that time, except to say there *will definitely* be some impact and you probably won't like it.

✔ In comparison, most Frontier Markets don't have this level of debt or future unfunded liabilities (with a couple of exceptions such as Argentina and Venezuela). With a few exceptions, we can also say the same for most Emerging Markets.

✔ Declining birth rates in developed markets and the questionable job picture for college and university graduates mean fewer individuals coming into the workforce and paying taxes, buying consumer goods, and otherwise generating wealth.

In comparison, many Emerging and Frontier Markets have exactly the opposite conditions, with youthful populations, little in the way of outstanding consumer or corporate debt, and small numbers of retirees with the attendant pension and healthcare costs.

✔ At the time of writing in late 2013, the Euro-zone crisis appeared on the wane but any hope of a truly sustained recovery in southern European countries such as Greece, Italy, Portugal, and Spain appears unlikely for several years to come. While the Euro-zone emerged from six quarters of recession in the middle of 2013, it still has very high levels of unemployment and its austerity programs seem unlikely to allow it to generate rapid growth that would reduce this anytime soon.

Bottom line #1: Work with a financial advisor

The first bottom line operates in the individual investor's *relationship* with his or her financial advisor. Generally, we suggest that you devote between 5 percent and 10 percent of your international equity investment dollars to Frontier Market investments. However, we see that as a general across-the-board average.

Explore the concepts we discuss here, along with your own financial situation, investible dollars, retirement horizon, risk tolerance, place in the life cycle (such as whether you plan to have children), and anticipated cash needs with your financial advisor.

Regardless of the type of investment, tell your advisor everything in the same way that you would tell your doctor everything. You cannot hold the doctor or the advisor responsible for a professional and comprehensive decision unless you give either professional all the relevant information.

If you do not have any spare dollars for new Frontier Investments, look over your Emerging Markets investments with your advisor and consider switching some of those investments to finance your first foray into Frontier Markets. If you've held these Emerging Market investments for a few years, you likely have some reasonable profits.

If you don't have any Emerging Markets investments and Frontier Markets investments, consider whether you might first invest in Emerging Markets and then move onto Frontier Markets when you have established your comfort level.

If you have neither Emerging Markets investments nor available cash, consider parking a small but fixed amount in a money market fund and build it up to a Frontier Fund deposit.

However, check your own outlook and the view of your advisor at the same time. Broadly speaking, as a result of the Financial Crisis of 2008–2009, retail investors fall into one of two categories in their attitudes towards professional financial advisors:

- Some feel that they want and need professional advice more than ever and appreciate the value of professional financial advice.
- Others feel that the professionals let them down during the financial crisis.

Many of the individuals in the latter group understand that the forces that led to the crisis exploded outside of their grasp and beyond what any advisor could have ever anticipated.

However, they believe that their advisors should have communicated more frequently during the darkest days of the crisis. They have come to distrust their advisors and in some cases have decided to handle their own investments.

Others have decided that the financial world has become so complex and changeable that they have more faith in their advisors — and more appreciation for the ways in which an advisor can help solidify their financial health — than ever before.

Are you in that category? If so, then proceed and start discussing Frontier Markets with your advisor.

If you don't consider yourself a member of that category, consider joining it! Professional advisor associations in your area will assist you in finding the kind of professional advice that most suits your needs.

As much as we encourage you to embark on Frontier investing, we also encourage you *not* to go it alone and instead strike up a relationship with a trusted professional. The bottom line here is that the growth potential in Frontier Markets that we have discussed, combined with the outlook in developed markets that we discussed earlier in this chapter, make it in your own best interests to diversify into Frontier Markets, depending on what stage you are in your life.

Bottom line #2: Look at your retirement plans

The other bottom line for investors involves retirement plans. If you have a pension plan at your place of employment and if it has a Frontier Markets component, discuss with your pension administrators their plans for it. Ask whether they plan to expand the Frontier Markets component and to what extent. If the pension plan at your place of employment has no Frontier Markets component, ask the administrators about their intentions. (You can show them this book to back up your point!)

In either case, the common bottom line is that it is in your best interests to diversify some portion of your investments outside of developed markets, and while Emerging Markets have done well over the last decade, the chances are that Frontier Markets will repeat their performance over the next decade. Even if they don't all do as well as we anticipate, because they are not correlated with each other or with developed or Emerging Markets, a small portion of your portfolio should be invested in Frontier Markets.

Chapter 3

The Lay of the Land: Mapping Frontier Markets

*M*ost people reading this book will be familiar with the term "Emerging Markets," even if they can't give a hard and fast definition. There's a general understanding that Emerging Markets are those economies which are less developed than the wealthier countries of North America, Western Europe, Australia and New Zealand, and Japan.

This means that their average incomes per head of population are lower than those in more developed countries, which means that they're poorer, but also have the opportunity of growing faster than the more mature economies, where the majority of the population already enjoy a relatively prosperous existence.

Put simply, Frontier Markets are a subset of Emerging Markets, having in general lower incomes per head than the more established Emerging Markets such as the four BRIC nations (Brazil, Russia, India, and China). In essence, Frontier Markets are where the major Emerging Markets were 15 to 20 years ago, and we believe that they have the capacity to grow as rapidly as the first generation of Emerging Markets.

Of course, there's a lot more to Frontier Markets than simply classifying them as the poorer and less developed Emerging Markets. Included among the countries in Frontier Markets indices compiled by major financial firms such as MSCI and S&P are a number of very wealthy Middle Eastern states such as Saudi Arabia, Kuwait, and Oman, which restrict foreign investment in their stock markets, as well as some countries such as Iran that have quite well developed markets but are under sanction by the US and other western powers.

In this chapter, we describe the income levels at which countries are considered Emerging and Frontier Markets, look at which ones feature in the various indices, and consider what factors most of them have in common. Finally we will look at Exotic Frontier Markets, which are currently still too poor or too difficult to access by foreign investors but which may be included in the indices in a few years.

Characterizing This Subsegment of Emerging Markets

Emerging Markets as an investment concept have been on investors' radar screens for over a quarter of a century. Antoine van Agtmael, an economist at the International Finance Corporation, an arm of the World Bank, first coined the term in the early 1980s. As you might expect from an economist, the definition was made in economic terms — Emerging Markets were countries with low to middle income per capita.

Each year on July 1, the World Bank divides countries into four categories, based on annual gross national income (GNI) per person in purchasing power parity (PPP) terms. In 2012, the categories were split as follows:

- ✔ **Low income:** below \$1,025
- ✔ **Lower-middle income:** \$1,026–\$4,035
- ✔ **Upper-middle income:** \$4,036–\$12,475
- ✔ **High income:** \$12,476 or more

The World Bank notes that low-income and middle-income countries are often referred to as *developing economies,* but goes on to say that while the term is convenient, it does not imply that all countries in the categories have reached similar stages of development.

In effect, Emerging Markets are low- and middle-income countries and Frontier Markets are a subset of Emerging Markets. In 1992, the head of the IFC's Emerging Market database, Farida Khambata, was the first person to use the term *Frontier Markets.* They are investable, but have lower market capitalization and liquidity or more investment restrictions than the more-established Emerging Markets, or both. These traits make them unsuitable for inclusion in the larger Emerging Markets indices.

Emerging Markets have been a recognized asset class for the last quarter century, since MSCI Incorporated launched the first comprehensive Emerging Markets index in 1988. Meanwhile, the various other index compilers such as the IMF, Standard & Poor's (S&P), FTSE, and Dow Jones still include different lists of countries in their versions.

Emerging Market countries

Twenty-two countries are included in the Emerging Market indices from MSCI and S&P, two of the most popular. They are:

Asia:

- ✔ China
- ✔ India
- ✔ Indonesia
- ✔ Malaysia
- ✔ The Philippines
- ✔ South Korea
- ✔ Taiwan
- ✔ Thailand

Europe, the Middle East, and Africa:

- ✔ Czech Republic
- ✔ Egypt
- ✔ Greece
- ✔ Hungary
- ✔ Morocco
- ✔ Poland
- ✔ Russia
- ✔ South Africa
- ✔ Turkey

Latin America:

- ✔ Brazil
- ✔ Chile
- ✔ Colombia
- ✔ Mexico
- ✔ Peru

Here are a few notes about this list:

- Egypt is under review for a possible downgrade to Frontier Market status by MSCI as of November 2013.
- Greece was downgraded from developed to Emerging Market status by MSCI in November 2013.
- Morocco was downgraded from Emerging to Frontier Market status in November 2013.
- Colombia, Egypt, Morocco, Peru, and the Philippines are included in the MSCI Frontier Emerging Markets Index, as "crossover" markets, which have elements of both classifications.

Frontier Market countries

MSCI and S&P have Frontier Market indices, and the 40 countries that are included in both are:

Sub-Saharan Africa:

- Benin
- Botswana
- Burkina Faso
- Ghana
- Kenya
- Ivory Coast
- Mauritius
- Namibia
- Nigeria
- Senegal
- Zambia

Asia:

- Bangladesh
- Kazakhstan
- Pakistan
- Sri Lanka
- Vietnam

Europe:

- ✔ Bulgaria
- ✔ Croatia
- ✔ Estonia
- ✔ Latvia
- ✔ Lithuania
- ✔ Romania
- ✔ Serbia
- ✔ Slovakia
- ✔ Slovenia
- ✔ Ukraine

Latin America:

- ✔ Argentina
- ✔ Colombia
- ✔ Ecuador
- ✔ Jamaica
- ✔ Panama
- ✔ Trinidad and Tobago

Middle East and North Africa (MENA):

- ✔ Bahrain
- ✔ Jordan
- ✔ Kuwait
- ✔ Lebanon
- ✔ Oman
- ✔ Qatar
- ✔ Tunisia
- ✔ United Arab Emirates (UAE)

There are another 45 to 50 countries that are not included in the index providers' lists and are termed *Exotic Frontier Markets*. They have smaller market capitalizations, lower liquidity, and lower valuations than the principal Frontier Markets. They also include some large stock markets that are difficult or impossible to access by foreign investors. We deal with them in more detail later in the chapter.

PPP and Big Macs

Purchasing power parity (PPP) is an attempt to account for the fact that the same basket of goods costs different amounts of money depending on where the costs are calculated. To take a domestic American example, Des Moines, Iowa, is cheaper to live in than Los Angeles or New York City. Similarly, living in a developing economy is cheaper than living in a developed economy and adjusting dollar costs to take this fact into account results in an adjusted GNI per capita, so that a comparison can be done on an apples-to-apples basis.

In a similar vein, the Big Mac Index, first developed by *The Economist* magazine back in 1986, compares the cost of the same item — a Big Mac hamburger, around the world, to find out whether a country's currency is over- or under-valued. You could view the PPP-adjusted GNI per capita as the inverse of the Big Mac Index. In fact, *The Economist* calculates a raw index, which just compares Big Mac prices and a GDP per person index, reflecting the fact that you would expect a Big Mac to cost less in poorer countries as labor costs are lower. A Big Mac cost $4.56 in the U.S. in July 2013, so in Norway, where it costs $7.51, the krone appears over-valued. In India where it costs $1.50, the rupee appears seriously undervalued against the American dollar.

The Major Characteristics of Frontier Markets

Frontier Markets are where the major Emerging Markets were 12 to 15 years ago in terms of GDP growth, structure of their economies, and valuations. The largest and poorest frontier economies have very young populations, a low level of urbanization, and are generally embracing economic reforms. They are involved in the removal of trade barriers, similar to the path followed by the Emerging Markets over the last two decades. Furthermore, they sell at attractive valuations and sometimes provide dividend yields double those available from either developed or Emerging Markets. We believe that, as with the Emerging Markets, Frontier Markets are poised to deliver superior absolute returns over the next decade, albeit with some volatility along the way.

The major advantage of Frontier Markets that makes it likely that they will perform as well as Emerging Markets have over the last 10 to 15 years is that they have the same characteristics now as the major Emerging Markets had earlier but still sell at reasonable valuations.

These characteristics include, but are not limited to:

- ✔ Young populations that are growing rapidly
- ✔ Birth rates, that, while still healthy have declined somewhat
- ✔ Low levels of urbanization leading to migration from the countryside to the cities
- ✔ Growing middle classes as incomes rise
- ✔ Rapid economic growth producing rising living standards
- ✔ Low levels of internal and foreign debt
- ✔ Governments pursuing policies of liberalization and reform
- ✔ The removal of trade barriers through the free trade agreements and reductions in tariff and customs duties
- ✔ Low valuations

The 40 countries in the MSCI and S&P Frontier Markets indices represent 14 percent of global population and 7 percent of global gross domestic product (GDP) on a PPP basis, but less than 1 percent of the world stock market capitalization.

Expanding that definition to include the Exotic Frontier Markets such as Myanmar (Burma), Iran, Iraq, and Saudi Arabia, Frontier Markets then represent 25 percent of global population and 11 percent of global GDP on a PPP basis. However, they still represent less than 2 percent of global stock market capitalization.

If Frontier Markets' stock market capitalization just grows to represent the same percentage as their present share of global GDP, then their capitalization could rise by five or six times. Of course not all of this would be achieved by share prices rising, as many new companies would be listed on their stock markets, but nonetheless, the opportunity exists for the Frontier Markets to repeat the strong performance of the Emerging Markets over the last 15 years.

Market capitalization in the way we use the term here has two definitions:

- ✔ The total value of publicly traded shares in a country
- ✔ The total value of an individual company's publicly traded shares

In the next few sections, we look at these factors in order to see which regions look most attractive and likely to produce superior returns over the next 10 to 15 years.

Population, age, and growth

The regions that look most interesting from the perspectives of population, age, and growth are in Asia and Africa as well as a couple in South America and Eastern Europe. Table 3-1 shows the countries with the largest populations (greater than 20 million) that have young median ages (the point at which half the group are older than that point and the other half younger), and almost all of which have positive birth rates above 1 percent.

Table 3-1	Frontier Markets with the Largest Populations		
Country	*Population (m)*	*Median Age*	*Birth Rate (% p.a.)*
Pakistan	193.2	26.7	1.3
Nigeria	174.1	17.9	2.5
Bangladesh	163.6	23.9	1.6
Philippines	94.9	23.8	1.8
Vietnam	92.5	29.0	1.0
Colombia	45.7	30.3	0.8
Ukraine	44.5	40.3	-0.6
Kenya	44.0	18.9	2.3
Argentina	42.6	31.0	1.0
Peru	29.8	26.7	1.0
Venezuela	28.5	26.6	1.4
Ghana	25.2	20.7	2.2
Romania	21.8	39.4	−0.3
Sri Lanka	21.7	31.4	0.9

You can draw several conclusions from this table. The African nations (Nigeria, Kenya, and Ghana) have by far the youngest populations, all having populations half of whom are younger than 21. The East Europeans (Ukraine and Romania) not only have the oldest populations but negative birth rates. That means shrinking populations, as is the case with virtually all the other East European countries with smaller populations.

Asia and Latin American frontier countries tend to fall in between these two extremes, with median ages in the mid to high twenties on average. The principal difference is the higher birth rates among the Asian countries as opposed to birthrates only averaging 1 percent in Latin America.

A large population is an important factor when considering whether a country will likely enjoy a sustained period of economic growth. Quite apart from providing economies of scale because its population is large enough to support an expanded infrastructure and effective provision of services, a large population also means a large domestic market, giving the country some insulation from the vagaries of the trade cycle.

Most of the Asian tiger markets had small domestic markets, with city-states Hong Kong and Singapore having only 7 and 5.5 million people, respectively, leaving them very vulnerable to variations in global growth. Generally, once a country has more than 25 million inhabitants, it has a big enough market to support sizeable local industries.

The largest populations on this list are all in Asia and Africa. Pakistan, Nigeria, and Bangladesh are among the top ten countries in the world by size of population, and the Philippines and Vietnam are in the top fifteen.

Colombia, Ukraine, Kenya, and Argentina are in the top 30, but their lower birth rates (negative in Ukraine) mean that they will fall down the rankings during this decade.

Populations in the future

Estimates from *The Economist* of the world population rankings in 2050 still have China, India, and the United States as the three largest countries in the world. Meanwhile India has overtaken China due to its "one-child policy." Of the frontier economies, Nigeria will be fourth, Pakistan sixth, and Bangladesh and the Philippines are eighth and ninth largest respectively.

Exotic Frontier Markets, are Frontier Markets that are extremely illiquid or have barriers to foreign investors. Four exotic African markets are in the top 20 by population in 2050, starting with the Democratic Republic of the Congo (DRC) at tenth, Ethiopia eleventh, Tanzania thirteenth, and Uganda nineteenth.

When added to the other frontier economies of Vietnam and Kenya at seventeenth and eighteenth and Egypt, under review for downgrade to frontier status, at fifteenth, this means that Frontier Markets of various types are forecast to have 11 of the 20 largest populations in the world in 30 years.

Even though Yogi Berra famously said, "It's hard to make predictions, especially about the future," demographics is about the most predictable of subjects to forecast, as populations change very slowly. Unless birth rates absolutely plummet in sub-Saharan Africa and South Asia, these countries' populations will definitely be among the largest in the world in a few years. Some of them have already reached that category.

Urbanization and the rise of the middle class

The proportion of a country's population that lives in cities is an important factor when considering the sustainability of high economic growth over the next one or two decades. When people move from the country to the towns and cities, they contribute disproportionately to economic growth because human beings are more productive in an urban setting than down on the farm.

That occurs because of the creation of a critical mass of workers and consumers in a small enough area to allow economies of scale and frequent productive interactions.

From agriculture to industrialization

All the industrial revolutions that have occurred following the first one in 18th-century Great Britain saw a movement of people from the countryside to the towns, which provided the workforce and consumers necessary for the takeoff phase of the industrial economy.

In an agricultural society, the vast majority of the population work on the land, and towns are small and essentially act as markets for the exchange of agricultural surplus goods for manufactured products. Technology is confined to a few simple functions such as mills and foundries, and changes very slowly.

When agricultural techniques change and lead to a similar or greater output with fewer workers, as happened with the Agricultural Revolution that preceded the Industrial Revolution in Great Britain, the surplus laborers move voluntarily or involuntarily into the towns and cities.

While the process can be prolonged (it took until 1950 for city dwellers to exceed agricultural inhabitants in France, compared to 1850 in Great Britain) and usually involves suffering for the forced migrants, it is an indispensable element in an economic takeoff since it provides the necessary labor.

China's changing population

In China between 12 and 15 million inhabitants each year have moved into the cities since Deng Xaio Ping began economic reform in 1979. In 2012 China had over 60 cities with a population of more than 1 million, a number estimated to grow to 220 by the year 2020. In all, 380 million people have moved to the cities in the last 20 years, meaning that 633 million out of its 1.3 billion population (just over half the population) are now urban dwellers.

This process has helped make China the second largest economy in the world within 30 years. Having a big population helped; however, China had been the largest country in the world for many centuries, but had remained economically weak. Having a big population is not enough to make an economy grow or become successful, as proven by the large, poor countries that make up many of the Frontier Markets.

However, in China, Deng's reforms allowed peasants to retain any surplus they grew above a minimum quota and that led to sharp increases in agricultural output.

Moreover, the knowledge that growth was much faster in the coastal cities and that working for a couple of years in factories in Shenzhen or Shanghai could provide enough money to return home, buy a house, and the goods to furnish it encouraged individuals to make the move that that led to rapid GDP growth.

Urbanization equals growth

Urbanization proves that the economy is starting to grow faster, and perhaps as important, that reforms leading to higher output are taking place in the countryside. This is especially true in sub-Saharan Africa, where most agriculture is subsistence level, and a drought, flood, or plague of locusts can lead to famine and drastic drops in incomes.

Table 3-2 shows the largest Frontier Markets by population ranked by their percentage of urbanization from lowest to highest, GDP per capita in purchasing power parity (PPP) terms, and GDP growth in 2012.

Table 3-2   Frontier Markets Ranked by Percentage of Urbanization

Country	Urbanization (%)	GDP per Capita ($000)	GDP Growth (%)
Sri Lanka	14	6,100	6.0
Kenya	22	1,800	5.1
Bangladesh	30	2,000	6.1
Vietnam	30	3,500	5.0
Pakistan	36	2,900	3.7

(continued)

Table 13-2 *(continued)*

Country	Urbanization (%)	GDP per Capita ($000)	GDP Growth (%)
Egypt	43	6,600	2.0
Nigeria	50	2,700	7.1
Ghana	51	3,300	8.2
Romania	57	12,800	0.9
Ukraine	69	7,600	0.2
Colombia	75	10,700	4.3
Peru	77	10,700	6.0

Source: World Bank, IMF, CIA World Factbook

Several obvious conclusions emerge from this table. The South Asian markets, Vietnam, and African markets have the least urbanized populations, lowest GDPs per capita (except for Sri Lanka), and fastest growth, while Eastern Europe and South America have much higher urbanization rates and are wealthier. Finally, Eastern Europe economies are slower growing.

Liberalization and reform of economies and removal of trade barriers

High customs duties and quotas on imports are among the major barriers preventing emerging and frontier economies from growing faster, but foreign trade helps generate hard currency earnings and increases specialization in agriculture and the manufacturing industries. Those changes help improve quality and achieve critical mass and reduce waste and spoilage caused by inadequate storage and transit facilities.

There are various means of overcoming these barriers. The simplest of these, a customs union, lowers, or removes completely, tariffs and customs duties on a range of traded goods between neighboring states.

Early examples of such customs unions include the Zollverein in early 19-century Germany, which reduced duties on goods traded between the various independent states in Germany and acted as a precursor of political union.

The United States also abolished interstate tariffs shortly after independence, although not without some struggles. The European Economic Community (EEC), a predecessor to the European Union (EU) in the 1950s and 1960s, initially started as a free trade area. Its goal was to allow the exchange of German iron, steel, and coal for French and Italian agricultural products, and it was known as the *Common Market* for its first 25 years. Other European customs unions include the European Free Trade Area (EFTA), comprised of European states such as Switzerland and Norway that are not part of the EU but enjoy free trade privileges with it and each other, and the North American Free Trade Agreement (NAFTA), signed in 1988, which permits effective free trade between the U.S., Canada, and Mexico.

Among Emerging and Frontier Markets, free trade areas have also become popular. The best known and one of the longest established of these is Mercosur (Mercado Comun del Sud), the customs union covering Brazil, Argentina, Uruguay, Venezuela, and Paraguay. Launched in 1991 as a free trade area between Brazil and Argentina, it has expanded since then to become a full-fledged customs union for the southern cone countries of South America, with Venezuela joining as a full member in 2012.

The members of the Andean Community (Communidad Andina in Spanish or CAN) customs union, Bolivia, Colombia, Ecuador, and Peru, are associate members of Mercosur. Formerly known as the Andean Pact, it began in 1969 and allows free trade between the four Andean nations.

In Africa, Kenya, Uganda, Tanzania, Burundi, and Rwanda are members of the East African Community (EAC), revived in 2000 after its predecessor organization collapsed in 1977.

It established a common market for goods, services, and labor in 2010 and is affiliated with the longer-established Southern African Customs Union, which is the oldest existing customs union in the world, founded in 1910.

The Southern African Customs Union is comprised of the five states of South Africa, Namibia, Botswana, Swaziland, and Lesotho and provides for a common external tariff (customs) and common internal excise duties. The revenues from these duties are administered by South Africa and distributed according to a revenue-sharing agreement.

The South Asian Free Trade Area is comprised of India, Pakistan, Bangladesh, Sri Lanka, Nepal, Bhutan, and the Maldives and came into force in 2006 with the aim of reducing customs duties of all traded goods in the area to zero by 2015.

Reductions in customs duties have occurred, although countries were able to place certain goods on a "sensitive list" which excluded them from reductions. Bangladesh has over 1,200 such goods on its list, but India only has 25 items on its list for imports from Pakistan and Sri Lanka, although it lists 695 for the other less-developed countries.

Other such customs unions or free trade areas affecting Emerging and Frontier Market economies include:

- ✔ The Common Economic Space (CES) of Russia, Belarus, and Kazakhstan
- ✔ The Central European Free Trade Area (CEFTA) of Bosnia, Serbia, Albania, Macedonia, Montenegro, Moldova, and Kosovo
- ✔ The Gulf Co-operation Council of Saudi Arabia, Bahrain, Kuwait, Oman, Qatar, and the United Arab Emirates (UAE)
- ✔ The ASEAN (Association of South East Asian Nations) Free Trade Area (AFTA) comprised of Brunei, Indonesia, Thailand, the Philippines, Malaysia, Singapore, Vietnam, Laos, Cambodia, and Myanmar

While belonging to a free trade area or even better, a customs union, is not an invariable guarantee that the country is willing to embrace reform (Myanmar was admitted to ASEAN as long ago as 1997), it does usually serve as a reliable indicator that the rulers of a country can see the connection between reduced customs barriers, economic growth, and reforms.

Low valuations

Perhaps the most important factor to consider when looking at Frontier Markets from an investor's point of view is that they are reasonably valued. In fact, you could argue that they're pretty cheap, as many stock markets sell for Price/Earnings (P/E) ratios of around ten times last year's earnings and have a dividend yield of over 4 percent.

We give this definition of valuation a couple of times in this book, but it's worth explaining it here because valuation is a major part of the argument in favor of investing in Frontier Markets.

A company is usually valued by dividing its share price by its earnings per share (EPS), which are found by taking its net earnings (profits) after paying taxes and dividing that by the number of shares the company has in issue. Thus if a company earned $100 million in 2012, and had 100 million shares in issue, its EPS would be 100/100 = $1.00 a share. You can find these numbers in a company's annual or quarterly report, or on its website, which will usually provide earnings and EPS for the last few years.

Then you take its share price, which for the sake of argument is $15, and divide that by its EPS. Thus 15/1 = 15, and the company has a P/E ratio of 15 times last year's (historic) earnings. This suggests that it is fairly valued; generally companies find it difficult to grow their earnings more than 15 percent per annum on a sustainable basis.

If a stock has a P/E ratio of 20 or higher, it will usually be a fast-growing company in a fashionable industry such as technology or healthcare. If the P/E ratio is ten times or less, it generally means that the company is in a slow growth sector such as utilities or pipelines, or is in a cyclical industry such as airlines or energy and materials. That kind of industry experiences sharp fluctuations in its revenues and earnings and therefore is not as attractive to investors.

Frontier Markets generally sell at attractive valuations, because until 2012–2013 they had not risen much after their sharp fall in 2008–2009. Meanwhile their underlying economies and the companies operating in them had seen strong increases in GDP, sales, and earnings.

The MSCI Frontier Markets 100 Index had a P/E ratio of 15.9 times 2012's earnings at the end of September 2013, a dividend yield of 4.1 percent, and a P/B ratio (Price/Book Value) of 2.6 times. Compare this to a P/E ratio of 18.0 times for the MSCI Emerging Markets Index, a dividend yield of 1.8 percent, and a P/B of 3.0 times. Thus the MSCI is selling at a discount of 15 percent of the slower growing Emerging Markets index and with a dividend yield more than twice as high.

Furthermore this valuation is inflated by the high weight in the Frontier Index of Qatar, the UAE, and Kuwait, which rose more than 50 percent between September 2012 and September 2013. That occurred partially in anticipation that Qatar and the UAE would be upgraded to Emerging Market status. This new status was confirmed in May 2013 and becomes effective in May 2014.

Looking at some of the largest stock markets remaining in the Frontier Index at the end of September 2013, Pakistan was selling at a P/E of 9.8 times 2012's earnings and 1.8 times P/B, Sri Lanka at 11.5 times P/E and 1.5 times P/B, and Vietnam at 12.3 times P/E and 1.7 times P/B. The Guggenheim Frontier Markets ETF, which has an 85 percent weight in Latin American markets, had a P/E ratio of 10 times at the end of September 2013 and a P/B of 1.5 times.

The Next Eleven (N-11) Nations and the CIVETS

Goldman Sachs economist Jim O'Neill coined the well-known BRIC acronym in a research paper in 2003 to describe the four largest Emerging Market economies of Brazil, Russia, India, and China. In 2005, he came up with another and less memorable acronym (sometimes called a *numeronym*), the N-11 (Next Eleven). It described the next group of emerging economies that Goldman Sachs believed had a high potential, along with the BRICs, to become the world's largest economies in the 21st century.

The Next Eleven (N-11) are the following economies:

- Bangladesh
- Egypt
- Indonesia
- Iran
- Mexico
- Nigeria
- Pakistan
- Philippines
- South Korea
- Turkey
- Vietnam

These countries all have large, generally young populations, hence large domestic markets. They also have sizeable stock markets and are embracing economic reforms.

As we have been discussing, Frontier Markets such as Bangladesh, Nigeria, Pakistan, and Vietnam have small stock markets with limited liquidity, so attempting to move even reasonable amounts of funds into and especially out of these countries would present lots of difficulties.

MIST (Mexico, Indonesia, South Korea, and Turkey)

The MIST countries — Mexico, Indonesia, South Korea, and Turkey — are the four largest members of the Next Eleven by size of GDP. At the end of 2011, the MIST countries had 73 percent of the N-11 GDP, at $3.9 trillion, which amounted to almost 30 percent of the BRICs' $13.9 trillion GDP.

Comprised of two advanced democracies, Mexico and South Korea, which are members of the Organization of Economic Development (OECD), a high level Emerging Market in Turkey and a mid-level Emerging Market in Indonesia, there is not a great deal of similarity between these four countries. That makes any attempt to put them together as an investment theme even less sensible than the BRICs.

Turkey, Mexico, and South Korea are all geographically close to major economies in the European Union, the United States, and Japan. A large number of Mexican and Turkish citizens work in the larger economies so the first two countries benefit from inward investment from their larger neighbors. Indonesia and Mexico both have large natural resources, especially oil and gas, while Turkey and South Korea are resource importers.

Coining catchy acronyms or *numeronyms* is a good way to get publicity and attract investors' attention to an investment sector that may have been unfairly neglected or ignored. As an investment thesis, however, an actively managed global Frontier Markets fund gives the manager the flexibility to invest in those countries he or she feels are attractive rather than ones that go into making a neat acronym.

CIVETS

A great example of what the desire to coin a catchy acronym can produce is the CIVETS (Colombia, Indonesia, Vietnam, Egypt, Turkey, and South Africa). This gem was coined by Robert Ward, global director of the Global Forecasting Team of the Economist Intelligence Unit and publicized by Michael Geoghegan, president of HSBC Bank in a speech in Hong Kong in 2010.

In case you aren't familiar with the civet, it's a carnivorous mammal found in Indonesia that eats and partially digests coffee cherries. When excreted they fetch a high price due to the transformation that has occurred while going through the civet's digestive system. The idea behind using the civet as a an acronym presumably is that the process of industrialization and urbanization occurring in these developing markets transforms their existing natural resources into something worth a lot more, despite the messy process involved. A similar phenomenon was described during the Industrial Revolution by Yorkshire industrialists who observed, "Where there's muck (dirt) there's brass (money)." In other words, it required the pollution produced by factories and mills to create wealth.

These countries have somewhat more commonality than the N-11, with four of them being natural resource producers and only one (Vietnam) considered a Frontier Market rather than an Emerging Market. There is still not much more in common between them other than young populations, fast-growing econo-mies, and some intellectual capital, especially in Colombia, Egypt, Turkey, and South Africa.

Exotic Frontier Markets

Do you feel that Frontier Markets are fairly risky and volatile and that you need a long-term approach to allow you to benefit from the excellent prospects in these economies? Well, welcome to Exotic Frontier Markets, which are generally described as Frontier Markets that don't have even the same limited liquidity and regulation possessed by regular Frontier Markets!

In addition, this group of markets also includes a number of countries which actually have fairly large liquid and well-developed financial markets, but that for one reason or another are off-limits to foreign investors. In essence, it would be fair to describe these countries as those where there are barriers to entry, due to poverty, small size, lack of a stock market, or government restrictions.

Table 3-3 list some of the larger Exotic Frontier Markets and then examines which category they fall into.

Table 3-3	The Larger Exotic Frontier Market Countries (2012)		
Country	*Urbanization (%)*	*GDP per Capita ($000)*	*Stock market Capitalization ($bn)*
Iran	79.8	13,100	107.2 (2011)
Myanmar	55.2	1,400	NA
Tanzania	48.3	1,700	1.5 (2011)
Iraq	31.9	4,600	4.0 (2011)
Saudi Arabia	26.9	25,700	338.9 (2011)
Angola	18.6	6,800	NA
Cambodia	15.2	2,400	NA
Zimbabwe	13.2	500	10.9 (2011)
Laos	6.7	3,000	NA
Cuba	11.1	10,200	NA

Of these ten countries with a population of almost 300 million, the two which stand out in terms of stock market capitalization are Iran and Saudi Arabia, while five countries have no investable stock markets at all.

Overcoming barriers to entry

All of these Frontier Markets and others not included here, such as the Democratic Republic of the Congo, Belarus, Ethiopia, Bolivia, Ivory Coast, Mozambique, Mongolia, Kyrgyzstan, and Algeria, have barriers to entry.

A number of sub-Saharan African nations and Communist and Former Soviet Union countries have no stock markets. Some have very few companies listed, such as Laos and Sierra Leone, each of which have only two listings. In cases such as Saudi Arabia, foreigners are not permitted to own shares in local companies.

Limited stock markets

It's no surprise that Communist countries shouldn't have stock markets. After all they don't believe in capitalism and private ownership of property. The fact that two of the four remaining Communist countries — China and Vietnam — *do* have vibrant stock markets goes to show that pragmatism often trumps politics. It should be noted that several different Asian stock exchanges are bidding for the chance to establish a stock exchange in Myanmar now that the junta is loosening control. Observers expect that Cuba will rapidly establish a stock market should the Castro brothers ever step down.

Restrictions on foreign purchases of equities

Saudi Arabia is the crown jewel in this category, as it has by far the largest stock market among Frontier Markets with a market capitalization of over US$330 billion at the end of 2012. However, foreign investors are not permitted to own shares in Saudi-domiciled companies directly, so Saudi Arabia is classified as an Exotic Frontier Market.

Some investment banks have found a way to permit foreign investors to own Saudi companies through *Participation certificates* (P-certs or P-notes), which give the foreign investor the performance of the underlying share by buying shares through their Saudi subsidiaries. This has allowed some foreign investors and global and Middle East frontier funds to buy exposure to Saudi stocks.

There are constant rumors that the Saudi authorities will open up the Tadawul, as the Saudi stock market is known, to let foreigners buy stock directly. However, at the time of writing in November 2013, this has not occurred. One of the issues delaying matters is the need to set up settlement of shares on a two- or three-day basis after the trade, rather than overnight, as is the case at present.

When the Tadawul does finally open up, Saudi Arabia will immediately become the biggest stock market in the Frontier Market universe and should expect to see large foreign inflows.

Sanctions

The major market affected by sanctions is Iran, one of the N-11 markets identified by Jim O'Neill at Goldman Sachs. Due to its program of developing nuclear weapons capacity facilities over the last decade, it has been subjected to sanctions from the United States, Canada, and the European Union. These restrictions have prevented citizens of these countries from conducting business with the Iranian regime.

Given its large, youthful, and well-educated populace and its enormous reserves of oil and natural gas, Iran is an attractive economy from a long-term investment perspective. A tentative agreement was signed in November 2013 between Iran and the major western countries such as the United States and the European Union, along with Russia. In this agreement, the western powers agreed to temporarily suspend some sanctions for 6 months, in exchange for Iran committing not to develop weapons grade plutonium from its nuclear program. If this initial rapprochement leads to further relaxation of sanctions, Iran could become one of the largest Frontier Markets in the next few years.

Low levels of development or income

The obvious candidates for the Exotic Frontier Markets category are those countries which are even less developed and poorer than the investable Frontier Markets. Some of these may combine this status with an unwelcoming attitude to foreign investments. Bolivia, despite a GDP per capita of $5,200 per annum in PPP terms, is regarded as an Exotic Frontier Market largely due to President Evo Morales's nationalization of numerous industries during the last decade.

Of the countries listed in Table 3-3, Zimbabwe, Myanmar, Tanzania, and Cambodia have GDPs per capita of less than $2,400 per annum (p.a.), making them lower middle income by the World Bank definition. We can accurately classify any country in the low (less than $1,025 p.a.) or lower middle income $1,026–$4,035) with a stock market capitalization below US$10 billion as an Exotic Frontier Market.

This doesn't mean, as with Angola and Iraq, that there aren't countries with higher GDPs per capita also included in this category, just as larger countries with lower GDPs per capita, like Pakistan, Bangladesh, Nigeria, and Vietnam, are included in the more mainstream and investable Frontier Markets. This is largely a function of the size of their stock markets.

Anticipating growing investment appeal

As these countries become wealthier and climb up the GDP per capita tables, they will almost certainly become reclassified as mainstream Frontier Markets and become included in the MSCI and S&P Frontier Market indices. The formula for doing so is well known and the path is well traveled these days.

Most of Sub-Saharan Africa, the Former Soviet Union states in central Asia, parts of Eastern Europe and the Balkans, and most of North Africa are still considered no-go areas for even experienced Frontier Market investors.

Some might ask why go to the bother of researching a country that doesn't even have a stock market, since there is no easy way to play it? Mostly because once the first companies start to trade even in small volumes, analysis becomes possible. With a suitably long-term horizon, you will probably be seeing companies from some of the countries from Table 3-3 in your frontier fund in the next five years.

Monitoring the most promising Exotic Frontier Markets

It's worthwhile keeping an eye out for news items on the countries from the list that are nearest to being investable. At the time of writing, that includes Saudi Arabia, where shares in the form of P-certs or the equivalent are already in the Top 10 holdings of the Templeton Frontier Markets Fund and HSBC Frontier Markets Fund. Should the Iranian regime ever change its tactics on the nuclear issue, as seems a possibility with the November 2013 agreement, Iran could find its way in as well.

Meanwhile in Iraq, mobile telephone companies must list 25 percent of their shares on the stock market, which has already doubled in size to over US$10 billion in market capitalization in 2013. Several Frontier Markets funds own a Singapore-listed Cambodian casino and hotel operator. Should Myanmar open a stock exchange, it would likely also land on the specialist frontier managers' radar screens as well.

Chapter 4

Reasons to Tackle the Frontier — Or to Flee

M ost people have heard the opening voiceover from the first *Star Trek* series. James T. Kirk, a.k.a. William Shatner, intones the mission of the starship *Enterprise* and its crew ". . . to boldly go where no man has gone before." "Space," he declares in his inimitable fashion, is "the final frontier."

Going beyond a frontier can be exciting because it brings with it the feeling of doing something new, different, and out of the ordinary. That applies to your investments as well as other areas of your life. Certainly, you do need ordinary investments, such as blue chip equities like banks, insurance companies, recession-proof retailers, and reliable mutual funds. Most likely, these holdings will form the core of your portfolio. However, combined with that core, we recommend some frontier holdings that you can leave in place for at least five years so that you can profit from the factors such as the opportunities for growth and the lack of correlation between developed and Frontier Markets that we discuss in other chapters.

Certainly going into any frontier region anywhere at any time requires a certain amount of boldness. We believe in investing in Frontier Markets for all the reasons that we outline throughout this book but we also want you to sleep at night. And we want you to feel positive about your investments.

Going boldly means having a good guide — in this case, your financial advisor. It also means going carefully, and that means using our baseline weighting of 5 percent to 10 percent of your total international investments for your frontier holdings. As we explain in other chapters, you can adjust the baseline up or down depending on factors such as risk tolerance, age, and retirement horizon. Generally, the greater your risk tolerance and the longer your retirement horizon, the higher you can go with the baseline; while the lower your risk tolerance and the shorter your retirement horizon the lower you might need to go with it.

With very few exceptions, though, we believe that most investors should have at least some global frontier equity holdings in their total portfolio. In other chapters, we discuss the different financial products with which you can invest in Frontier Markets, ranging from equities to bonds to exchange-traded funds, or ETFs, and (our preferred approach) Global Frontier Funds. In this chapter, we look at what Frontier Markets offer to your portfolio.

Frontier Markets: Viable for the Average Investor

Perhaps we should start this section by pointing out that at time of writing, the "average investor" doesn't have Frontier Markets in his or her portfolio. In fact, there really is no such thing as an "average investor." We are not average authors (perish the thought) and you are not an average employee or average self-employed professional. So we're directing our comments to the individual investor or pension manager who now has more access to more financial products including frontier investments than we could have dreamt in the late 1980s.

Until that time, investors had several main choices: the proverbial shoebox under the bed, bank accounts, government and municipal bonds. A lucky few had enough money to command a stockbroker's attention and could go that route.

However, beginning in the early 1980s, all that changed with the explosion of mutual funds offering every conceivable combination of holdings, ranging from core equity funds investing in blue chip stocks to funds investing in sectors such as resources and technology or telecommunications to international equity funds.

Embracing What Frontier Markets Offer to Your Portfolio

Embracing what Frontier Markets offer your portfolio means appraising the potential impact of the lack of correlation, the rising consumer class in these countries, their extensive natural resources, their increased political stability, and the unleashing of the economies in the former Communist bloc countries and then having the payoff in your portfolio!

Consider that these factors require an expert juggling act, which can most effectively be executed within the framework of an actively managed fund in which the portfolio manager has the freedom to make the necessary asset allocation decisions. When, for example, a war breaks out, he or she can quickly decide the best course of action. That isn't the case in a passive investment such as an exchange-traded fund designed to track a market capitalization weighted index.

Diversification

The principle of diversification is one of the concepts at the center of any discussion of asset allocation and asset allocation is at the center of any well-constructed investment plan. Put simply, asset allocation means not having all your eggs in one basket and frontier investments means that you can have more different types of eggs.

Lack of correlation

A lack of correlation may be the single most difficult concept for a non-professional investor. When we say that Frontier Market investments have a *lack of correlation* to developed markets and to each other, we mean that they don't move in sync with investments in developed markets and with each other.

You may remember (but you might like to forget) the political wrangling in Washington that occupied headlines and everyone's attention during the fall of 2013.

While the American stock market gyrated every time a news report suggested that the Republican Party and Democratic Party chieftains and the President had started edging closer to or further from a settlement on the issue of the debt ceiling, the markets in most frontier countries generally went unscathed. This occurred for two main reasons:

✔ Some of the Frontier Markets (generally regarded as a subset of the Emerging Markets) were isolated from the forces shaking the American market.

✔ Much of the economic strength of these markets is generated internally by their domestic consumption, which continued regardless of what was happening to the US economy.

The fact that things were weird in the United States and that many experienced commentators were deeply concerned about the chances of a default on its debt by the American government didn't mean that the same things were happening in Frontier Markets. Arguably, there was some overall nervousness in these markets during the American events of fall 2013, but little perceivable direct impact.

Reduction in volatility

Volatility is one of three things that work against what we call the *sleep at night* factor; the other two are political and economic risk (which is often confused with volatility), and the constant stream of headlines in the media, especially the ones that concern companies, regions, countries, or industries in which you have invested.

Put simply, volatility is the percentage change in your holdings on a daily, weekly, or monthly basis (those ups and downs you see in market charts), while risk refers to the possibility of permanent loss of your capital caused by the underlying factors that create some of the ups and downs.

Because Frontier Markets do not correlate with each other and with developed markets, you can reasonably expect that if part of your portfolio zigs, the other part will remain stable or even zag in the opposite direction.

Faster growth

In these markets, there are more opportunities for faster growth than available in the developed markets. This is due to a number of factors that differentiate the Frontier Markets from the developed economies and even from the more advanced Emerging Markets:

✔ **The attractive demographics.** Most of these countries have high birth rates and young populations. In contrast, the birth rates in some of the developed markets are negative (meaning that each couple is not necessarily having two children). This has worrisome implications for the future of developed economies and their ability to generate sufficient income and sales taxes to pay their bills.

- ✓ **The rising consumer class.** Most frontier economies have a growing consumer class that wants — and has become increasingly able to afford — the same consumer goods that individuals in developed nations enjoy.

- ✓ **Natural resources.** Many frontier countries have extensive natural resources, most notably oil, but also metals and minerals and food products that developed nations require in huge quantities.

- ✓ **Improving political stability.** With some obvious exceptions, many frontier countries, such as formerly war-torn African nations, are now peaceful and democratic or at varying stages of evolution toward democracy.

- ✓ **Growth in former Communist blocs.** Most of the former Communist bloc countries are at various points along the long road between a tightly planned, state-controlled economy and an open market economy. Many of them, such as Kazakhstan, with its oil reserves, have extensive natural resources. This is a historic time in the development of these countries and if you have a long-term investment horizon, you can share in the profitable journey of societies undergoing an evolution on a scale unlike anything else you are likely to see in your lifetime.

Increasing Your Familiarity with Frontier Markets

Do you remember when you were in grade school and some of the countries that we discuss here seemed so far away and perhaps a little hard to imagine? Those days have long since ended and you can now become familiar with Frontier Markets in any one of a long list of ways. Certainly we hope you will start with this book. We've written another book entitled: *Investing in Frontier Markets: Opportunity, Risk, and Role in an Investment Portfolio* (published by John Wiley & Sons), and we also produce a radio network program called *Emerging and Frontier Markets Investing.*

Everyone is different, of course, but you may find that your comfort level with Frontier Markets increases as you utilize these sources of information. It's not a question of how "familiarity breeds contempt"! It's more a question of how familiarity breeds comfort!

Other sources of information about Frontier Markets include:

- ✓ Television networks and their web portals.
- ✓ Web searches.
- ✓ Cable channels and their web portals.

- Mainstream publications such as *The New York Times, The Wall Street Journal, Financial Times,* and *Barrons* increasingly carry material on these markets.

- Some wire services allow public access to much of their material.

- Online libraries such as the one provided by the British Broadcasting Corporation.

- Radio networks such as National Public Radio.

- Publications such as *National Geographic* magazine.

- Materials from brokerage and financial planning companies.

- Universities often have non-credit evening classes in investing.

- Library videos.

- Consulates and embassies of these countries are often happy to send out materials.

- International conferences such as those held by the International Monetary Fund devote large portions of their time to Frontier Markets; they also provide detailed analyses throughout the year.

- Specialized financial and investing websites such as the one run by Morningstar Research.

- Fund companies such as Franklin Templeton have huge amounts of material on their websites.

Don't set yourself up for information overload. Settle on several sources and concentrate on them for as long as they seem satisfactory. After all, you want to do other things besides read about Frontier Markets. Still, your investment in these markets should include some of your time as well as your money. Look upon doing some of this reading as protecting your investment.

The impact of the Internet

There is little about the impact of the Internet that we can say here that has not been said already but it has a few specialized dimensions to add to the Frontier Markets investment equation:

- Even in the most remote of countries such as Sierra Leone and others, the populations have Internet access and they see and want the same consumer goods and technologies that we take for granted in the developed nations; that drives demand and therefore revenues of companies servicing those needs.

✔ The populations of Frontier and Emerging economies are also able to get information and disseminate different views through social media and instant messaging. The theory that the Arab Spring protests of 2011 were driven by social media on the Internet is an arguable — but popular — political concept. Certainly the authorities' suspension of wireless coverage in such countries as Iran and Egypt during the protests indicates that they thought the web was a major factor contributing to the unrest.

✔ The Internet means that frontier countries are no longer the hazy faraway images that we knew in grade school. You can get access to all manner of information at any time.

✔ The Internet also makes many sources, such as the online library of the British Broadcasting Corporation, instantly available.

✔ Immediacy means you know what's happening as it is happening. In the 1960s, immediacy meant hustling news film to a waiting airplane — how quaint by today's standards. Now you can see a political disturbance as it is actually happening.

As we stress in other chapters, the availability of on-the-spot news can also be a detriment if it unduly colors an investor's view of a faraway investment destination. Immediacy is one thing but balance is quite another thing.

The effect of the 24-hour news cycle

Many of the previous points about the impact of the Internet apply equally to the effect of the 24-hour news cycle. Additionally, the cycle leads to constant repetition of the same explosion in the same distant location, and for some, that may make a frightening tragedy even more frightening. No one disputes the tragic and historic nature of much of what you might see on tonight's newscast, but it is possible that the 24-hour news cycle works against keeping a perspective on what is happening thousands of miles away.

The wall-to-wall coverage of a tragedy, while it may boost ratings and provide the most exhaustive detail and while intellectually interesting, challenging, and largely accurate, may not provide the best basis for investment decisions.

The Rise of Indices: Appreciating Their Importance and Limitations

You've probably heard or read references to one or more stock indices in the news and often without an explanation of their role and function. Put simply, a stock index amounts to a list of stocks assembled in a group with their weighting assigned by the market capitalizations of the entities involved. The market capitalization is simply the number of shares issued by a company multiplied by their stock price. These stocks can vary by type, including:

- By size of company, such as *large cap,* which refers to large capitalization, or mid-cap, small cap, and micro-cap

- By sector or industry group, such as technology, construction, energy, and so forth

- By theme, such as agriculture

- By issue, such as sustainability

- By style, such as value, growth, return on equity, and so forth

- By country and region, such as developed markets, Emerging Markets, and Frontier Markets

Companies that create these indices are called index providers and major examples include:

- **MSCI Inc.,** which compiled the first global and international stock indices

- **FTSE,** the index compiler owned by the Financial Times of London

- **Dow Jones,** the creator of the venerable Dow Jones Industrial Index, started in 1896 and now part of media conglomerate News Corporation, which also owns *The Wall Street Journal* and *Barron's*

- **Standard & Poor's,** the credit rating group

- **Russell Investment Group,** one of the leading pension consultants

The terminology of indices crops up in newscasts often without clear explanation:

- When an index is rising or falling, it simply means that the sum total of the market capitalization of all the stocks in the index, whether the 30 companies in the Dow Jones or the 500 in the S&P 500 Index, is going up or down.

- ✔ When a newscaster says that a specific stock *outperformed* the index, he or she means that a company's shares performed better the than sum total of all the companies in the index. If shares in a company appreciated by 3 percent but the index (or collection of stocks) appreciated by 2 percent, the newscaster might have said that these shares outperformed the index by 1 percent.

- ✔ When a newscaster says that "S&P futures are pointed up before the market opens," he or she is referring to the sum total of the stocks within the S&P indices.

An exchange-traded fund, or ETF, tracks or mimics an index, meaning that with the exception of some nuances, in individual cases, the contents of the ETF reflect the stocks or countries mandated by the company that constructed the index. That leads to our statement that ETFs are passively managed — that they are designed to track the index after the payment of their (usually very low) fees, with nearly zero room for decision-making by a fund manager. By contrast, we term conventional mutual funds *actively managed,* meaning that the fund manager can actively change the holdings and weightings within the fund provided that the changes do not contravene the provisions of the fund's prospectus.

For purposes of understanding the concepts in this book, the most important indices are:

- ✔ The MSCI Emerging Markets Index
- ✔ The MSCI Frontier Markets Index

However, please note that the countries listed in the indices vary between index providers, a function of the judgments of their analysts. When a fund company selects an index on which to build its ETF, it may use an existing index or may contract with a provider for a custom-designed index. That in turn reflects the fund company's own analyses of economic forces combined with what it believes will interest the market — that is, *you* the investor. However the choice is made the central fact remains: When a fund such as an ETF is based on an index, the individuals running the fund have nearly zero room to change either the selection of equities or their weightings in the ETF.

The MSCI Emerging Markets Index

Not all indices rate all countries as either emerging or frontier.

Like other index providers, MSCI rates countries outside of developed nations as either emerging or frontier, depending on a series of factors that include the liquidity of its markets, the creditworthiness of the companies and governments, and the quality of reporting and governance.

At the time of writing, the MSCI Emerging Markets Index included the following countries:

- ✔ Brazil
- ✔ Chile
- ✔ China
- ✔ Colombia
- ✔ Czech Republic
- ✔ Egypt
- ✔ Hungary
- ✔ India
- ✔ Indonesia
- ✔ Malaysia
- ✔ Mexico
- ✔ Morocco
- ✔ Peru
- ✔ Philippines
- ✔ Poland
- ✔ Russia
- ✔ South Africa
- ✔ South Korea
- ✔ Taiwan
- ✔ Thailand
- ✔ Turkey

Here are a few things to keep in mind about this list:

- ✔ Colombia, Egypt, Morocco, Peru, and the Philippines are included in an expanded version of the MSCI Frontier Markets Index, known as the MSCI Frontier Emerging Markets Index.
- ✔ Effective November 2013, Morocco has been classified as a Frontier Market.
- ✔ Egypt has been put under observation from May 2013 by MSCI for a potential downgrade to Frontier Market status due to its political and financial crises.
- ✔ As of November 2013, Greece moves from developed status to emerging status due to its financial problems.

The MSCI Frontier Markets Index

At the time of writing, the MSCI Frontier Markets Index included the following countries:

- Argentina
- Bahrain
- Bangladesh
- Bulgaria
- Croatia
- Estonia
- Jordan
- Kazakhstan
- Kenya
- Kuwait
- Lebanon
- Lithuania
- Mauritius
- Nigeria
- Oman
- Pakistan
- Qatar
- Romania
- Serbia
- Slovenia
- Sri Lanka
- Tunisia
- Ukraine
- United Arab Emirates
- Vietnam

Here are a few notes about this list:

- ✔ Effective May 2014, Qatar moves from the Frontier Markets Index to the Emerging Markets Index.
- ✔ Effective May 2014, the United Arab Emirates move from the Frontier Markets Index to the Emerging Markets Index.

Approaching with Caution: Frontier Market Risks

Frontier Market investments — and investment destinations — do have risks. But those risks have much to do with our suggestion that these markets comprise between 5 percent and 10 percent of your total international equity holdings as a baseline weighting.

Before going into the types of risk, check out two of the most commonly confused words in the investment lexicon: *risk* and *volatility.* They are often used interchangeably. We can understand the confusion, but take a look at the two terms.

Volatility, in this context, signifies the extent of uncertainty about the value of a company, expressed by daily, weekly, or monthly movements in its share price. A variety of factors affect volatility, ranging from the political climate of the company's country of domicile; how liquid or illiquid its shares are due to how many are freely traded or how many trade each day; the tax treatment of its profits and dividends and how often it changes; and major financial developments in one or more of its major markets. These developments could include changes in interest rates, property prices, profits, or business confidence.

Risk is the extent to which the value of a company's shares might permanently erode, leading to a permanent loss of the investors' capital. A variety of factors, ranging from changes in the company's finances to its ability (or lack thereof) to roll with the punches in its product sector and to stay ahead of changes in technology, generate higher or lower degrees of risk. Unfavorable political changes such as nationalization, revolution, or the expropriation of foreign-held assets can lead to a sharp increase in risk. Where they occur, ineffective or harmful economic policies such as export taxes, money printing leading to high inflation, and punitively high levels of taxation add to the list of dangers.

The one thing that both risk and volatility do have in common is their impact on the sleep-at-night factor.

There are four main types of risk baked into many types of investments, including those based in Frontier Markets and elsewhere: investment risk, political and social risk, currency risk, and liquidity risk. The following sections take a look at each type of risk.

Investment risk

Investment risk refers to the hazards specifically connected to the shares of a specific company, such as:

- The quality of management
- The company's preeminence (or lack of it) in its product sector
- The effect of the company's debt load
- The company's relationships with its stakeholders, such as unions and customers
- The presence or absence of barriers to the entry of competitors
- The company's ability to keep a healthy pipeline of products being readied to come to market
- The company's risk management capabilities

Political and social risk

Political and social risk refers to factors that are not directly connected to the company but are sufficiently strong in the surrounding environment to have an impact on its fortunes. These include:

- **The rule of law.** Knowing that the rules that govern how your investment is treated will be followed and that contracts signed by the company in which you've bought shares will be honored is one of the most important factors to consider when investing in a country or region. It's noticeable that the majority of the Frontier Markets considered attractive usually have common law systems like the United Kingdom and the United States.
- **The country's stability.** Formerly unstable African nations are now considered much more stable than decades earlier.
- **The presence or absence of militant groups.** If we use the Middle East as an example, at the time of writing, Egypt, Syria, Lebanon, and Libya were embroiled in political crises but the United Arab Emirates, Qatar, and several other nations in the region are stable investment destinations.

✔ **The proximity to countries in crisis.** At the time of writing, Turkey was relatively stable politically and socially but its economy appeared threatened by the influx of refugees from Syria.

✔ **The presence or absence of corruption in senior levels of government.**

Currency risk

Currency risk refers to the potential for costs when transactions involve more than one currency. These risks can occur in several ways:

✔ Through the company's own transactions

✔ Through whether it retains revenues in a foreign market or repatriates them to its home market, such as the United States

✔ Through charges levied by financial institutions involved in the transactions

✔ Through the exposure of a country's currency to speculation

Liquidity risk

Liquidity risk refers to the ease or difficulty, speed, and complexity involved in transactions. Most Frontier and some Emerging Markets are still relatively illiquid, meaning that it is difficult to buy large amounts of equities quickly and almost impossible to sell them quickly. One of the major issues for investors in these markets is the settlement of trades on the stock market. Many countries lack a central electronic market, and trades have to be settled by the movement of physical stock certificates between parties to the transaction.

A month-long systems delay

Gavin was managing funds investing in Indonesia when it began opening up to foreign investors in 1989. He received a request from his main broker dealing in that market to stop trading for the next month. When he asked why, he was told that the sudden increase in the volume of trades in the Jakarta stock exchange had totally overwhelmed the settlement systems of the local brokers who were dealing for the various foreign investors. The broker had to send a couple of extra staff from its Singapore office to sit in the bank vault of its custodian bank and sort out all the unsettled trades, which they estimated would take them a month!

Incidentally, one of the extra staff was a gentleman named Nick Leeson, who later became famous (or notorious) for helping effectively bankrupt his employer, Barings Bank, through unsuccessful futures trades in 1995.

Then there are issues with finding suitable custodian banks to hold the shares in the company once they have been bought. Usually it is not practical for investors to begin trading in these markets until a major international bank such as Citigroup or HSBC provides a custodian service, which guarantees that investors actually have ownership of shares that they have purchased.

The liquidity of the stock markets, even of relatively advanced nations such as Kazakhstan and Nigeria, is much lower than that of developed markets or even the major Emerging Markets such as China, India, and Brazil. As a result, many companies choose to list their shares in the form of ADRs and GDRs, not only locally but also on developed markets such as New York and London. They not only have a higher investor profile and have their report and accounts audited to international standards, but also they are often more liquid and trade more shares than they do on their local stock markets. Some Exotic Frontier Markets such as Sierra Leone and Laos only have a couple of stocks listed and they may only trade a few days a week, an activity level much less than we expect in developed markets.

Recognizing the Hurdle of Home Bias

Perhaps one of the most serious hurdles that you may have to overcome is the hesitation to invest outside your home turf. Getting over the hurdle of home bias means getting past the comfort and implied restriction of choosing investments solely based on whether they are familiar and based in your country. Investing only in a well-known company whose products you have used for most of your life is *home bias*. The investor who doesn't overcome the hurdle of home bias is, by definition, canceling out the investment yields provided by the Frontier Markets of Africa and some of Asia, most of which had high growth during the last decade. That leads to opportunity cost, which is an estimate of the number of dollars missed by not putting some money into those markets.

A first step to overcoming some of this home bias may be to invest in an Emerging Market fund such as the Templeton Emerging Markets Fund. While it is likely that the period of greatest out-performance against developed markets may have already occurred, as they effectively did twice as well as the MSCI World Index over the decade ending in 2012, they still offer many attractive opportunities for investors and contain many world class companies, some of which may be familiar to you.

Such groups as technology companies like Samsung, HTC, Acer, and Lenovo, software and outsourcing leaders like Infosys or Wipro, or automotive manufacturers like Hyundai, Jaguar/LandRover (owned by India's Tata Group), or Volvo (owned by China's Geely group) are among the leading global companies in their fields. Owning an Emerging Markets fund gives an investor exposure to these success stories and some insight into how the process of economic development can transform a country within a generation. Seeing the process at work gives you confidence in the ability of other less-developed countries to follow in their footsteps.

You may also find yourself able to deal with the home bias hurdle by making greater use of the sources of information that we list in "Increasing Your Familiarity with Frontier Markets." Your comfort level with Frontier Markets investing will increase in proportion to your familiarity with it.

Part II
Examining Issues Affecting Frontier Market Performance

Top Three Questions to Ask Yourself Before Investing Overseas

- ✔ Will I be able to invest my money freely?
- ✔ Will I be able to get my money back when I want it without restrictions on when I get it?
- ✔ How much will I lose in taxes and charges?

Visit www.dummies.com/extras/frontiermarkets for more information on evaluating Frontier Markets.

In this part. . .

- ✔ Get a handle on the politics of Frontier Markets.
- ✔ Spot the key players in Frontier Markets.
- ✔ Understand different banking systems.
- ✔ Discover your foreign allies.
- ✔ Understand the risk of corruption in some Frontier Markets.
- ✔ Learn about the relationship between income disparity and consumer consumption.
- ✔ Examine laws about foreign investment.
- ✔ Find out why currencies and exchange rates matter in the Frontier Markets equation.
- ✔ Use audited reports when making investment decisions.

Chapter 5

Political Systems and Market Players

C onsidering the political system of a country in which you are thinking of investing would seem to be a basic precaution. Yet as in Emerging and Frontier Markets, the political complexion of the government doesn't necessarily dictate how well the economy and stock market perform. Ordinarily, an investor would expect that a democratic regime, with its ability to change governments and the free flow of information, would do better than more autocratic regimes such as monarchies and dictatorships. This isn't always the case.

Thus, among the frontier economies that appear to be the most attractive, and which we list at the end of the book, you find one of the few Communist regimes left standing as well as several democracies. The wealthiest frontier states with the largest stock markets are the emirates of the Persian Gulf, while several countries that were considered to be developed economies half a century ago but have since fallen to frontier status are democracies.

It doesn't make good investment sense to exclude certain countries from consideration simply because of the nature of their ruling regimes. In this chapter, we show you that just as there are good airlines in a sector that's known as having been a dreadful industry for investors, even regimes that officially disapprove of the idea of private property can prove to be rewarding investments. Just think about China. It all depends on the attitude of the ruling elite. Do they want the economy to grow, and therefore willing to surrender some control, or are they determined to retain power even if the country is reduced to poverty, as has been the case in Myanmar (formerly Burma) and Zimbabwe?

Parsing a Nation's Politics

The political system of a Frontier Market is one of the most important factors that investors have to consider when deciding where it makes sense to invest their hard-earned dollars. As with all such decisions about investing overseas, the underlying questions are:

- ✔ Will I be able to invest my money freely?
- ✔ Will I be able to get it back when I want it without restrictions on when I get it?
- ✔ How much will be taken in taxes and charges?

These are pretty basic matters and any country that makes it difficult to invest money and freely reclaim it falls to the bottom of the list of potential investment destinations. With all the other uncertainties that accompany investing in Emerging and Frontier Markets, the last thing investors need are concerns over whether they can retrieve their funds or whether their holding will be taken away from them against their will.

We should distinguish between the normal difficulties of investing money in Emerging and Frontier Markets, such as finding a local stock broker, setting up a local bank account, getting access to company reports and accounts in a timely fashion, and the costs of doing transactions. Some Frontier Markets can run as high as 3 percent or even more. It's a long way from $9.99 trades with your online discount broker!

These factors, however, are part and parcel of dealing in these markets. They go with the territory and are one of the reasons that these countries' stock markets sell at cheap valuations. These factors also partially explain why these markets are not correlated with major markets, meaning that they don't move in line with them. Thus, adding some Frontier Markets to your portfolio can reduce its overall volatility, even though they are quite volatile.

In this chapter, we cover the effect that different types of political regimes can have on your investments, and the possibility of losing substantial amounts of money due to the actions of the local government.

Appreciating the importance of freedom

When you live in a prosperous democracy like the United States, it can sometimes be easy to take the basic democratic freedoms, such as freedom of speech, of religion, and of free assembly, for granted. American investors need to remember that these freedoms were hard won, need to constantly be maintained against erosion, and don't exist for a large percentage of the world's population, including some of the largest and most economically successful nations.

Transparency of information

The basis of capitalism is transparency due to freedom of information. If investors cannot trust the numbers produced by companies in which they are investing, the market system would grind to a halt. How do you know how to value a company, or what its shares are worth, if you have no reliable means of ascertaining its revenues and profits or assets and liabilities? The information also needs to be timely; it's no use finding out that the company you just invested in plunged into losses nine months or a year ago.

The situation in many frontier economies is similar to what happened on Wall Street or in the City of London a century ago. Company insiders and well-connected parties such as their banking contacts, friends, and relations had much better and timelier information than the outside minority shareholders. Companies were not required to do more than publish their balance sheets, not their profit and loss accounts, and then only once or twice a year and then many months after the actual date to which the published balance sheets referred.

Because reports weren't required, share prices could easily be manipulated. Histories of the Roaring Twenties, such as John Brooks' *Once in Golconda,* are filled with stories of how well-connected insiders formed what were known as "blind pools." The pools bought positions in a company, usually a thinly traded one, spread rumors that a takeover or major positive piece of news was imminent, and then unloaded their stock on the unsuspecting small shareholders after the price had been run up. More recently, viewers of *The Sopranos* may recall Tony and his friends using the same tactics with a dodgy technology company during the NASDAQ bubble in 1999–2000.

Free elections

More importantly, political freedom means that the citizens of a country have the opportunity to change their government in a free election, so that the incumbents in power get challenged over instances of incompetence, corruption, or brutality. Human nature dictates that if there is no chance of being caught or punished for wrongdoing, people will continue to behave badly. This is perfectly logical behavior; after all, if you know that the consequences of taking bribes, allowing monopolies to continue or ignoring violent actions by the police or armed forces were, at worst, a metaphorical slap on the wrist and possibly some minor embarrassment, then chances are high you won't change your ways.

The exceptions in India and China

This is not to say that democracies are always the most efficient and successful form of government. There is a long-standing debate about the courses followed by the two most populous countries in the world, China and India, with the former an autocratic, officially Communist state and the latter a vibrant, noisy, and turbulent democracy.

China, with its one-party status and impressive physical infrastructure, but constrained human rights, is an example of how an autocratic regime can overcome opposition to necessary reforms from powerful vested interests that benefit from existing low-growth economic arrangements. In this view, the owners of property and facilities, including trade guilds and monopolies, have little or no interest in encouraging faster growth and function essentially as rent-takers (*rentiers* in Marxist terminology), who can exact high fees for the use of their land or resources.

However, as readers and viewers of *Spider-Man* know, with great power comes great responsibility. The Chinese regime has shown a willingness to override the wishes of its people when it deems it necessary, even if this involves widespread use of force. Such events as the suppression of the student protests in Tiananmen Square in 1989 or the forcible dispossession of several million local inhabitants to build the Three Gorges Dams in the 1990s or the effective banning of such Internet search engines as Google illustrate the downside of such an approach.

India, on the other hand, has a democratic system of government where power has changed hands several times in the last 30 years, a free press, and an independent, if somewhat slow and corrupt, legal system. However, this has allowed vested interests to obstruct or delay the building of necessary physical infrastructure, and the country suffers from a chronic shortage of power, ports, roads, and railways.

Some observers have remarked that while China has an impressive physical infrastructure in the form of new cities, railways, airports, and power stations, it lacks an intellectual infrastructure in the form of rule of law, respect for property rights, and the free flow of information. India is almost a mirror image, and it's notable that its export industries tend to include higher valued-added products in areas such as generic pharmaceuticals, software, and service outsourcing compared with China's low value-added exports of basic goods such as textiles and footwear, electronics, and steel and aluminum.

Polishing your political savvy

Although we all might consider a functioning democracy the best and most transparent form of government, many Frontier Markets don't belong to the club of democratic nations. Some are still officially Communist, such as Vietnam, Laos, and Cuba; some are ruled by autocracies, which usually means a one-party state with varying degrees of political freedom. This category includes many of the members of the Former Soviet Union. It also includes some Middle East nations, some of which are still ruled by kings or emirs and some of which may be democratic in form, but have elements of one-party or one-tribe rule, such as much of sub-Saharan Africa.

This shouldn't dissuade you as an investor from considering putting money into these countries, either directly via a single country fund, or through a global Frontier Markets fund. What it does mean is that an awareness of the political background in the areas in which your fund invests is needed, so that a change of government due to popular protest as occurred in Egypt, Libya, and Tunisia during the Arab Spring is not a complete surprise.

In Chapter 3, we note the political nature of the regimes in the various frontier economies, and in Chapter 6, we discuss corruption and income disparities which may lead to political unrest. Putting this information together should help you to get some feel for which regions have a higher likelihood of experiencing regime change in the near future.

Monarchies

It may come as a surprise to many North American investors, but there are still a few countries outside of the United Kingdom, Japan, Scandinavia, and the Low Countries (the Netherlands, Belgium, and Luxemburg) where what someone described as "being a member of the lucky sperm club" is enough to qualify you to be the ruler of your country.

These countries still have monarchs, whether described as kings, sultans, or emirs, and are all concentrated in the Middle East and North Africa. The islands of the Pacific which still have monarchs have economies that are too small to be investable.

Table 5-1 lists the countries with hereditary rulers (leaving out North Korea and the Kim dynasty and Cuba with the Castro brothers).

Table 5-1	Frontier Market Countries with Monarchies		
Country	*Population (m)*	*GDP per capita ($000)*	*Market Capitalization ($bn)*
Saudi Arabia	26.9	25.7	338.9 (2011)
Morocco	32.6	5.4	60.9 (2011)
UAE	5.5	49.0	93.8 (2012)
Kuwait	2.7	43.8	100.9 (2012)
Qatar	2.0	102.8	125.4 (2012)
Jordan	6.5	6.1	27.0 (2012)
Bahrain	1.3	29.2	17.1 (2011)
Oman	3.2	29.6	19.7 (2011)

The major features that emerge from this table are that with the exception of Morocco and Saudi Arabia, all these countries are fairly small in terms of population and with the same exceptions are all fairly wealthy. In fact, Gulf Co-Operation Council members Kuwait, Qatar, and the United Arab Emirates (UAE) rank among the wealthiest countries in the world.

They also all have reasonably sized stock markets, and Kuwait, Qatar, and the UAE comprise over 60 percent of the MSCI Frontier Markets Index, as the large size of their markets offsets their small populations. Saudi Arabia is not included in the MSCI Frontier Markets Index because it does permit direct investment by foreigners, but would immediately become the largest weight in the index when and if it's finally included.

Just to show that nothing is set in stone, Morocco was classified by MSCI as an Emerging Market until November 2013, and Qatar and the UAE will be upgraded from Frontier to Emerging Market status in May 2014.

All monarchies classified as Frontier Markets are located in the Middle East and North Africa, a legacy of the colonial era when the ruling powers of Britain and France chose ruling through local leading families as the simplest way of maintaining control. Saudi Arabia and Morocco were never directly colonized and Jordan and the GCC countries were effectively British protectorates, but not colonies. While these regimes have proved surprisingly resilient, there is no reason why monarchs cannot be overthrown, as occurred with King Faisal in Egypt in 1952, King Faisal II in Iraq in 1958, King Idris in Libya in 1969, and most famously and recently, the Shah of Iran in 1979. Although it had been 35 years since the last dethroning of a king in Saudi Arabia, Islamic rebels seized the Great Mosque in Mecca in 1979, a direct threat to the Saudi royal family whose claim to the throne depends at least in part on their role as defender of the holy places. Likewise, unrest by Shiite inhabitants of Bahrain in 2011 as part of the Arab Spring led to a crackdown by the security forces.

The legitimacy of the regimes in Saudi Arabia and the Gulf is due to their ability to provide improving living standards to compensate for a lack of democratic rights, although all these states have councils or parliaments which allow some expressions of popular feeling. Jordan and Morocco are much poorer and less able to buy off their populations, but the ruling family has been established for almost a century in Jordan and over two centuries in Morocco and has generally been competent and efficient in running the country.

Communist regimes and autocracies

The other group of nondemocratic countries are those that still have Communist regimes, which, despite holding elections, only permit election of members of the Communist ruling regime or those who are affiliated with them. You can see the list in Table 5-2. This group also includes some regimes best described as autocratic — that is authoritarian or one-party but not officially Communist, such as the military junta that has ruled Myanmar (formerly Burma) since 1962, or the members of the FSU like Kazakhstan and Belarus which have a dominant leader.

The fact that a country is officially Communist does not prevent it being a suitable investment. You only have to look at China's progress over the last 35 years to see that. Thus Vietnam is probably one of the most attractive Frontier Markets, given its large young population, large domestic market, and its well-established stock exchange which has been in existence for over 20 years. Laos's economy is much smaller and its stock exchange only has two stocks at the time of writing, but it is right next door to Vietnam and tends to follow its example, so it too may prove a rewarding investment.

Table 5-2	Frontier Market Communist Regimes and Autocracies		
Country	*Population (m)*	*GDP per capita ($000)*	*Market Capitalization ($bn)*
Vietnam	92.5	3.5	38.2 (2012)
Myanmar	55.2	1.4	NA
Kazakhstan	17.7	13.9	35.6 (2012)
Cuba	11.1	10.4	NA
Laos	6.7	3.0	NA
Belarus	9.6	15.9	NA
North Korea	24.2	1.8	NA
Eritrea	6.2	0.8	NA
Iran	79.8	13.1	107.2 (2012)

The first point to note about these countries is that Communism is not generally good for your wealth. Although some countries, such as Vietnam and Laos, have gross domestic product figures equivalent to those of their neighbors at the same stage of economic development, North Korea is one of the poorest countries on Earth. Myanmar is even worse off, proving that you don't need to be Communist to run an economy into the ground.

Cuba's relatively high GDP per capita can be attributed to the fact that Castro did not take over until 1959, and its popularity as a tourist destination for wealthy European, Canadian, and Latin American countries. Belarus benefits from its status as an East European economy with natural resources, a factor that also accounts for Kazakhstan's and Iran's high levels of personal income.

Only Vietnam, Iran, and Kazakhstan have stock markets of any note, making this group of countries almost impossible to access for the investor. It should be noted, however, that several different countries are bidding to develop a stock exchange for Myanmar, now that the junta has begun to liberalize by releasing opposition leader Nobel Prize winner Aung Sang Suu Kyi in 2012 and allowing relatively free elections for some of the seats in parliament.

While this group of countries contains a couple of attractive possibilities in Vietnam and Kazakhstan, over all, their isolated economies are too poor or the regimes running them too unwilling to surrender control by permitting economic growth through liberalization to make the others worth considering at this stage. It's worth keeping an eye on Myanmar, where the recent opening up by the junta could lead to a flowering such as that seen in Vietnam in the early 1990s and China in the 1980s. Iran would be by far the largest of these stock markets and economies if it became open to foreign investors, pending resolution of sanctions due to its nuclear development program.

Socialist governments

Socialist governments are those regarded as left wing by observers in their approach to the economy. This usually means they are in favor of tight regulation of businesses in order to rein in perceived exploitation of the consumer, high taxes to redistribute income, and high social spending to address inequalities such as poor schooling and substandard housing.

In general those in power are elected in free elections, surrender power when defeated, and attempt to follow the course of many western European governments over the last century. In the U.K., for example, between 1945 and 1951, the post-World War II Labor government introduced the National Health Service, nationalized a number of industries such as coal, steel, electricity, railways, and road and air transport and took over the Bank of England, the country's central bank. In France under Francois Mitterrand in 1981, the socialist party partially nationalized the banking industry and the French state owns stakes in such industrial firms as automaker Renault, as well as the gas and electricity industries. Of course, the American government did the same thing with General Motors in 2008 (Government Motors)!

Therefore, just as with Communist countries, socialist regimes are not an ideal investment destination, and worth watching closely because their instincts are to regulate and tax, which is not an environment that encourages investment or growth. If the economy is not performing well, there may be a tendency to blame foreign investors and expropriate their holdings such as happened in several South American economies like Argentina, Bolivia, and Venezuela, and described in more detail in Chapter 6. Socialist Frontier Markets are listed in Table 5-3.

Table 5-3	Frontier Market Countries with Socialist Governments		
Country	**Population (m)**	**GDP per capita ($000)**	**Market Capitalization ($bn)**
Argentina	42.6	18.2	43.6 (2012)
Venezuela	28.5	13.2	5.1 (2012)
Ecuador	15.4	8.8	5.8 (2012)
Bolivia	10.5	5.2	7.7 (2012)
Nicaragua	5.8	4.5	NA
Costa Rica	4.7	12.8	1.4 (2012)
Zimbabwe	13.2	0.6	10.9 (2011)

Almost all the countries in Table 5-3 are located in South or Central America, a wealthier continent than either Asia or Africa. It includes several fallen giants such as Argentina and Venezuela, which were regarded as developed countries a generation or two ago. Indeed Argentina was one of the wealthiest countries in the world a century ago, as wealthy as France and ahead of Sweden and Denmark in income per capita.

Its decline to Frontier Market status, discussed in more detail in Chapter 6, is a sad story of bad government from Juan and Eva Peron in the 1940s onward. Similarly, Venezuela, despite being a major oil producer, has been reduced to importing oil. That occurred as its infrastructure crumbled over the last 15 years under the late Hugo Chavez's populist regime. Both countries, as well as Bolivia, have nationalized large portions of their economies as a means of diverting attention from their economic failures by blaming the foreigners and the wealthy for their problems.

Some socialist regimes such as Costa Rica have successfully carried out their programs of social reform and sharply reduced poverty and inequality while addressing the lack of education and sanitation. However, regimes such as Costa Rica's neighbor Nicaragua have struggled to deliver on their promises and carried out divisive social policies of redistribution at the expense of economic growth.

Ironically, the poorest country on the list, and one of the poorest in the world, Zimbabwe, has the second biggest stock market among the socialist countries, owing to its experience of hyperinflation in 2007–2009. The stock market, as in Weimar, Germany, between 1922 and 1923, was the only asset that maintained the real value of savings as inflation soared to 6.5 sextillion percent in November 2008. (Don't even try to guess what that number means!) Today, Zimbabweans still use the U.S. dollar, the South African rand, and the Euro as means of exchange.

Printing money in Zimbabwe

The government of former guerilla leader (and University of London graduate with a law degree) Robert Mugabe came to power in Zimbabwe's first election in 1980. When a policy of taking over white-owned farms and giving them to untrained and inexperienced supporters of his ZANU-PF party in 1999–2001 caused farm output to fall 45 percent, the economy and the banking system collapsed. Industrial output fell by 25 percent for three successive years between 2005 and 2007, unemployment soared to 80 percent, and even life expectancy fell.

The government reacted by printing money to make up for the collapse in export earnings from agriculture and to pay for its involvement in the civil war in the Democratic Republic of the Congo (DRC) in the early 2000s. This led to hyperinflation, with the annual inflation rate reaching 11.2 *million* percent in June 2008 and 79.6 million percent a *month* in November 2008. At that point, the government abandoned the national currency and replaced it with foreign currencies. Playing with a printing press is great fun initially, just like drinking, but continued for too long, it can have disastrous effects.

Socialist or quasi-socialist economies are usually wealthy enough to afford the high taxes and income redistribution practiced by their governments, who almost always attain power peacefully via the ballot box. This doesn't prevent them from following policies that discourage growth and investment. While there are occasional success stories like Costa Rica, which abolished its army 60 years ago and spent the money on social reform, in most cases the countries have gone backward or at best marked time.

It's notable that Argentina, Venezuela, and Zimbabwe are all poorer than they were a decade ago, and Bolivia, Ecuador, and Nicaragua have about the same level of GDP per capita. The size of their stock markets tells its own story. Despite having populations in excess of ten million, Bolivia, Ecuador, and Venezuela have market capitalizations below $10 billion.

Democracies

It is difficult to generalize about Frontier Market democracies. They range in size from Nigeria, Pakistan, and Bangladesh with 170 million, 193 million, and 162 million inhabitants, respectively, ranking among the ten largest countries in the world by population. This group also includes such small though relatively well-off southern Africa states as Botswana and Namibia with just over 2 million people each, and the Baltic states of Estonia, Latvia, and Lithuania with 1.3 million, 2.3 million, and 3.5 million, respectively. None of the East European Frontier Markets has a population of more than 10 million except Romania (21.8 million) and Ukraine (44.5 million).

All these Eastern European states are democratic, although some of the FSU countries in the Caucasus region, such as Azerbaijan, Armenia, and Georgia, have been criticized for the conduct of their elections. The attraction for the former Soviet satellites is entry into the European Union and becoming associate members and trading partners before full membership. This requires a functioning democracy and ensures that elections are perceived as being free and fair by outside observers.

Other regions with democracies include South Asia, with Pakistan, Bangladesh, and Sri Lanka all being included in the list despite security concerns and violence around elections. South America has a number of countries which have emerged from populist periods in the 1970s and 1980s to be regarded as in good standing, such as Colombia, Peru, Paraguay, and Uruguay. The example set by Brazil in replacing a military government with a democracy and electing two former labor militants as President has helped validate the process.

Finally, sub-Saharan Africa has probably seen the greatest turnaround, with autocrats, military regimes, and Communist dictatorships being replaced by freely elected democracies that are encouraging investment and growth. This does not mean that There are not still a number of states that rank in the "failed" category. War-torn countries that have effectively ceased to exist like Somalia, artificial colonial constructions with rebel provinces like the DRC, or one-party states like Eritrea still appear, but the majority of the larger African nations are holding relatively free elections and experiencing peaceful changes in control.

There are too many democracies to list, which is an encouraging sign, but you will find the various types of regimes listed in the country statistical tables in the Appendix.

Most of the larger frontier stock markets outside of the wealthy Middle Eastern countries are found among the democracies, as one would expect. Pakistan, Bangladesh, Sri Lanka, Nigeria, Kenya, Colombia, Peru, Croatia, Romania, and Ukraine all had stock markets worth more than US$10 billion at the end of 2012, making them the largest among the Frontier Markets outside of the Middle East. It would be a reasonable conclusion that democracy and high stock market capitalization go together, although state-organized capitalism ("capitalism with Chinese characteristics" as it has been described) can also produce high stock-market-to-GDP ratios, as with Vietnam and China.

Staying informed to enhance your investment acumen

No one expects you to know the political ins-and-outs of relatively poor foreign countries. That's why we advise using an actively managed Global Frontier Markets fund to gain access. In this case, you let the fund manager and his or her team of analysts, many of whom will have been born or brought up in these countries, do the worrying about which minister has been found guilty of corruption or which tribe the head of the army belongs to and whether he's Christian or Muslim.

Nonetheless, being aware of the basic political story for a few of the larger countries in which the fund has holdings is not a bad idea. It means you're less likely to panic at news stories showing a riot or demonstration, like the ones in Turkey in 2013. A democracy like Turkey allows ventilation of frustration while autocratic regimes like Egypt or Syria have no such luxury and may stand or fall on how they deal with popular unrest.

Adding a couple of local English language newspapers to your search engine Favorites menu is a good way of becoming better informed about what's important to the locals. Newspapers such as the *Times of India*, the *Straits Times* in Singapore, *the South China Morning Post* from Hong Kong, or the *Nairobi Herald* in Kenya can give you a feel for the top issues in these regions. These publications can also alert you to something that the mainstream Western media may ignore or miss completely until it blows up on the front pages and news channels.

Spotting Other Key Players in Any Country

As observers of the North American political scene know, it's not just the political parties that set the agenda in politics. In Frontier and Emerging Markets, finding out the major players is an important step in working out what's driving legislation and who's behind the ascent and decline of various political parties and personalities.

Thus in Argentina, the legacy of the populist regime of Juan and Eva (Evita) Peron is still present 60 years after Evita's death, as evidenced by the stream of those wishing to pay their respects at her tomb in her father's family mausoleum in the exclusive Recoleta district of Buenos Aires. The present President, Cristina Kirchner, is a member of the Peronist party and succeeded her husband, Nestor Kirchner, just as Juan Peron's second wife Isabel did after his death in 1974.

The Peronist movement is hostile to foreign investment, and just as Peron nationalized several foreign industries like the railways, shipping, utilities, and public transportation in the 1940s, so Cristina Kirchner and her husband nationalized the national airline, the water utility, private pension funds, and the largest oil company between 2006 and 2012. Quite apart from discouraging foreign investment, this statist approach reflects the hostility of the labor-supported Peronist movement towards capitalism, whether local or foreign.

Therefore, you're sensible to look at companies which had funded or supported rivals to the Peronist candidate and anticipate that they would likely be subjected to intrusive tax audits, changes in regulation to disadvantage them, loss of licenses, reduced or difficult access to supplies and foreign exchange, and possible expropriation. Certain industries that the government sees as low priority because they don't provide much support to the government — particularly agricultural exporters — have found themselves hit with export taxes, the most damaging way for a government to raise funds.

Therefore, knowing where a company or sector stands in relationship to other major players in the political system can help you avoid some pitfalls. The following sections discuss areas where such knowledge is especially useful in working out what's happening.

Banking systems

Banks are essentially private-sector money creation machines. A bank can lend each dollar that it takes in deposits up to 12, 15, or even 20 times. Thanks to the magic of fractional banking, a bank is only required to keep a small percentage of its deposits in cash or short-term instruments to be available to pay out to customers who withdraw cash or need to have a check or draft paid out.

Therefore, the authorities tend to be pretty careful about whom they allow to have this privilege. Still, in the wild and woolly days of American banking in the 19th century, state-chartered banks were often allowed to set up freely during a boom since state governments valued anything that helped the growth of the commonwealth, such as ready access to liquidity to buy and develop land. Viewed from that perspective, the U.S. was an Emerging Market back then, and several states defaulted on their debts to international lenders in the 1830s.

Nowadays governments are more restrained in the manner in which they issue licenses, so a listed bank in an Emerging and Frontier Market will usually be well connected and have some important members of the ruling establishment on its board of directors. If the bank is state-controlled, as is the case with most of the Chinese banks and some of the Indian banks, there may be questions about its lending policies, as it may be required to lend to noncreditworthy but well-connected borrowers such as state-owned enterprises. This is why privately controlled banks are usually safer bets, as they still need to be in good order with the authorities, but don't have the state dictating their lending practices.

Powerful business dynasties

A family that has been successful enough in a developing economy to have control of a listed company will almost certainly have control of several other businesses. This doesn't mean that they're all listed on the stock market, and one of the issues dealing with family-controlled business groups is that the line between public and private companies is often blurred, usually to the benefit of the private companies, as the family doesn't have to share the proceeds with outsiders.

However, if the family is smart and competent, it will generally realize that playing fair with minority shareholders is good policy in the long run. They will grasp that this allows the family to return to the market for funds for expansion on a regular basis. In a fast-growing frontier economy, there are always new projects with a good rate of return that require funding, and while companies in Emerging Markets are obviously more dependent upon bank lending for a larger portion of their funding than those in more developed countries, family managements dislike having too much debt or allowing the banks to dictate their progress.

Family dynasties such as the Ayalas in the Philippines, whose flagship Ayala corporation has been in business since 1836, the Tata family in India, owners of Jaguar/Land Rover, whose original company was founded in 1868, are worthwhile investments. We would also include that of Li Ka-Shing in Hong Kong, listed as one of the ten wealthiest people in the world and whose businesses include utilities and real estate in Hong Kong, infrastructure in China, ports in Asia, Europe, and the Americas, and mobile phones everywhere through Hutchison (Wind), and whose eldest son, Victor, has taken over as chief executive officer.

Foreign allies and patrons

It's probably no consolation to former Egyptian President Hosni Mubarak that he fell through no fault of his own. His 30-year spell as ruler of Egypt came to an end in 2011 because his regime's foreign patron, the U.S., decided that it wasn't in its interests to continue supporting him. Once this had become apparent from the American response to the popular protests in Tahrir Square in Cairo, the military decided that it was no longer necessary to support an unpopular and aging leader who had been in power for so long that resentments had built up to a very dangerous level.

He should have remembered the fate of other US-supported leaders in regimes that lacked democratic legitimacy, thus making it difficult for a U.S. president to support them once unrest escalated. Both the Shah of Iran in 1979 and Ferdinand Marcos in the Philippines in 1986 found themselves leaving hurriedly on planes with only the members of their immediate family and closest supporters as company.

While regimes less concerned about their public image and not having to face the dangers of free elections can stick with autocrats for longer, as witnessed by the Chinese support for the Kim dynasty in North Korea and Russian President Vladimir Putin's propping up of Alexander Lukashenko of Belarus, even their patience can have its limits.

The Soviet Union supported Castro's Cuba by supplying it with cheap oil and buying its sugar exports at well above the world price. When it collapsed in 1991–1992, Boris Yeltsin's new Russian government decided its perilous finances would not allow it to continue subsidizing Cuba and cut off support. The Castro regime came close to collapse and was forced to liberalize and allow its citizens to earn foreign hard currency by running small businesses and renting out their homes to tourists.

Cuba found a new patron with cheap oil in Hugo Chavez's Venezuela in the last decade, supplying Chavez with Cuban experts such as doctors and security personnel to train the Venezuelan armed forces. Now that Hugo Chavez has died, it will be interesting to see how long Venezuela continues to subsidize Cuba, given its own poor finances.

In the Middle East, along with Russia, Iran is regarded as one of Syrian President Bashir Assad's major backers. Shiite Iran has supplied arms, personnel, and the support of the Hezbollah militia from Lebanon, to keep the Syrian regime in power. On the other side are Saudi Arabia and some of the Gulf emirates, particularly Qatar, which are Sunni, and which regard Iran as their major strategic threat.

Knowing which major power is the ally or backer of a developing economy is a very useful tool in assessing the political stability of a regime, especially if it is not democratically elected. As the examples of Egypt, the Philippines, and Iran demonstrate, having the U.S. as your principal backer is not always comforting.

Chapter 6

Corruption, Income Disparity, and Investment Restrictions

*I*nvestors considering investing in Frontier Markets have to consider such factors as corruption, income disparity, and restrictions on foreign investors when deciding whether to go ahead. These issues are real and in some cases can make certain countries higher risk than others, but be aware that wide variations exist even between countries even within the same region, let alone globally.

Having the local knowledge to assess whether these factors are too much of a negative, or are improving rapidly, is one of the reasons that this is *not* a field where going it alone is the best choice. Paying a manager with offices on the ground or good local knowledge is worthwhile in markets that are still inefficient and illiquid, so buying an actively managed Global Frontier Fund is a sensible choice. When scandals erupt or social unrest stirs, the manager will have a good grasp of what it means to long-term investing in these countries, or in some cases, not investing in these countries.

In this chapter, we look at whether it's possible to measure such factors as corruption and how equally or unequally wealth is distributed, and if so, whether different levels of corruption and income inequality make a difference to a country's economic growth and prospects. (Hint: Yes they do!). We also see whether a country's track record in paying or defaulting on debts provides a guide to future behavior.

Corrupt Governments and Markets

Corruption is one of the major concerns for investors looking at investing in developing economies. The popular stereotype of investing in so-called "third world" countries is the need to grease the palms of numerous corrupt officials, including, in many cases, the country's ruler. It usually is a man, although there have been a couple of presidential spouses who have gained notoriety. In the 1970s and 1980s, Imelda Marcos, the wife of the then-President Ferdinand Marcos, became notorious for her extravagance, including shopping trips to New York and Paris where she added to her amazing collection of shoes. Her collection eventually totaled over 3,000 pairs, at a time when most of the Philippine population was struggling just to get by.

This kind of extravagance does not necessarily make a country a bad place to invest but an investor is well advised to consider that a ruler with a cavalier attitude to their own country's money and resources may take the same view of foreign investors' property. On the other hand, sometimes leaders who are personally honest and upright may prove to be disastrous for the country with misguided policies, such as occurred in a couple of African countries after independence.

As is almost always the case with widely held beliefs, there is undoubtedly some truth in this stereotype of higher levels of corruption in poorer countries.

Some rulers of developing countries have regarded their nations as their personal possessions, believing they are entitled to take whatever they wish, regardless of whether it legally belongs to them. They have also shown little or no concern for the majority of the unfortunate citizens of their countries, except for their immediate families and members of their own tribal, political, or religious groupings.

You've seen such notorious examples of appalling behavior by leaders such as Idi Amin in Uganda, Muammar Gaddafi in Libya, Robert Mugabe in Zimbabwe, the various generations of the Kim family in North Korea, and the Assad dynasty in Syria. Regimes like these deliberately set back the development and growth of the countries they ruled or still rule to maintain their power and the privileges that come with control.

Corruption at lower levels of government and business is also believed to be much more prevalent in developing economies than in wealthier developed nations and for good reasons, especially with local officials. As in 19th-century North America and Western Europe, salaries for government positions are often extremely low, there are no pensions, and in the event of job loss, no unemployment benefits.

Corruption allegations in China

An acquaintance of Gavin was taking part in a vintage car rally in China a few years ago, when Bo Xilai was governor of Liaoning province in northeastern China. The route of the rally led through Liaoning and on the night before the rally was due to set off from Dalian, the capital city, Bo summoned the rally organizers. He reportedly demanded a large amount of cash in addition to the official fees already paid to permit the rally to proceed.

Bo Xilai was found guilty of corruption and sentenced to a long term in prison in late 2013, as Gu Kailai had already been.

In effect, these government officials often walk a high wire without a safety net. That makes it logical for a government servant (in this viewpoint) to exploit the profit-making opportunities from an official position. Only in this way can he or she build up a nest egg that will help provide income in the event of misfortune, such as illness, loss of employment due to a change of government, or being too obviously corrupt and getting caught.

In Communist China, changes of leadership in the Communist party hierarchy often bring a rash of corruption trials, as the losing rivals of the new leaders are brought to book for their past offenses. The trials in 2013 of former Chongqing regional party boss Bo Xilai and his wife, Gu Kailai (also accused of arranging the murder of her British-born investment advisor), revealed that Bo had demanded payments from businessmen for allowing them to conduct their operations. At his trial in 2013, a businessman testified that he had paid US$3.56 million to Bo Xilai that included US$3.23 million to Gu Kailai in 2000 to buy a villa in the south of France as well as paying for their son's travel and credit card bills. Ironically, Bo had risen to national prominence on promises of social equality and a series of campaigns against corruption while in charge of Chongqing.

As we discuss in the following sections, studies have found a strong correlation between lower levels of corruption and stronger GDP growth, so it is obviously good news when Frontier Markets improve their rankings in the Transparency International's Corruption Perception Index (CPI). Some of the largest and most populous have accomplished this over the last decade. However, just because a country has a low CPI ranking doesn't mean that it should be dismissed as a possible destination for investment.

A low CPI ranking merely means that an investor needs to be aware that there are issues with corruption or the perception of corruption when considering that country and not be surprised if shady dealings come to light. It does not and should not rule out investing in that market but does reinforce the conclusion that investors should invest via a fund with managers who are familiar with the local political scene and customs.

Corruption in the Philippines on display

Gavin visited the Philippines shortly after the People Power Revolution of 1986 that overthrew the corrupt and undemocratic regime of Ferdinand and Imelda Marcos. Imelda Marcos's shoe collection was put on display at the Malacanang Presidential Palace in Manila for viewing by the public. Taking several of the converted jeeps (known as "jeepneys") that act as taxis in Manila, the intrepid author arrived at the palace gates only to discover that the shoe display was closed on Saturday afternoons.

After her democratically elected successor, Cory Aquino, stepped down as President in 1992, Marcos's shoes disappeared from public view, although in 2001, around 800 pairs went to a shoe museum in Marikina, the center of Filipino shoemaking. Floods damaged several dozen pairs in 2009, but over 750 pairs are still on display at the museum. The Bata Museum in downtown Toronto, Ontario, also houses several pairs.

Investing without transparency

Obviously, factors such as a high degree of corruption and lack of transparency make investment decisions even more difficult than in developed markets. After all, stock markets depend on trust; if you can't believe the numbers, then how can you value a company and decide whether it is worth investing in?

For businesses, the problem is made more difficult by the Foreign Corrupt Practices Act of 1977, which made it illegal for American companies and individuals to offer bribes to foreign governments and their agents. It was introduced in the mid-1970s after investigations by the Securities and Exchange Commission (SEC) discovered that over 400 US companies had paid more than US$300 million in bribes to foreign governments. Even such well-known companies as Lockheed and Chiquita Bananas had paid bribes.

Getting to know the CPI

One way of finding out the level of corruption or honesty in developing economies is the annual index produced by Transparency International called the Corruption Perceptions Index (CPI). As its name suggests, the index is a comparative listing of corruption worldwide, produced by Transparency International, a nongovernmental organization founded in 1993 by Peter Eigen, an ex-regional director of the World Bank. The CPI ranks nations on the prevalence of corruption within each country, based upon surveys of business people.

The CPI has been criticized for poor methodology and for being unfair to developing nations, while at the same time, praised for highlighting corruption and embarrassing governments. As an example of its ability to influence decisions, some fund management companies adjust their risk scores for countries depending on how well (or badly) a country scores on the CPI.

A study in 2002 found a "very strong significant correlation" between the CPI and two other indicators of corruption, black market activity and an over-abundance of regulation, with all three having a strong correlation to real GDP per capita. Other studies in 2007 and 2008 found a correlation between a higher CPI (for example, less corruption) and higher GDP growth, with an increase of 1.7 percent in GDP growth for every unit increase in a country's CPI score.

The correlation between two items describes the relationship between two different types of investment or series of numbers. Thus when two stocks have a correlation of 1.0, one moves exactly as much as the other and in the same direction. When the correlation is below 1.0, and especially when it is below 0.5, investments are not particularly correlated with each other.

In other words, having two different sorts of investments with low or no correlation can be very useful when constructing a portfolio. This means decreased overall volatility of the total portfolio decreases because everything doesn't move at the same speed or even in the same direction. For example, if an asset has a negative correlation (for example, -0.5 or -1.0), it will move in the opposite direction to the first asset, thus reducing the overall volatility of a portfolio.

Reviewing the CPI rankings of various countries

How do various countries rank on the CPI? Do certain regions score better than others and are there any distinguishing features to help potential investors avoid problems?

The countries which rank as being regarded as the least corrupt by the CPI in 2012 are shown in order in Table 6-1.

Table 6-1	Countries with the Highest CPI Scores	
Ranking	*Country*	*Score*
1	Denmark	90
2	Finland	90
3	New Zealand	90
4	Sweden	88
5	Singapore	87
6	Switzerland	86
7	Australia	85
8	Norway	85
9	Canada	84
10	Netherlands	84

You're probably wondering where the U.S. ranks on the CPI. It comes in a very respectable 19th with a score of 73, just behind Japan and the United Kingdom, both of which tied for 17th with a score of 74.

The names of most of the countries ranked at the bottom of the CPI will probably come as no surprise to anyone who reads the newspapers or follows current affairs on the Internet. They are shown in Table 6-2.

Table 6-2	Countries with the Lowest CPI Scores	
Ranking	*Country*	*Score*
174	Somalia	8
174	North Korea	8
174	Afghanistan	8
173	Sudan	13
172	Myanmar (Burma)	15
170	Uzbekistan	17
170	Turkmenistan	17
169	Iraq	18
165	Haiti	19
165	Venezuela	19
165	Burundi	19
165	Chad	19

The list comprises several war-torn states where central government has either broken down or is ineffective in large parts of the country (Somalia, Afghanistan, Sudan, Iraq), three of which have had American and western military forces deployed in the last two decades. Also on the list are two reclusive Asian states with ruling juntas (North Korea and Myanmar), two former Soviet central Asian republics with autocratic governments, two Caribbean countries with a history of populist regimes, and two central African countries with ongoing insurgencies.

It would be fair to conclude that geography is not a determinant of corruption, except insofar as wealthy developed regimes with low levels of corruption are largely concentrated in Scandinavia, Australasia, and in small wealthy countries such as Switzerland, Singapore, and Luxemburg.

Similarly, the next few countries at the bottom of the CPI are concentrated in sub-Saharan Africa (six countries including Zimbabwe, the Democratic Republic of the Congo (DRC), and Angola), the Middle East (Libya, Yemen, and Syria), two South East Asian Communist or ex-Communist nations (Laos and Cambodia), and two more central Asian ex-Soviet republics (Tajikistan and Kyrgyzstan).

All these countries are either poor, formerly Communist, or have been involved in civil wars or rebellions — sometimes all three of these difficulties. They are almost impossible for an investor to gain access as most have no stock markets, although Iraq, Venezuela, and Zimbabwe all have markets with capitalizations over US$4 billion.

The first European country to appear at the bottom of the list is Ukraine at 144, the same rank as Syria, the Central African Republic, Cameroon, and the Congo. Russia, a member of the G-8 nations, is in at 133. Of the other members of the BRIC nations (Brazil, Russia, India, and China), India ranks 94, China 80, and Brazil 69, the same as South Africa and better than Italy, which has a rank of 72, and Greece at 94.

Table 6-3 shows the CPI rankings for the largest Frontier Markets in terms of population and GDP.

Table 6-3	The Top 30 Major Frontier and Frontier Emerging Markets' CPI	
Ranking	*Country*	*Score*
1	Qatar	68
2	United Arab Emirates	68
3	Botswana	65
4	Estonia	64
5	Slovenia	61
6	Bahrain	51
7	Turkey	49
8	Namibia	48
9	Croatia	46
10	Slovakia	46
11	Ghana	45
12	Kuwait	44
13	Romania	44
14	Saudi Arabia	44
15	South Africa	43
16	Bulgaria	41
17	Sri Lanka	40
18	Peru	38
19	Morocco	37
20	Colombia	36

(continued)

Table 6-3 *(continued)*

Ranking	Country	Score
21	Argentina	35
22	Philippines	34
23	Egypt	32
24	Indonesia	32
25	Vietnam	31
26	Kenya	27
27	Nigeria	27
28	Pakistan	27
29	Bangladesh	26
30	Ukraine	26

The disappointing aspect of these rankings from an investor's viewpoint is that all the highest-scoring countries from a corruption perspective are small, wealthy states such as those in the Persian Gulf like Qatar, the UAE, Bahrain, and Kuwait, or in Eastern Europe, such as Estonia, Slovenia, Croatia, Slovakia, Romania, and Bulgaria. The African countries of Namibia and Botswana rank highly but have resource-based economies with small populations. Turkey is regarded as an Emerging Market, although it is a gateway to other central Asian and Middle Eastern frontier economies.

Ghana, at number 11, is the first sizeable frontier economy with a young, relatively low-income population to show a respectable CPI score. Next come Saudi Arabia, which foreign investors cannot access directly and then South Africa, an Emerging Market. It's not until Sri Lanka at No. 17, that you begin to find numbers that most investors would consider typical Frontier Markets.

The five largest countries by population and with the most potential in terms of young populations, low income levels, and a high percentage of their citizens still in the countryside unfortunately have the lowest CPI scores. Vietnam, Kenya, Nigeria, Pakistan, and Bangladesh are probably the five most interesting Frontier Markets from a long-term perspective.

Spotting signs that corruption is being reduced (or ignored)

The easiest way to spot corruption being reduced is checking whether its ranking in the CPI improves over the years. If the ranking remains unchanged, or (even worse) declines, then it's a good sign the authorities are turning a blind eye to the situation. Even countries regarded as notoriously corrupt can improve and it's notable that China is ranked higher than democracies such as Colombia, India, the Philippines, and Indonesia, and substantially higher than the other remaining Communist regimes such as Vietnam, Laos, or North Korea.

If you compare 2012's CPI ranking with 2005 — a long enough period for there to be a meaningful change — all the five large Frontier Markets mentioned at the end of the previous section have improved their CPI scores. Bangladesh, which was ranked dead last in 2005 at 158/158 and with a CPI score of 17, is now 144/174 with a CPI of 26. Nigeria and Pakistan have improved from 19 and 21, respectively, to 27, Kenya from 21 to 27, and Vietnam from 26 to 31.

On the other hand, Venezuela (23 to 19), Iraq (22 to 18), Sudan (21 to 13), and Myanmar (18 to 15) have all experienced declines from their 2005 levels which were already depressingly low. In one or two cases, such as Myanmar, the increase in corruption perceptions may actually be a sign of liberalization, as a previously closed system begins to open up. The release of opposition leader Nobel Peace Prize winner Aung San Suu Kyi by the junta in Myanmar in 2010 led to free elections to some seats in the country's parliament in 2012. As the previous restrictions are lifted in a closed economy, the opportunities increase for making money legally or illegally.

Recognizing How Income Disparities Affect Investment Performance

One of the major factors affecting the economic performance of a country is the degree of income disparity; in other words, how big a gap there is between what the wealthiest 10 percent of the population and the poorest 10 percent earn. The larger the gap between these two groups, effectively the haves and the have-nots, the more likely it is that there will be high levels of poverty, social unrest, and the chance of political upheaval.

Take a look at the events that led to the Arab Spring of 2011. A series of seemingly stable states in the Middle East and North Africa (MENA) experienced outbreaks of popular unrest that led to the overthrow of the long-established regimes in Tunisia, Egypt, and Libya and the start of the ongoing Syrian civil war. It's possible to see what happens if the ruling elite allows too much wealth to be concentrated in the hands of its own small clique. As with high levels of corruption, too high a level of income disparity can be an indication that a country is more at risk for political or social unrest than countries with a more equal distribution of wealth.

Considering the quality of income measurement

As with corruption perceptions, there is a way to measure the inequality of income distribution. The Gini index — named for its developer, Italian statistician Corrado Gini — is a measure compiled by the World Bank, and is defined as "the extent to which the distribution of income . . . among individuals or households within an economy deviates from a perfectly equal distribution."

A Lorenz curve plots the cumulative percentages of income received against the cumulative number of recipients, starting with the poorest individual or household. The Gini index measures the difference between the Lorenz curve and a hypothetical line of perfect equality, expressed as a percentage. Thus a Gini index of 0 represents perfect equality, while an index of 100 represents perfect inequality.

The World Bank compiles the Gini index with primary household survey data from government statistical agencies or World Bank country departments. This means that some countries don't have a Gini index owing to insufficient (or nonexistent) data and not all countries have their Gini index calculated every year. Still, enough countries have a relatively recent Gini to make it a useful guide (see Table 6-4).

The Gini index for developed countries

Thus a Scandinavian or Northern European country with a long established tradition of social equality, a welfare state, and a highly progressive tax system would have scores around 25–30; for example, Sweden (25), Norway (25.6), and Finland (26.8). Germany (28.3), Austria (29.2), and the Netherlands (30.9) are a little less equal by this measure, while the United Kingdom and the U.S. come in at 36 and 40.8, respectively. All these scores date from 2000, but it would be a reasonable assumption that none of them have changed dramatically. Regimes with a high degree of inequality in their income distribution will score over 50.

The Gini index for developing, emerging, and frontier countries

The most recent Gini calculation for some major developing countries like Brazil, China, Colombia, the Philippines, Russia, and South Africa is from 2009, while for Bangladesh, India, Indonesia, Nigeria, and Sri Lanka, it is 2010. Given that income disparity changes relatively slowly, it is reasonable for investors to use these numbers to see how equal or unequal certain countries are.

Table 6-4	Income Disparity in Frontier and Frontier Emerging Economies (2010 Unless Otherwise Indicated)
Country	*Gini Index*
Ukraine	25.6
Romania	27.4 (2011)
Kazakhstan	29.0 (2009)
Pakistan	30.0 (2008)
Egypt	30.8 (2008)
Bangladesh	32.1
India	33.9
Vietnam	35.6 (2008)
Tunisia	36.1
Sri Lanka	36.4
Indonesia	38.1 (2011)
Turkey	40.0
China	42.1 (2009)
Philippines	43.0 (2009)
Argentina	44.5
Mexico	47.2
Peru	48.1
Nigeria	48.8
Brazil	54.7 (2009)
Colombia	55.9
Zambia	57.5
South Africa	63.1 (2009)

Despite the unrest that led to the Arab Spring, neither Egypt nor Tunisia is especially unequal compared to other developing economies. It therefore seems reasonable to suggest that a combination of factors, including corruption and particularly conspicuous consumption by the ruling elite (Imelda's shoes again), may be necessary ingredients to produce social unrest and lead to the overthrow of regimes. The removal of support by the major power that has been a supporter of the regime, such as the U.S. for Ferdinand Marcos in 1986 and Hosni Mubarak in 2011, and Russia for Muammar Qaddafi in 2011, may also be a contributing factor.

Also note that the former Soviet bloc states of Ukraine, Romania, and Kazakhstan are the most equal in income distribution. Meanwhile, the South Asian states of India, Pakistan, Bangladesh, and Sri Lanka have relatively low income inequality despite the conspicuous consumption of many of their wealthy elites, and note that the officially Communist regimes of Vietnam and China are mid-ranking in terms of income distribution.

The two regions that come out worst in terms of income inequality are Latin America and sub-Saharan Africa. All of the former Spanish and Portuguese colonies, including the Philippines, have Gini indices above 43.5, reflecting the stratified nature of colonial society and its continuation in their modern successors. Finally, Nigeria and the two southern African states of Zambia and South Africa itself are among the most unequal countries in the world in terms of income distribution.

When you consider that in 1994 and 1993 (the last time a Gini was calculated for them), Botswana and Namibia, two other southern African resource-based countries, scored 61 and 74.3, respectively, it becomes apparent that southern Africa is the home of the most unequal income disparity by a long shot.

The answer to why this income disparity exists is probably found in the apartheid (Dutch for apart-hood) system that South Africa operated under directly and its economic satellites of Namibia, Botswana, and Zambia operated under indirectly most of the last century, and officially between 1948 and 1994. With the gold, diamond, copper, coal, and uranium mines that were the foundation of the region's wealth manned by millions of tribal and migrant workers, the white ruling class retained the benefits of the country's growth. In fact, apartheid has been seen as a way to ensure that the Afrikaner blue-collar working class got its fair share of the economic pie at the expense of the native African inhabitants, whether from the Zulu or the Xhosa tribe.

This means that investors thinking about investing in African funds should be aware that South Africa has by far the largest stock market on the continent, and that most African regional funds will have a high weighting in South African stocks, unless their prospectus specifically states a limit on the percentage. With the high degree of income inequality that still prevails 20 years after the first free multi-racial elections in 1994, the recent violence due to police action caused by rivalry between different labor unions in the mining industry in 2012, appears likely to continue.

Similarly, the rising popularity of extreme views among sections of the ruling African National Congress (ANC), South Africa's ruling party since independence and for the foreseeable future, should give investors pause. Although the ANC under President Jacob Zuma in 2012, expelled Julius Malema, the former leader of its Youth League, who had called for the elimination of "counter revolutionary forces," Malema remains popular with many former ANC supporters and the striking miners and their families ahead of the next election in 2014.

Relating income levels to consumer consumption

One of the most attractive aspects of many Frontier Markets is their young and rapidly growing populations and the high percentage of them who still live in rural areas. The most rapid phase of GDP growth occurs in developing countries when a large percentage of the population is below age 15, which means that there will be plenty of new entrants to the labor force, keeping wage pressures under control but also creating many new customers for what are known as Fast Moving Consumer Goods (FMCG).

FMCGs include the obvious categories such as food, beverages, alcohol, tobacco, personal care (shampoo, toothpaste, feminine hygiene, and so forth), and baby food. They also include mobile phones, credit and debit cards, motorbikes, and utilities (electricity, water, heating) as the new consumers move from farms to factories and into houses and apartments in the rapidly growing towns and cities.

Obviously, countries with high levels of income inequality are less attractive long-term investments than those with a relatively flat income structure, although this may merely mean that virtually everyone is relatively poor together, as in some former Soviet successor states like Ukraine and Belarus. A good shorthand way of assessing consumer income levels is looking at the percentage of citizens in a country who own a mobile phone.

Cellphone penetration

Most developing countries don't have an extensive existing landline telephone network, so consumers have adopted mobile telephones as the convenient and cheap means of communication. As well as voice communications, texting is a very low-cost way of keeping in touch, especially as network coverage in such continents as Africa and South America can be pretty intermittent. Mobile telephones have also become a means of transferring money, especially in Africa, helping the growth of the cash economy. This occurred even before smartphones had become widely distributed, as most developing markets are still on 2G or at best early-stage 3G networks.

For all these reasons, even developing countries with relatively low levels of GDP per capita have surprisingly high levels of cellphone penetration. Even Bangladesh, with GDP per capita of only US$2,000 on a purchasing power parity (PPP) basis, had 51 percent mobile phone ownership at the end of 2012. Pakistan had 57 percent, India 73 percent, and Sri Lanka 84 percent. Remarkably, Vietnam, with a lower GDP per capita than India (US$3,500 versus US$3,900) had a 138 percent mobile penetration, and resource rich Kazakhstan had 142 percent, both much higher than the U.S. or Canada. Myanmar, on the other hand, is at a stunningly low 2 percent, because the junta has decided retaining control is more important than growth.

In Africa, Nigeria had 55 percent mobile phone penetration at the end of 2012, Kenya 64 percent, and Ghana 84 percent. The wealthier southern African states are all over 100 percent cellphone ownership; Namibia's stands at 102 percent, South Africa 133 percent, and Botswana 138 percent.

In South America, the Frontier Markets of Argentina, Colombia, Ecuador, Peru, and Venezuela, as well as Brazil, have mobile phone ownership over 100 percent. The same is true for the wealthy Gulf Cooperation Council (GCC) markets of Saudi Arabia, Kuwait, Qatar, and the UAE, while Egypt is at 98 percent. The eastern European markets and Russia also have well over 100 percent mobile phone penetration.

This gives an investor a handy guide to the relative level of consumer development among developing markets. Those with penetration below 100 percent are still at a relatively early stage of development, and the consumer goods that will be affordable and appeal to their citizens will be relatively basic and low cost, although they may well represent a substantial upgrade on what consumers have been using previously.

Alcohol consumption

As consumer development increases, beer companies benefit from customers switching from privately brewed or distilled liquor, which often has dangerous side effects (think bathtub gin during Prohibition). Governments are in favor of packaged alcoholic beverages because they receive the excise duty on their sale and it's safer for the drinkers who consume them than the moonshine they were previously drinking.

This effect benefits such brewers as SABMiller. The SAB stands for South African Breweries, which has over 95 percent of the South African beer market and has expanded into southern and eastern Africa by using its knowledge of African consumers. Similarly Guinness maker Diageo has locally listed subsidiaries in Nigeria and Malaysia, and sponsors local soccer teams. Its Irish stout is well liked by African consumers for its supposed ability to improve a drinker's performance with members of the opposite sex!

As consumers become wealthier and more sophisticated, evidenced by the likelihood that many of them have two cellphones, higher value and more up-market brands can be sold, including foreign luxury brand. Consumption of such products as Louis Vuitton bags, Gucci shoes, and Martell brandy supposedly indicate that you are a "cool" and "happening" type of person.

Gavin remembers seeing parties of Chinese businessmen in Hong Kong nightclubs in the 1990s with bottles of Johnnie Walker Black or Blue label whisky or Courvoisier brandy ostentatiously placed on the table, which was then mixed with Seven-Up to help to disguise the taste of the spirit. The important thing was being seen consuming an expensive foreign spirit and thus demonstrating how successful you were. The same scene is doubtless being repeated all over Africa and southern Asia, as consumers there also want to show, in the words of the old cigarette advertisement, that "You've come a long way, baby."

Understanding the relationship between income disparity and consumer consumption

As with corruption, extreme income disparity is a feature of many developing economies. Although it's worth being aware of income disparity, that should not alienate an investor from considering Frontier Markets. However, if corruption and income disparity are combined, then the possibility of social unrest spilling over into political protest will be high, such as what happened with some countries in North Africa during the Arab Spring of 2011.

If income disparities are very high, then it's likely the country you're considering will be less attractive as a possible investment destination because the majority of the population doesn't have a great deal of disposable income to spend. Therefore, looking for countries with lower levels of income disparity is one means of finding investments that will benefit from consumers moving from the countryside to the cities, and from barter to the cash economy, leading to rapidly rising sales of FMCG, as they will retain a larger percentage of their new incomes.

Consumer product companies are a good way to play this phenomenon, but many of them are global multinationals, as discussed in Chapter 10, whose stock prices are often more influenced by their own domestic stock market than by their exposure to Frontier and Emerging Markets. Investors should consider investing through a diversified Global Frontier Markets fund, whose managers can choose which countries have attractive levels of income disparity and which stocks are correlated with what's happening in Frontier Markets. Such a fund is the preferable way to gain access to these markets.

Looking at Laws Affecting Outside Investors

Despite their need for investment capital to help their countries grow and develop, many developing economies don't always welcome foreign investors with open arms. Memories of colonial exploitation or simply dislike of outsiders benefiting from the efforts of their own population has led many countries to put controls on how much foreigners can own of listed companies, or whether they can own them at all.

Controls may include restricting foreign investors to owning a certain percentage of shares in companies, as practiced by Thailand, the Philippines, Malaysia and China and used to be the case in Qatar and the United Arab Emirates. Or controlling powers may completely ban investors from ownership like Saudi Arabia at the time of writing, or they may expropriate companies, as occurred in Argentina from 2006 to 2012, in Bolivia from 2006 to 2012, and in Venezuela under the late Hugo Chavez from 2007 to 2010. In Africa, the Democratic Republic of the Congo (DRC) expropriated several mines owned by foreign companies in 2009 and 2010.

Getting familiar with restrictions on foreign investment

In many ways, investing in countries that restrict the percentage of companies that foreigners can own is exactly the same as investing in any other foreign country. The investor uses a broker to buy stocks, settle the account, and hold the shares. The foreign investor owns the shares, receives dividends, can take up rights issues, and can vote the shares.

The difference arises when the amount of stock held by foreign investors exceeds the percentage legislated by the country. This varies from country to country. In the Philippines, foreigners are allowed to own up to 40 percent of shares of any type (voting, non-voting, or preferred). In Thailand, foreigners can own up to 49 percent of any company except financial institutions such as banks and brokerages, where the limit is 25 percent. In Malaysia, the limit varies by industry, but foreigners can, for example, own up to 70 percent of brokerages and fund managers.

China's system is different and more confusing to a foreign investor. China has two classes of shares in domestic Chinese companies. One, the A shares, is reserved only for domestic Chinese investors. The other, the B shares, supposedly is reserved only for foreign investors, although in practice anyone with access to hard currency, such as American or Hong Kong dollars, can buy them if they have a foreign brokerage account.

China also has what are known as H shares, which are Chinese listed companies that are cross-listed on the Hong Kong Stock Exchange (HKSE) (hence H shares). These H shares have exactly the same rights as A and B shares, but are denominated in HK dollars and trading on a long-established stock exchange with what most observers agree are higher standards of regulation and reporting. China has tended to only list its largest, highest-quality companies on the HKSE, such as its energy companies like PetroChina, China National Overseas Oil Co. (CNOOC), China Petroleum and Chemical (Sinopec), mobile telephone operators such as China Mobile and China Unicom, and all its major state-controlled banks.

The FTSE Xinhua China 25 Index, which has an iShares ETF (NYSE:FXI) that tracks it, is essentially comprised of H shares because the top 15 holdings in the ETF are all H shares, except for three HK-listed Chinese large capitalization companies. The three HK-listed companies are instant messaging service Tencent, property investor China Overseas Land & Investments, and women's shoe retailer Belle International. The top 10 holdings in the ETF are shown in Table 6-5.

Table 6-5	iShares FTSE Xinhua China 25 Index (End August 2013)
Stock	%
China Mobile-H	10.2
China Construction Bank-H	8.7
Tencent	8.4
Ind. & Comm. Bk. China-H	7.5
Bank of China-H	5.9
CNOOC-H	4.3
China O'seas Land & Inv.	4.0
China Life Insurance-H	3.9
Sinopec-H	3.8
Ping An Insurance-H	3.8

When the foreign portion of a company's shares is fully taken up, because all of the 40 percent or 49 percent shares available have been purchased, then the foreign shares will begin trading at a premium to the local shares. That occurs because the only way new foreign investors can buy shares in that company is by persuading existing foreign holders to sell their shares. If the country's economy is growing strongly and the stock market is doing well, then the premium a foreign investor would need to pay to obtain shares can rise to more than 20, 30, or sometimes over 40 percent above the price of the local shares. This is what happened in Thailand in the 1990s when it was one of the booming "Tiger" economies in South East Asia.

Unfortunately, when the economy's growth slows or the stock market stops performing well, then foreign investors can be hit by a double whammy because the price of the underlying local shares goes down and the premium above the local price starts to shrink as other foreign investors decide to sell out of the country.

The same issue affected China B shares because supposedly only foreigners could legally own them. As a result, liquidity in these shares has always been very low as there were only other foreign investors involved. Also, when investors soured on Chinese investments, there were very few buyers willing to purchase B shares, since foreign investors do tend to hold similar views on how attractive the stock market looks.

You shouldn't sidestep investing in the foreign shares of companies in developing countries. However, do be aware that when foreign shares are trading at a premium to local shares, there is the risk of the premium shrinking or even disappearing completely if other foreign investors become more bearish about the outlook for that country.

Understanding resource nationalization

Nationalization is the compulsory purchase of a company's shares or assets by a government regardless of the wishes of the shareholders and other stakeholders. Nationalization was employed by developed market governments such as the British Labour party after World War II when it nationalized the coal, steel, road and rail transportation, and electricity industries between 1945 and 1951 and the French Socialist party after 1981 when it nationalized private banks. Nationalization or expropriation has been a favorite tactic of Latin American regimes in the post-World War II era.

Resource nationalization, a subset of nationalization, is the compulsory purchase of natural resource assets, such as oil and gas, precious metals, and other commodities as well as agricultural land, which are regarded by many nationalist parties as "belonging to the people." There is some logic to this view in that these are generally raw materials being extracted from the soil, and they are limited resources, with the exception of agricultural crops, so when they're gone, they're gone. Furthermore, the environmental side effects of mining and drilling are often harmful to both the country and its local inhabitants.

After nationalization, however, the profits from these extractive industries tend to go to the ruling regime and its favored groups or business partners, rather than to the people. The foreign investors, who in many cases have invested large amounts of capital to develop the resource, either receive compensation well below the real value of the assets or often, nothing. That happened during the Communist takeovers in Eastern Europe after World War II and in Cuba after Castro came to power in 1959. Furthermore, often nationalized assets are run with much worse environmental records or lower safety standards for the workforce due to underinvestment in equipment and training.

Nationalization in South America

Just in the last decade, in three South American frontier nations, Argentina, Bolivia, and Venezuela, nationalization has been pursued as a consistent policy. Regimes generally use nationalization as a means of diverting the local population's attention from deteriorating living standards by blaming foreigners, usually "Yanqui imperialists," but, as in the case of Argentinean energy company YPF, the blame is placed on Spanish energy company Repsol.

The Kirchner government in Argentina renationalized the Buenos Aires water utility in 2006, pension funds in 2008, the national airline in 2009, and YPF, its largest oil and gas company, in 2012.

In Bolivia, President Evo Morales nationalized the gas industry upon his election in 2006, the largest telecom company in 2008, the largest hydroelectric plant in 2010, and the electric grid in 2012.

In Venezuela, the late Hugo Chavez stripped major international oil companies of their control of the massive Orinoco oil fields in 2007, nationalized the cement industry in 2008, steel plants in 2008 and 2010, the rice processing industry in 2009, and supermarkets and glass plants in 2010. The latter moves were intended to bring inflation under control by seizing the companies that made consumer products. That provided a great example of treating the symptoms rather than the underlying cause, which was the rapid expansion in money supply caused by Chavez's own policies.

Those policies included providing the cheapest gasoline in the western hemisphere, at 5.8 cents a gallon. No, that's not a misprint; gas is so cheap that in April 2013, *The Wall Street Journal* reported a taxi driver paid less than half the price of a cup of espresso coffee to fill up his Nissan Sentra taxi. And that's at the official exchange rate; at the unofficial rate, gas costs 1.5 cents a gallon. As a result of the subsidies to maintain gasoline at this price, Venezuela's budget deficit in 2012 was estimated by Moody's to be 12 percent of GDP, worse than troubled Euro-zone economies. Compared to next-door neighbor Colombia, where market prices for gasoline prevail, Venezuelan consumption of fuel is seven times higher per capita.

Nationalization in Africa

Several African governments have also nationalized mines owned by foreign investors, including the Democratic Republic of the Congo (DRC), which seized Canadian miner First Quantum's Kolwezi and Frontier copper mines in 2010, accusing the company of contract violations. In 2009, First Quantum was reportedly the DRC's largest taxpayer, accounting for between one-eighth and one-quarter of its total tax revenues. Having taken the government to international arbitration proceedings, First Quantum subsequently sold its Congolese mines to Kazakh miner Eurasian Natural Resources Corporation for US$1.25 billion in January 2012.

This financial drama followed in the footsteps of the late President Sese Seko Mobutu, who helped stage the "Rumble in the Jungle" between Muhammad Ali and George Foreman in 1974. In 1967, he expropriated, without compensation, the copper mines operated by the Belgians, who had run the country in a particularly brutal fashion when it was their colony. The DRC was cut off from international aid until it paid some compensation to the Belgian miners.

Other African countries such as Ghana and Zambia nationalized their mining industries after independence in the 1960s with disastrous consequences for output and government finances. Now they have adopted other methods, such as doubling the 3 percent royalty to 6 percent on revenues in Zambia in 2012. Ghana has the right to take a 10 percent free equity stake in any new mine or oil project and the right to buy another 20 percent at market prices, as well as charge a royalty that fluctuates between 3 and 12 percent, depending upon the operating margin.

Knowing how governments respond to financial turmoil

What emerges from a study of developing countries' reactions to financial turmoil is that there is no one model that applies to all countries. Some, such as the South American and African countries which nationalized businesses either after independence or during the financial crisis of the last few years, have reacted in ways that have resulted in heavy losses for foreign investors, deterred foreign investment, and created a legacy of distrust.

After the Asian financial crisis of 1997 to 1998, which saw many countries like South Korea, Thailand, Indonesia, the Philippines, and Malaysia forced to devalue from their fixed exchange rate regimes pegged to the US dollar, many Asian economies have liberalized, floated their currencies, and opened up their financial markets to foreign investment.

Latin America

Basically, looking at how governments have reacted in the past will usually provide a good guide to how they will react in the future, although sometimes a traumatic event such as the Asian Crisis will lead to a major reassessment of policy. Argentina has consistently defaulted on its foreign debts on a regular basis, going back over a century to 1890 to 1891, the first time Baring's Bank had to be rescued because it owned too much Argentinean debt that no longer paid interest. In 1991, Argentina had the world's biggest default (Greece surpassed it in 2012), when it stopped paying interest on US$82 billion of its international debt. It now looks as though Argentina may end up trying to restructure its debt again.

In general, we can reasonably say that Argentina, Bolivia, Ecuador, and Venezuela in Latin America have a track record of debt restructurings or defaults and nationalizations, while Chile, Colombia, Peru, and for the last 20 years, Brazil, have been more reliable destinations for foreign investment.

Asia and Eastern Europe

In Asia, most countries have a strong record of respecting foreign investment, although investors suffered dramatic losses in 1997 to 1998 when a number of countries devalued sharply but didn't default. The Philippines is the only country that has suspended interest payments in recent times (1983 under the Marcos regime), although Pakistan restructured some of its debt in 1999.

Eastern Europe

The largest debt default before Argentina was Russia, which defaulted on US$73 billion of its debt in the aftermath of the 1997 to 1998 Asian Crisis and the plunge in oil prices, which provided most of the government's revenues, to $10 per barrel. Ukraine and Moldova also defaulted on their debt in 2000 and 2002. Eastern Europe in general, however, has been respectful of foreign investors, partially due to the desire of many countries to join the European Union.

The Middle East and North Africa

The Middle East and North Africa (MENA) countries have made substantial borrowings owing to their strong revenues from energy resources. Foreign investment in the region has been relatively low because the largest countries, such as Saudi Arabia and Iran, do not permit foreign investment or are under sanctions. However, in November 2009, Dubai, a member of the United Arab Emirates (UAE), had to declare a moratorium on its debt after its property boom collapsed. Dubai had to restructure its debt with the help of fellow UAE member Abu Dhabi.

The rest of Africa

While several African countries have had to restructure their international debts or suspend payments, in general funding has been provided by development banks or multinational institutions such as the World Bank, African Development Bank, or the IMF rather than private investors. When private firms have invested, certain countries, such as Ghana and Kenya, as well as South Africa, Namibia, and Botswana, have been welcoming to properly structured investments. Others such as the DRC, Zimbabwe, and countries affected by civil wars like Sierra Leone, Liberia, and the Sudan, have proved difficult. Outside of Southern Africa, the track record is too short to permit generalizations.

Chapter 7

Currency Considerations, Exchange Rates, and Accounting Standards

*Y*ou may be asking why you have to bother with technical stuff like currency exchange rates and accounting standards. Besides understanding that the details will affect your returns, you probably won't have to bother in the real sense of the word if you invest in Frontier Markets through a global frontier fund or an exchanged-traded fund. The fund manager is "bothering" with it and the net value of your units reflects the end results.

However, if you decide to trade directly, you will certainly have to pay attention to these details. Either way, they affect your net returns and so they're important. Please keep in mind that these are very volatile times and factors such as exchange rates are also volatile.

You can reduce your exposure to the volatility of exchange rates by confining your trading to a single currency. Many readers of this book will find it easy and convenient to confine their trading to American-dollar-denominated assets, including mutual funds, exchange-traded funds, and equities traded as American Depositary Receipts (ADRs). Of course, ADRs are US$-denominated versions of the underlying foreign company, so they will be exposed to changes in exchange rates between the US dollar and the Euro, pound sterling, yen, and so on.

Remember that the very nature of Frontier Markets means an added set of complications and unless you consider yourself a math whiz or can devote large amounts of time to Frontier Markets trading, you are probably going to get better results on a net-net basis if you trade through a Global Frontier Fund. As we have stated, we don't sell these funds or have any direct financial stake in your decision, but we do believe that the added complexity makes these funds the best way to go. This doesn't necessarily mean that you shouldn't do online trading for your developed market holdings. The advantages and disadvantages of online trading in developed markets amount to a separate set of considerations best left to another book!

Being Wary of Small Illiquid Currency Markets

As a general rule, the liquidity of an asset is a function of how quickly it can be sold to a willing buyer at a mutually agreed price. Viewed from that perspective, shares in Ford Motor Company have complete liquidity.

Carrying that line of reasoning over to currencies, many readers of this book can easily change currencies for major developed markets, although comparison shopping is every bit as important with currency conversions as with any other necessity. However, with some exceptions, you can't easily and inexpensively change dollars into Emerging Market currencies and you certainly can't easily and inexpensively change dollars into Frontier Market currencies.

When you do make the trade, it *will* be expensive since what is known as the *bid-ask spread* will often be fairly wide.

That factor alone justifies going the ADR route. Remember that in order to be listed in the United States as an ADR, the listing company has to comply with the reporting requirements of American listed companies.

The same general principle applies to companies listing as Global Depositary Receipts (GDRs). These certificates trade on exchanges such as the London Stock Exchange, Frankfurt Stock Exchange, and Luxembourg Stock Exchange.

If you want to make money as a Foreign Exchange Trader or Forex Trader you can probably do that if you devote the time and research. But that's a different book.

Some of the world's most illiquid currencies include the Thai *baht,* Uruguay *peso,* Iraqi *dinar,* Serbian *dinar,* Saudi Arabia *riyal,* and some African currencies. This is not to suggest that you can't obtain them, just that doing so comes with difficulty and at extra expense.

For the sake of comparison, the world's most liquid currencies include the American dollar, the Canadian dollar, the British pound sterling, the Euro, the Japanese yen, and the Swiss franc.

Illiquid currencies can be a separate concern from illiquid assets although the two factors are not mutually exclusive. Illiquid shares are those for which a ready buyer cannot necessarily be found, such as shares of a small corporation on the stock exchange of a former Communist bloc country. The common characteristics between the illiquid currencies and illiquid shares are that they are thinly traded, cannot be easily transacted, and generally have higher trading costs.

Opening a local bank account if you invest directly

Opening a local bank account if you invest directly is not something that we would recommend with one possible exception: If you are an expatriate of the country in which you are considering such an account and still hold valid citizenship in that country, it is possible that you will have fewer problems. However, that exception aside, opening a local bank account in a distant nation may set you up for problems. It would simply not be worth the time, trouble, expense, and risk to set up a local bank account in a former Communist bloc country such as Kazakhstan for the purpose of trading Kazakh equities, some of which can be less liquid than the GDRs linked to them and that trade freely on the London Stock Exchange. (Setting up a bank account in a Frontier Market in which you carry on business and to which you travel regularly would be a separate set of considerations.)

The random factor in this equation is the amount of help you can expect from your government in the event that the authorities in the distant country freeze your account.

Granted, the world is changing and everything, including money flows, is being globalized. Perhaps if we write another edition of this book in five years, we might make a different argument but we can only describe the situation as we see it at the time of writing.

We would not go so far as to say that you *must* restrict your Frontier Markets investing trading to Global and Regional Frontier Funds and ETFs, ADRs, and GDRs, but we can assure you that you'll save yourself a lot of trouble if you use that strategy.

Finding out if a local bank account is susceptible to confiscation

As a general statement if you want to open an account in a foreign country, check with your own financial institution for its advice. If you bank with a large financial institution it may have operations in your target country and opening a bank account through your own institution gives you the least problematic approach. Such global banks as Citigroup (NYSE:C) and HSBC (NYSE:HBC; LSE:HSBC) have retail banking operations in many emerging countries around the globe. In fact, HSBC styles itself as "The world's local bank." However, note that these banks' local operations follow the laws of the country in which they are based, not the country of the parent company.

The specter of possible confiscations of depositors' funds flared up in March 2013 during the Cyprus bank crisis. Initially, all bank depositors on the small island in the Eastern Mediterranean were informed over one weekend that 6.7 percent of their deposits up to Euro 100,000 ($137,500 at December 2013 exchange rates) and 9.9 percent on deposits above that level would be confiscated. The move was styled as necessary to help bail out the banks as a condition of Cyprus receiving a Euro 10 billion bailout from the European Union, European Central Bank, and the IMF.

After massive protests, the authorities retreated from this bright idea and instead decided that depositors in the worst-affected bank, the second largest in Cyprus, Cyprus Popular Bank (known as Laiki Bank), up to Euro 100,000 would be protected and transferred to Bank of Cyprus. Every other depositor in Laiki Bank and those in the Bank of Cyprus above Euro 100,000 would have their assets frozen, with losses for large depositors in Laiki determined by how much of Laiki's assets could be recovered. Large depositors in the Bank of Cyprus also face losses dependent upon how big its recapitalization turns out to be.

At the time of writing, some analysts held out the possibility that the next European country to require a bailout, widely thought to be Portugal, will also have to require its banks to confiscate a portion of depositors' funds in a form of "bail-in." Cyprus's experience shows that opening local bank accounts is not without its dangers, even in relatively wealthy countries in western Europe.

Looking for bank guarantees? Don't expect them

Remember that you cannot assume that the same safeguards we enjoy here in the United States, such as detailed regulatory surveillance and bank guarantees, apply equally in a foreign country. You can start by checking the International Association of Deposit Insurers (ADI) website at www.iadi. org to see whether the country you're considering is a member.

At the time of writing, 112 jurisdictions have deposit insurance systems in place, according to the association. Among Emerging Markets these include Brazil, Indonesia, India, Mexico, and Taipei. At time of writing, the ADI list does not include China.

Also at the time of writing, Frontier Markets with deposit insurance systems in place include Kazakhstan, Nigeria, and Vietnam. Several countries, including Mozambique and Zambia, have deposit insurance systems under construction while countries such as Ethiopia, Qatar, and the United Arab Emirates are studying these systems. This is a partial list included to provide examples. For a complete list, see the Association website at www.iadi.org.

Do not assume that the deposit insurance provisions of a specific country resemble the provisions that exist in the U.S. You would have to check the specific provisions of your intended country as well as the procedures for laying a claim, which could be quite complex if you're working from a distance. If you decide to go this route (and we generally wouldn't recommend it), go beyond ascertaining the existence of a bank guarantee system and check the processes that you would have to follow if necessary.

Finding out about foreign exchange controls

As a general statement, historical factors such as the disintegration of the Union of Soviet Socialist Republics (USSR) and the trends toward globalization and trade liberalization have meant a decrease in the number of countries still imposing exchange controls. Only the Communist regimes of Cuba and China, and the occasional populist regimes such as Argentina and Venezuela still impose foreign exchange controls.

As with other issues in foreign countries, one image held by some individuals of foreign exchange controls comes from old movies where a shady-looking character approaches an innocent tourist and offers to do a quick currency exchange in a tourist café or a similar environment.

Modern exchange controls are less hilarious and more complex:

- ✔ Some countries place restrictions on the amount of a currency that can be imported or exported (this is the one that led to those hypothetical transactions in the cafés).

- ✔ Some countries ban citizens of a country from owning foreign currency (this one also led to those meetings in cafés).

- ✔ Some countries have restrictions on currency exchanges, perhaps restricting access to foreign currency to government operations.

- ✔ Some countries have fixed official exchange rates as opposed to free-floating rates. Just a few examples include Cameroon, Panama, Venezuela, Bulgaria, and Saudi Arabia.

Becoming an Exchange Rate Expert

Each of the factors in this section indirectly affects the cost of your Frontier Markets investments. You need know that they exist, but you don't have to worry about calculating them if you invest through a Global Frontier Markets fund. The fund manager has included them in the fund's costs. You only have to become deeply familiar with these intricacies if you're trading directly on a foreign exchange, an approach that we would rarely recommend.

Becoming a real exchange rate expert would mean putting so much time into the study of exchange rates that it would in effect become a part-time job. Each of the potential variations can change frequently.

Exchange rates can be quoted in several ways:

- ✔ The official rate

- ✔ The rate including a service charge by a financial institution

- ✔ The rate plus the extra charge levied by credit card companies when you travel abroad

Studying swings in rates

Becoming an exchange rate expert means coming to grips with at least three factors:

- ✔ Rates change daily and hourly.

- ✔ Currency swings are caused by a huge variety of factors ranging from the stability of a government to the economy to oil prices. Factors influencing the relationship of the American dollar to the Canadian dollar include both "made in the U.S.A." factors such as the economy and "made-in-Canada" factors such as commodity prices.

- ✔ Currency swings can be an instrument of monetary policy, such as when a government wants to tighten or loosen the money supply, or an economic tool, such as when the government wants to increase exports by influencing the exchange rate between its own and other currencies.

Somewhat surprisingly, black market rates can become instruments of economic policy.

At the time of writing, Reuters reports that black market currency transactions are not necessarily furtive arrangements in North Korea. Once reserved for official exchange only in zones aimed at attracting foreign investment and in illegal underground market deals elsewhere, black market rates are being used more frequently and openly in North Korean cities.

Publicly advertised prices at rates close to the market rate — around 8,000 yuan to the dollar versus the official rate of 96 — could signal Pyongyang is trying to *marketise* its centrally planned economy and allow a burgeoning "grey market" to thrive. This could boost growth and capture more of the dollars and Chinese yuan circulating widely so that North Korea can pay for imports of oil and food.

Put more simply the article suggests that North Korea sees allowing a currency black market as a means to an end. In this scenario, the end is bringing in more foreign currency.

Being prepared for trading costs

When you buy or sell foreign currency at the foreign exchange booths in an airport or in a hotel, very often you will see signs saying "Buy from us — no commission!" Then you examine the difference between the rates at which the booth will *buy* the currency and that at which it will *sell* to you (known as the spread). You can also compare the rates at some airport booths and the rates available in less pressured situations and you realize why they don't charge commission.

Spreads on exchanging foreign currencies, even those of developed countries with highly liquid issues like the United States, Canada, the Eurozone, Japan, and the United Kingdom, can be as wide as 5 percent or even 10 percent when you, as an individual, change your money. Of course, rates for larger sums are much better, and spreads narrower and your bank will usually give you a reasonable rate if you give it sufficient notice.

When dealing in smaller less liquid currencies, such as those of Emerging and Frontier Markets, the same problem applies in spades. Spreads even for large transactions can be very wide, and the costs of exchanging money are higher because there is little competition for the banks that deal in these currencies. That's why using ADRs and GDRs is almost always preferable to buying shares listed in the local currency. Although the movement of the currency against the U.S. dollar will still be reflected in their price, trading in ADRs and GDRs means that the investor doesn't have to deal directly with spread and the charges. It's rather a "what you see is what you get" proposition.

Anticipating bank charges

Bank charges are a fact of life in almost every type of financial transaction except for cash arrangements. Those transactions aside, there is usually a real or hidden bank charge in other transactions.

You aren't necessarily avoiding a bank charge levied by a foreign bank by doing your investing through a Global Frontier Fund but you are saving yourself the complexity of dealing with the bank itself.

Eyeing Differences in International Accounting Conventions

International accounting conventions provide the reassurance of an apples-to-apples comparison of financial results. Portfolio managers use accounting reports (and analysis of them) as one of a series of decision-making tools for investment decisions.

As long as you know that differences in accounting conventions exist from country to country you don't have to become deeply immersed in the complexities of accounting systems unless you become involved in direct trading in a frontier country. You've probably seen by now what we think of going that route!

Grasping the fundamentals of accounting conventions

Accounting conventions are those terms found in the notes to financial statements, usually at the back of financial reports, generally known as *accounting standards* or *standard accounting practice.* These include the standards, terminology, and rules that accountants follow in recording and summarizing information for financial statements. Using the apples-to-apples analogy, they will often tell you which kind of apples you need to take into account when reading the report. This information allows all financial statement users to understand how a report's authors calculated its key items and totals. That in turn allows readers of financial statements to make the apples-to-apples comparisons.

Generally Accepted Accounting Principles (GAAP)

It would be difficult for someone outside of the accounting profession to become truly conversant with the complexities of each accounting convention. Once during a journalists' conference, an extremely articulate accounting executive explained the intricacies of the Generally Accepted Accounting Principles (GAAP) and then asked for questions, perhaps expecting an onslaught from a roomful of professionals who spend their working days asking questions. Strangely, he faced row upon row of glazed expressions and no one had any questions. And that happened in a roomful of financial media specialists who always have questions!

The puzzling GAAP complexities comprise a set of core accounting concepts that are so firmly entrenched that in some cases, an accountant who deviates from them can be considered at fault professionally. Briefly stated these principles include:

- Separation of accounting between business transactions and those of the owner
- Clear distinction and separate treatment of business and personal expenses
- Valuation of business assets at typically cost or other clearly disclosed basis
- Conservative estimations
- Importance of objectivity
- Equal length of fiscal periods for measuring financial progress
- Recognition of revenue at the time of the completion of a transaction

✔ Accounting for purchases initially at cost price, and continued on that basis unless specifically varied and clearly disclosed

✔ Consistency of reporting from period to period

✔ Comprehensiveness of disclosure

✔ Depreciation of assets, and on what basis it is being calculated

International Financial Reporting Standards (IFRS)

The International Financial Report Standards (IFRS) contains some of the core principles of GAAP but has several marked differences, including changes to asset reporting requirements which led to a more complex and detailed reporting regime.

Since a major incentive for changes came from the market freeze in 2008–2009 connected to asset-backed securities, the IFRS standards include new requirements mandating better disclosure of risk, especially counter-party risk.

The new requirements include a fair value measurement designed to reflect asset values more accurately than before the crisis (although these requirements were in the design phase before the crisis).

The rule of thumb to use when thinking about GAAP and IFRS reporting standards is that North American companies use GAAP and those outside North America use IFRS.

Confusing matters further, Canadian publicly traded companies currently use IFRS and historically, the application of the American GAAP was not always identical to the Canadian GAAP — a difference that those individuals at the lecture could not have contemplated.

At time of writing, IFRS continues evolving with interpretation pronouncements coming out regularly.

Appreciating how accounting differences affect investment information

Appreciating how accounting differences affect investment information means focusing on areas such as fair market value of assets that vary between the GAAP and IFRS accounting systems. Given the nervousness of advisors and investors over issues such as asset values as a result (among many other results) of the financial crisis, we can reasonably suggest the importance of a greater focus on a company's asset values.

IFRS reporting focuses on fair market value reporting to drive increased disclosure of reporting of gains and losses, including those connected to some financial assets. In this perspective, fair market value can influence results more than historical cost reporting, meaning major shifts in how things are reported.

The IFRS emphasis on fair market value means that there can be wide swings in how certain items are reported, especially in areas of unrealized gains or losses.

Seeking out audited reports

An auditor's report provides investors with an auditor's opinion, perhaps including disclaimers as to the veracity of statements and figures contained in a company's annual or quarterly report. This report telegraphs to decision makers with a stake in a company's fortunes an evaluation of the statements contained in the report. The report may contain a combination of assurances, caveats, and warning flags.

Financial reports are the basis on which investors, whether professional or individual, make their investment decisions. The aim of the company's report and accounts is to provide a stakeholder or potential stakeholder, such as an investor, the ability to see whether the company is profitable, the size of its assets and liabilities, whether they are long-term or short-term, and how the company is doing compared to the previous period, preferably the previous five years.

After reading the profit-and-loss section, the balance sheet (assets and liabilities), and the cash flow statement, an observer with a basic knowledge of finance should be able to understand whether the company is making money and turning that money into cash, how many assets it has, and how they were financed (with profits, equity, or debt). On that basis, they will then decide whether the share price is cheap, fair value, or expensive compared to the underlying business.

For Frontier Markets, the quality of reports and accounts may not be quite as good as those in the United States, Europe, or Japan. However, a number of frontier companies have ADRs and GDRs listed on established exchanges, meaning that they comply with North American or European standards. The reports of subsidiaries of global multinational companies listed locally will also often be of an international standard, which provides some reassurance. Still, if they have been audited by one of the Big Four accountants or a local affiliate, then the standard should be respectable.

Again, we recommend leaving the details of analysis to the manager of a Frontier Markets fund.

Part III

Approaching Frontier Market Investments with Savvy

Top Seven Questions to Determine Your Risk Tolerance

- ✔ Do sharp portfolio swings trouble you?

- ✔ If your portfolio declined tomorrow by 15 percent, would you lose sleep?

- ✔ Would that decrease have a major effect on your financial health?

- ✔ If the portfolio declined tomorrow by 15 percent and you considered the decline temporary, would you still feel a strong temptation to sell the depreciating assets?

- ✔ If the decline appeared permanent, would you have lost too much maneuvering room in your finances and have to make major sacrifices?

- ✔ Would the decline have an irreparable effect on your plans for your beneficiaries?

- ✔ If you lost your job or business tomorrow, would you have to liquidate investments to pay ongoing expenses?

Visit www.dummies.com/extras/frontiermarkets for more information on researching Frontier Markets.

In this part. . .

- ✔ Understand risk, volatility, and correlation.

- ✔ Gauge your ability to deal with risk and volatility.

- ✔ Understand the significance of correlation and non-correlation.

- ✔ Separate the bad news from the news you need for investment decision-making.

- ✔ Check your current investments for exposure to Frontier Markets.

- ✔ Work with an advisor to calculate your ideal exposure.

- ✔ Develop your investment timetable.

Chapter 8

Getting Clear about Risk, Volatility, and Correlation

*W*hen embarking on the study of anything new and unknown, it helps to square away the terminology at the outset. In that way, everyone can read for the proverbial same page.

Frontiers, by their very definition, divide the known from the unknown, and straddle the limits between what is familiar and unfamiliar.

That's a good short description of the place that Frontier Markets occupy in most investors' portfolios. The developed countries' stock markets form the majority of most international portfolios, with Emerging Markets having been gradually added to many portfolios over the last 15 years. It is rare nowadays to find an international or global fund that doesn't include at least a few stocks from China and Brazil, Russia, or India, especially as some companies in these countries are now among the largest in the world by market capitalization. (Market capitalization refers to the total value of the number of shares in circulation.)

Now Frontier Markets are beginning to appear on investors' radar screens, as awareness of the size of the opportunities available becomes known. There are also some easily accessible avenues opening up to allow the average investor to gain access to these countries, such as exchange-traded funds (ETFs) and mutual funds, most of which were not available as recently as five years ago.

So in this chapter, we continue laying the groundwork, or more specifically, increasing your understanding of the terminology and the things that you need to consider as you embark on frontier investing.

One of the most important factors to consider is the fact that despite being volatile, Frontier Markets, like Emerging Markets, are not necessarily riskier. Investors understandably confuse the two, but the fact that share prices move around a lot doesn't mean that there is a higher chance of losing money. Investors should consider Frontier Markets as similar in character to technology stocks; the fact that they can be very volatile hasn't made them an unsuccessful investment. You obviously need to be selective about which companies (or countries) you choose, but that's why using an actively managed fund for investing in volatile asset classes makes good sense.

One of the major attractions of these markets is that they don't move in sync with developed or even major Emerging Markets, so adding even a small percentage to your portfolio reduces its overall volatility. They are noncorrelated, to use the investment terminology. Having assets that don't move in the same direction is very valuable when constructing your investment portfolio.

Distinguishing Risk from Volatility

Many investors have been deterred from investing in Emerging or Frontier Markets due to their perceptions of the high level of risk. That leads investors to make the common mistake of confusing *volatility,* or how much the price of a stock market index or company's share price moves around, with *risk,* which is the degree to which the share price might erode permanently.

Due to Emerging and Frontier Markets' sharp rises and falls, potential investors believe they run a high risk of losing some — or even all — of the capital that they have invested in these countries.

This belief confuses volatility with risk, an error widely made and entirely understandable, given typical investor psychology. However, that error often prevents people from enjoying the benefits of undervalued investments which happen to be volatile.

Studies of behavioral psychology by numerous observers, including Daniel Kahneman, winner of the Nobel Prize for Economics, conclude that the inherent mental biases that all of us possess make us bad investors. The human habit of using mental shortcuts (sometimes called *heuristics*) has three effects that combine to make most investors prone to failure.

The three major biases that Kahneman and others identified are:

- Investors are bad at correctly judging the attractiveness of different investments. The "fight or flight" responses that kept our ancestors safe from saber-toothed tigers in the prehistoric era do not make us well-equipped to judge an investment correctly.

- Once we have made our decision, we are very overconfident in our judgments to the extent of ignoring any contrary evidence that might contradict our original thesis.

- We are very reluctant to incur losses if our decisions turn out to be incorrect. Kahneman and others found that the emotional pain of realizing a loss is between two and three times as great as the pleasure of booking a profit, so we tend to sell our winners and keep our losers, the exact opposite behavior to that required to become a successful investor.

These traits are reinforced by a natural dislike of sudden changes, which the rational part of the human brain is ill-equipped to handle effectively. Studies find that during times when lots of things are happening, or large amounts of information are received in a short time, the instinctive part of the human brain, sometimes known as the *lizard brain,* automatically takes over.

Lizard brain often results in actions that are devoid of any logical basis but which satisfy the instinctive brain's need to reduce the information overload and simplify the situation.

Thus, high levels of volatility, such as occur in these markets, make it difficult for investors to behave rationally when considering investments that tend to be more volatile than more-developed markets.

Furthermore, high volatility levels tend to reinforce the desire to take counterproductive actions, such as selling after markets have fallen sharply. While this may appear to be contrary to the human failing of keeping our losers, in fact it reinforces the losses caused by doing so, because investors tend to give up on losing positions at the worst possible time — after they have fallen sharply.

This behavior is reinforced by another behavioral quirk, which is known as *unfamiliarity bias.* Stock markets that are unfamiliar to investors, as is usually the case with Emerging Markets, and especially with Frontier Markets, are vulnerable to frightened overseas investors dumping their holdings over unfavorable headlines.

In many cases, the country at the center of events is many hundreds or thousands of miles distant from where the fund in which they are invested has holdings, with a completely different political, religious, or economic history, and the unrest or violence filling the headlines is being driven by completely different factors. However, even this knowledge doesn't prevent foreign investors from withdrawing their money.

Examining the Nature of Risk in Frontier and Emerging Markets

The first comment anyone looking at Frontier Markets usually makes is, "These seem like very risky markets. Why should I bother with investing in them?" We believe that these countries are now where the major Emerging Markets were 15 years ago, and offer investors the same opportunity to make superior returns. If the risk, which for investment purposes is defined as volatility, is balanced by the possibility of making superior returns then Frontier Markets should become worth considering as an investment.

As Frontier Markets have a relatively short history, it's more useful to look at what happened to Emerging Markets over the last couple of decades. Despite the widely held perception among most investors that Emerging Markets (including Frontier Markets) are much more volatile than developed markets, the evidence shows that the difference between them has been narrowing over the last decade.

The volatility of developed markets, as measured by the standard deviation of annual returns of the MSCI World Index, was 17 for the decade ended in 2009, while the volatility of the MSCI Emerging Markets Index was about 45 percent higher at 25.

The volatility of returns is measured by what is known as their standard deviation. Officially, standard deviation represents the statistical measure of the degree to which an individual value in a probability distribution tends to vary from the mean of the distribution. So for indices and stocks, volatility becomes how much returns in any one year are likely to vary from their long-term mean average. The greater (higher) the standard deviation, the more volatile the series being measured will be. Standard deviation doesn't care which direction the variance is occurring, merely how large the variance is.

Since 1980 as stock markets have grown and trading has boomed, the volatility of both developed and Emerging Markets has risen. However, the volatility of developed markets has risen much faster, from a standard deviation of 11 in the early 1980s to 17, while that of Emerging Markets has also risen, from 19 to 25, a much lower percentage increase. Thus both developed and Emerging Markets are a lot more volatile than formerly but the difference between them has narrowed a lot. Interestingly, the standard deviation for Frontier Markets was lower than that of Emerging Markets over the five years ending November 30, 2012, at 24.1 against 29.6 for Emerging Markets. This period includes the Financial Crisis, but does emphasize that, because of their small size and lack of liquidity, Frontier Markets tend to be less volatile than the bigger, more liquid Emerging Markets.

While individual Emerging Markets such as China, India, and Brazil remain much more volatile than individual developed markets (32.5 versus 23.5 over the decade ended in 2009), they have a lot less volatility than in the 1980s. But individual developed markets have actually become more volatile, rising from 20 in the 1980s to 23.5 today.

A team of professors at the London Business School, Elroy Dimson, Paul Marsh, and Mike Staunton, have studied the long-term returns from stock markets over the last century, and the role played by Emerging Markets in a portfolio. They point out that "For global investors, the high volatility of individual (emerging) markets does not matter, as long as they hold a diversified portfolio of Emerging Markets."

They go on to note that investors need not even be concerned by the higher volatility of the Emerging Markets index, noting "What matters is how much an incremental holding in Emerging Markets contributes to the risk of their overall portfolio."

Although the correlation (how closely one asset matches the performance of another asset) of Emerging Markets to developed markets has risen over the last decade, it still doesn't track the latter completely. Therefore, adding even a small position in Emerging Markets to your portfolio will disproportionately reduce its volatility.

Put another way, a 1 percent allocation to Emerging Markets will reduce portfolio volatility by more than 1 percent. With the correlation of Frontier Markets to developed markets being much lower than that of Emerging Markets, the case for including a small allocation to them in a portfolio is even more compelling. We examine correlation in more detail later in this chapter.

Dimson, Marsh, and Saunders state that a higher beta implies a higher expected return to compensate investors for the higher risk they are undergoing. Given that the long-term expected return from developed markets over the last century has been 3 percent to 3.5 percent per annum above the return from cash, investors should expect a modestly higher extra return of 1 percent to 1.5 percent P.A. from Emerging Markets, given their beta of 1.3 (3 to 3.5 to 5 is 1.3). In other words, investors are being logical in requiring higher returns for being willing to accept higher risks.

TECHNICAL STUFF

What's with the Greek symbols?

Like any discipline with pretensions to academic stature, economics uses Greek letters to describe important concepts. In portfolio management, alpha is the value added by a fund manager above the return that would be expected from just investing in an index. Beta measures the risk of the fund compared to the market benchmark. Statistically it is the co-variance of fund and the benchmark, divided by the variance of the benchmark.

If a fund or index has a beta of 1, it is just as risky as the benchmark; if it has a higher beta, as the MSCI Emerging Markets Index does, compared to the MSCI World Index, with a beta of 1.3 times, then it is more risky (volatile). Obviously, an investment with a beta below 1 is less risky.

Anticipating Volatility

The structure of Emerging and Frontier Markets reinforces their inherent volatility. In developed markets, by far the largest investors in equity or bond markets are institutions with a very long time horizon, such as life insurers or pension funds.

They receive regular inflows every two weeks or every month from their policyholders or members and the same pattern is seen for individuals using tax-sheltered savings and pension plans such as 401(k)s and individual retirement accounts (IRAs) in the U.S. Similarly in Canada, the United Kingdom, Australia, Singapore, and Hong Kong, there are individual, institutional, and government-run schemes regularly investing large sums of money into the capital markets, providing a base to support the markets.

This is emphatically not the case in most Emerging, and particularly, Frontier Markets. There are no, or very few, institutional investors to offset the actions of individuals and foreign investors. Therefore, bull and bear markets in Emerging and Frontier Markets tend to be more violent than those in mature developed markets, as they tend to become self-reinforcing.

This means that domestic individual investors tend to watch what the large foreign investors, such as Emerging or Frontier Market funds, are doing, piggyback on their inflows on the way up, and attempt to exit before the foreigners on the way down.

For this reason, one of the major elements investors need to examine when assessing the attractiveness or otherwise of Emerging and Frontier Markets is foreign investor inflows and outflows and the premiums at which shares available to foreigners (foreign shares) have traded recently. If there have been sustained inflows and foreign shares are at a big premium to local shares, it's safe to assume that most of the good news is already reflected in the price. You may have heard financial analysts use the expression *baked in* to the share price, referring to these factors.

One other fact to keep in mind when thinking about investing in Emerging or Frontier Markets is that many countries have regulations that either prohibit domestic institutions from investing in equities or limit the amount that they can invest to some fairly low percentage, usually 15 percent or less. This means the domestic institutions are required to invest the vast majority of their assets in government bonds, a requirement that helps the government to fund its deficits and keeps interest rates artificially low, a policy known as *financial suppression.* If you think this sounds similar to what is happening in the U.S. at the moment, with the Federal Reserve buying $85 billion of bonds a month, interest rates effectively being kept at zero, and banks being required to have high levels of capital that are kept in safe (government) assets, you wouldn't be far from wrong.

Gauging your ability to deal with risk and volatility

A questionnaire asking investors how risk tolerant they are in an attempt to assess how they would react if the stock market fell 10 percent or 15 percent is one of those exercises that, while not doomed to failure, is very dependent upon how the stock and bond markets have been performing over the previous two to three years.

This is one of the reasons why we advise you to find a financial advisor with whom you feel comfortable to help you realistically assess your tolerance for risk and volatility. Although many investors felt that they could handle a decline of 15 percent or more when they asked that question in the pre-Financial Crisis days of 2006–2007, they discovered that in fact their risk tolerance was much lower than they had realized when markets spiraled down in 2008–2009.

Right up until the Great Financial Crisis of 2008–2009, many individuals didn't recognize the old maxim "a rising tide lifts all boats," and that made them overly confident in their ability to handle downturns in the market. Prior to that the indices had been rising for over five years and the S&P 500 and NASDAQ had more than doubled over the same period.

When the stock markets started falling in late 2007, Bear Stearns had to be rescued in early 2008, mortgage giants Fannie Mae and Freddie Mac had to be bailed out in September 2008, and Lehman Brothers was allowed to go bankrupt later that month. Investors saw markets falling almost 50 percent within a year, and many were understandably horrified and sold shares in a panic.

Some of those who sold had overestimated their risk tolerance when the markets provided good returns before the crisis, and found to their dismay that their real tolerance was much lower than they had believed earlier.

In order to avoid a mismatch between risk tolerance and the nature of the investments they suggest to their clients, advisors should walk investors through a self-examination that focuses on several questions:

- Do sharp portfolio swings trouble you?

- If your portfolio declined tomorrow by 15 percent, would you lose sleep?

- Would that decrease have a major effect on your financial health?

- If the portfolio declined tomorrow by 15 percent and you considered the decline temporary, would you still feel a strong temptation to sell the depreciating assets?

- If the decline appeared permanent, would you have lost too much maneuvering room in your finances and have to make major sacrifices?

- Would the decline have an irreparable effect on your plans for your beneficiaries?

- If you lost your job or business tomorrow, would you have to liquidate investments to pay ongoing expenses?

If you answer "yes" to all or most of these questions, you have a low threshold for risk and volatility, and need to redefine your risk tolerance and the structure of your finances.

This obviously applies to an investor's entire portfolio. Any advisor will try to ensure that a client has a mixture of assets including cash, government and corporate bonds, and stocks and equity mutual funds. Not all of these assets move in the same direction at the same time, as some are not correlated with each other. When they are negatively correlated, they move in the opposite direction. Thus, those investors who owned Treasury bonds or government bond funds saw them rise in value during the crisis as investors fled equities for the safe haven of government-guaranteed obligations.

Understanding the risk and volatility in Frontier Markets

For investors considering Frontier Markets, risk tolerance becomes less important because these investments will only form a small part of a portfolio, probably less than 5 percent of the international equity portion. Furthermore, as we discuss in the next section, they are not correlated with developed or Emerging Markets and so are unlikely to move in line with them.

This doesn't mean that they aren't volatile; in fact, their illiquid nature and small market size means they are more volatile than either of the other two equity classes. In 2008–2009, the MSCI Frontier Markets Index fell by over 50 percent. However, given that investors considering Frontier Markets should have a time horizon of at least five years, and that they will have discussed the reasons for selecting them with an advisor, they should not be put off including Frontier Markets in their portfolio simply because they are volatile.

In fact, including Frontier Markets in a portfolio will reduce its overall volatility, even though these markets are quite volatile. The solution to this paradox is contained in the next section on correlation.

Seeking the Elusive Lack of Correlation

Perhaps the most important reason for including Frontier Markets in your portfolio is that because of their small size and illiquidity, they don't move in line with either the developed markets like the U.S., Europe, and Japan, or major Emerging Markets like China, India, and Brazil. In other words, they are not correlated with either of the two main types of equities. Therefore, adding a small percentage of Frontier Markets to your portfolio will reduce its volatility, as these markets will tend to zig while the other markets zag.

Defining investment correlation

Correlation in statistics is defined as the degree of association between two random variables. The correlation between the graphs of two data sets is the degree to which they resemble each other, so that a correlation coefficient of 0 means the two are absolutely independent while a correlation of 1 means they always occur together (or never occur together).

Thus there is an obvious high positive correlation between scholastic aptitude and college admission or smoking and lung cancer. Frontier Markets, because of their small size, limited liquidity, and the difficulty and high costs of trading, tend to have low correlations with developed markets such as the U.S., Europe, and Japan.

Emerging Markets had a low correlation with developed markets a couple of decades ago, but as they have developed and globalized, their correlation has risen. Over the decade to 2009, the correlation between the MSCI Emerging Markets Index and the MSCI World Index rose from 0.75 to 0.91. All market correlations have risen over the last few years, partially due to the Financial Crisis in 2008–2009.

Frontier Markets, however, have much lower correlation with developed markets. Research by pension manager Russell Investments shows that they have low correlation with Canadian and US equities similar to the situation with Emerging Markets in their infancy. Prior to the global financial crisis, the rolling correlation between them was generally below 0.30 and similar to Emerging Markets, even negative at times.

Although the crisis caused correlation to briefly spike to over 0.60 in 2008–2009, it has since trended downwards toward its historical range of 0.20 and lower. Russell goes on to say that it would not be surprising for correlations to have periodic spikes due to ongoing uncertainty.

Frontier Markets also have very low correlations with other asset classes, making them a great diversifier in traditional portfolios. In fact, Russell found the highest correlation among developed markets was only 0.44 (the Russell Developed ex-North America Index).

Surprisingly, Frontier Markets, although they form a subset of the Emerging Markets universe, also have a low correlation with them, at 0.41, perhaps reflecting the increased globalization of the major Emerging Markets like the BRIC countries (Brazil, Russia, India, and China).

As you might intuitively expect, the least-developed Frontier Markets, such as Africa, as represented by the MSCI Frontier Markets Africa Index, have the lowest correlations with developed (0.39) and Emerging (0.36) Markets.

Finally, Frontier Markets not only have low correlation with developed and Emerging Markets but also very low correlations with each other, given that what happens in Estonia has little connection with Nigeria or with Bangladesh.

Realizing why correlation is a crucial investment factor

Finding noncorrelated assets is the Holy Grail or philosopher's stone of portfolio construction. Putting together different asset classes that don't move in the same direction means that a portfolio manager can reduce the overall volatility of the portfolio while also increasing its return.

The traditional balanced fund comprised of 60 percent equities and 40 percent bonds is a shorthand way of constructing such a portfolio. Investment grade bonds, whether issued by governments or corporations, do not move in line with stocks. In fact, they may on occasion be negatively correlated, as occurred during the Great Depression, when a deflationary environment meant that government bonds rose steadily in value as stocks fell almost 90 percent.

Even in less extreme economic situations, such as the Financial Crisis, government bonds again held and even increased their value while stocks and corporate obligations fell, in some cases by as much as 50 percent.

In general, however, the different asset classes add value in different ways. Bonds are less volatile, reducing the overall volatility of the portfolio while providing income; at the same time, stocks provide exposure to growth and some degree of inflation protection as they can pass on price increases and preserve their real value.

Finding an asset that isn't correlated with the other main asset classes is therefore extremely valuable. When high-yield bonds (otherwise known as "junk" bonds) became popular in the late 1980s, one of their attractions, apart from the higher yield, was that they tended to act more like equities than bonds. Because the companies that issued them were not investment grade, their prices tended to rise when the economy was doing well and stocks were doing well. That was the exact opposite of traditional bonds, whose prices declined due to fears of rising inflation.

By adding some high-yield bonds to a traditional bond portfolio, the yield would rise but the portfolio's volatility would decline as the high-yield bonds were not correlated with the traditional bonds; in some cases, they were actually negatively correlated.

Similarly, when Emerging Markets were first introduced into international equity portfolios in the late 1980s, they too were not correlated with developed markets and reduced the volatility of portfolios while providing higher returns.

Today, both of these invaluable asset classes have become much more correlated with mainstream assets: high-yield bonds because their yields have fallen so much, and Emerging Markets investments because globalization has increased the correlation between them and developed markets.

Therefore, Frontier Markets represents an asset class that is not correlated with either developed or Emerging Markets and whose individual countries are not highly correlated with each other. They provide you with the opportunity to add an element to your portfolio that offers the chance of higher returns while at the same time lowering its overall volatility because of its low correlations.

Recognizing the increase in correlation that happens as economies connect

Perhaps we can suggest some basic economic concepts here that will prevent confusion.

As economies grow, they inevitably become more connected to each other with increases in trade. When a country is isolated from the world, as in the case of Communist regimes like Cuba and North Korea or autocracies like Myanmar, they will be too poor to be able to afford many imports and will not produce anything that anyone else wants to buy, except for raw materials, which generally have low value.

Once liberalization begins, trade starts to flow, incomes rise, manufacturing adds value to the inputs it processes, and the country's population can afford to buy more foreign goods. Access to foreign goods allows its population to discover what other countries and cultures are doing, wearing, riding, watching, or using.

This leads to more volatile markets, as foreign capital flows into or out of the country, and increased correlation as the developing nation becomes more aware of and more influenced by global economic expansion.

As recently as 30 years ago, adding European stock markets, such as those in the United Kingdom, France, and Germany, to a domestic United States portfolio was a good way to reduce volatility because the correlations between Europe and the U.S. were relatively low at around 0.5 to 0.6. Japan was an even better diversifier, as its domestic market was still heavily protected, making its domestically oriented stocks virtually immune to global economic conditions, although its blue chip exporters in the auto and electronics industries were obviously affected.

Nowadays, not only are developed markets essentially trading as one, but even the Emerging Markets have become essentially a high beta version of the developed world. China, Russia, and Brazil (and to a lesser extent India) have become among the largest economies in the world and the marginal buyers that determine the price and supply for many commodities.

The Bottom Line on Risk and Volatility

You should not confuse volatility, or how much a stock or an index moves up and down, with risk, which is the chance that you might suffer a permanent loss of your hard-earned capital. It's a difficult distinction to keep in mind when stock markets are plummeting, riots are breaking out in some of these countries, and you're watching the chaos on the nightly news or on your Internet feed while experts suggest dumping mutual funds that have exposure to these markets.

Nonetheless, simply because a stock market index moves up and down a lot does not mean it's risky. It simply means it moves around a lot; it's volatile. This is because Frontier Markets are small by comparison with the developed markets and major Emerging Markets. Few of them are worth more than US$40 billion in total, less than 15 percent of the market capitalization of Wells Fargo Bank alone. They're also not very liquid, given low volumes of shares traded, partially because of the absence of participation by any institutional investors like local pension funds and insurance companies.

Therefore, any buying or selling tends to make prices move much more than would be the case in a sophisticated market with ultra-fast trading systems and thousands of professional investors like endowments, hedge funds, and big mutual fund complexes based in the United States, Japan, and the United Kingdom.

These considerations don't mean that investing in these markets is a bad idea; they're just a reminder that volatility comes with the territory. Make sure you're comfortable with this concept. Discuss it with your advisor and set an appropriate percentage that enables you to sleep at night. We'd suggest no more than 5 percent to 10 percent of your international equity allocation.

They're also not correlated with each other, because what happens in Kazakhstan stays in Kazakhstan, unless Borat makes another movie. Events — even within the same region — don't necessarily have any impact on other countries, which are often hundreds of miles away and have very different histories and economies and are at different stages of development.

This combination of rapidly growing countries with young populations, low levels of urbanization, rapid industrialization, and growing trade flows that don't move in line with other major economies makes Frontier Markets an attractive element to add to your portfolio. Make sure you invest with a suitable time horizon in mind because there will be bumps along the road (there's that higher volatility coming in). But as with Emerging Markets, these countries will gradually become more correlated with the rest of the world, reducing the benefit of their present noncorrelation.

Chapter 9

Becoming a Bad News Connoisseur

In This Chapter

▶ Evaluating temporary and permanent bad news

▶ Examining bad news in the Middle East

▶ Trading successfully after bad news

Watching the nightly barrage of riots, shootings, bombings, and political protests can try your outlook on life, your political views, your feelings about our civilization, your business decisions, and perhaps even your vacation travel choices.

We certainly do not see any problem with you basing your business travel choices on what you see on tonight's newscast. In your business decisions, you have to consider several factors, such as:

✔ The safety of employees

✔ The company's business targets

✔ The safety of facilities in other countries

✔ The most cost-efficient deployment of expensive and limited resources

Depending on your position, those may be professional obligations. Your continued employment and possibly your advancement at your company, or even the success of your own company, may depend on how correctly you make these decisions, how effectively you execute them, and the positive or negative impacts that follow them.

Those harsh realities may run through your mind when you watch news footage of a riot in a country in which your employer or your own company has employees, facilities, business interests, or sales targets.

However, don't base your investment choices on the riots, shootings, bombings, and political protests that you see on the news. And certainly don't base investment choices on the imagery in a blockbuster Hollywood film populated by bumbling assassins, incredibly beautiful spies, and even breathtaking scenery.

Rather, you should base these decisions on the advice of your financial advisor, reputable books (such as this one, frankly), your own careful research over a period of time, your risk tolerance (which is reflected in your asset allocation), and the other factors we discuss in this book.

Moreover, we also don't believe there is anything wrong with the news media (though many might make that inference from this commentary). In fact one of us is a longtime financial journalist and the other an experienced media commentator.

We do submit, however, that the nightly newscast does not necessarily provide the best platform for investment decision-making.

Separating Bad News from Market News

By the time the traumatic events have made headlines, the financial markets have often anticipated them, fulfilling their role as predictors of future events. Studies have demonstrated that equity and bond markets often anticipate changes in the economy by six to nine months. That leads to situations in which bad economic news has often become "baked into" equity values by the time of broadcast or publication. The result is that by the time you hear or read the bad news, it may be too late to make a profitable — or even loss-saving decision based on it.

We understand that you may feel surrounded by information, much of it bad news at worst or confusing news at best. The 24-hour news cycle, countless Internet news portals, satellite radio, mobile news screens, conventional radio, television, newspapers, and magazines combine to keep us instantly and perhaps unrelentingly informed of developments in every news event.

The "All News All the Time" format satisfies news junkies, shift workers, and others who need constant updating on the minutiae of a news story as well as the core details.

As a part of the 24-hour news cycle, seemingly endless news footage of explosions and flames rivets the attention more than color-coded bar charts showing investment opportunities. A shouting correspondent ducking from gunfire telegraphs more drama than a thoughtful analysis of a foreign economy. Airplane crashes and blackened wreckage attract more attention than thoughtful analysis of airline stocks.

How did we become news junkies?

As a fact of contemporary life, what we now call the 24-hour news cycle started with the launch of the Cable News Network, which became known as CNN in 1980 and accelerated with the launch of CNN2 in 1982.

CNN later renamed CNN2 to CNN Headline News and later renamed it again to HLN. The success of those networks led to other 24-hour operations in television and radio in the United States and Canada. It also led to the all-news format at the United Kingdom's British Broadcasting Corporation and Sky News as well as operations in Europe and the Middle East.

The all-news-all-the-time radio format followed these developments and network executives skewed it to individuals rushing to work and needing basic news, weather, and traffic information with a short-and-sweet approach.

Dramatic or tragic events — whether natural or man-made — make gripping news stories and provide front-page headlines and lead stories on television and radio news. Wars, riots, rebellions, demonstrations, strikes, earthquakes, hurricanes, fires, and medical emergencies provide great pictures and dramatic stories and the 24-hour news cycle means that we cannot help but stay constantly informed on the bad news.

However, notwithstanding both authors' many years of involvement with professional media, we know that constantly informed does not necessarily amount to *fully informed*.

The genre of news sometimes called *hit-and-run* journalism, while honest, accurate, and perhaps more professionally intended than suggested by critics, doesn't always deal well with the economic aftermath of today's news.

News media and their audiences tend to focus on these front-page stories, but should investors shape their worldviews and decisions accordingly? That's an understandable move from a human nature perspective but a very faulty move when it influences investment decision-making.

Distinguishing Between Temporary and Permanent Bad News

Most bad news that affects investment is temporary in nature, although the word *temporary* is certainly open to interpretation.

A few examples of recent temporary downturns

In an easily recognizable and recent example, the American housing industry plummeted during the darkest days of the recession and took with it equities connected to it, such as Home Depot. At the time of writing, the housing industry appears to be recovering and Home Depot trades in the US$76 range — over $30 per share above its recessionary lows.

After the darkest days of the so-called European crisis (which was actually several crises that converged at the same time), some European mutual funds and equities have recovered to their pre-crisis levels. (Many European countries derive large proportions of their revenues from Emerging and Frontier Markets.) Those who sold out their European holdings took losses that could have been avoided. Those who stayed the course often avoided losses — not to mention otherwise unnecessary trading costs!

In a third example, the prices of some commodity producers such as Potash Corporation of Saskatchewan dropped dramatically when China announced in mid-2013 that its commodity requirements would decrease. But at the time of writing, share prices have started recovering.

Also during 2013, share prices of Las Vegas Sands dipped each time rumors of scandal broke in the news, but at time of writing, shares trade in the $66 to $67 range, approximately US$27 above the one-year low price.

(To be fair, some share prices, such as those of some financial institutions, have not recovered to pre-recessionary levels and may never completely recover.)

These and other example do not mean that restraint comes easy. The shareholders in all these companies most likely had some heart-stopping moments during the dark days of the recession.

Considering bad news leading to broad investment judgments

When considering bad news leading to broad investment judgments, the conversation often turns to *buying opportunities,* referring to shares for which valuations have become eroded but remain likely to recover. Bear in mind though, not every depressed stock qualifies as a buying opportunity. Whenever a market crisis occurs, sooner or later an analyst will suggest that it may have created a buying opportunity. Often that analysis proves correct. Still, *buying opportunity* is a very overused phrase.

For example, while those who bought Home Depot at depressed prices at the bottom of the recession may have financed a cruise with their proceeds if they retained their holdings until 2013, shareholders in several American financial institutions have yet to regain pre-recession share price levels.

The solution — as with any other area of life — is to avoid across-the-board generalizations.

The Arab Spring and Other Middle Eastern Tumults

Throughout most of 2012 and 2013, we would have understood if you concluded that the entire Middle East had disintegrated into flames, protests, riots, shootings, and bombings. Throughout this period, much of the electronic print and online news media regularly focused on crises in Libya, Syria, Lebanon, and other Middle East locales. That could have led some to conclude that the entire region had disintegrated into chaos and to mentally dismiss any question of investment.

That would have meant possible costs including taking a loss if you liquidated an investment prematurely and an opportunity cost if you had some cash ready to invest and decided to avoid the region altogether.

Opportunity cost refers to potential gains not realized due to inability, hesitation, or unwillingness to proceed. For example, if you have US$10,000 in a shoebox under the bed that could produce a gain of 5 percent over a year's time, your opportunity cost is US$10,000 x 5% = US$500 minus applicable taxes.

But try to keep this discussion of bad news in the media in context. In the big picture, what we are discussing here is one of a series of factors on which you and your advisor base investment decisions.

Besides not making investment decisions based on last night's newscast, also consider the fact that bad news in one part of a region doesn't necessarily mean bad news in *all* countries of the region.

The various crises in the Middle East provide the most obvious example of this principle at the time of writing. The Middle East doesn't represent one homogenous region any more than all of Europe consists of one homogenous region or all of North America constitutes one homogenous region.

Making flat statements about the Middle East seems as questionable as making flat statements about the entire continent of Europe or South America. The Middle East itself is comprised of the larger North African states of Tunisia,

Libya, and Egypt, which is where the Arab Spring began in 2011, all of which have changed governments recently. The states of the old Fertile Crescent — Lebanon, Syria, Jordan, and Iraq — and the wealthy Arab monarchies of Saudi Arabia and the Gulf Cooperation Council states each have had a different experience.

Tunisia

The series of political upheavals that have become known as the "Arab Spring" began in Tunisia, long regarded as one of the more stable North African regimes. It had been ruled by President Abidine Ben Ali and his family through their Constitutional Rally Party (sometimes known by its francophone initials, RCD) for over a quarter of a century. After the semi-immolation of a poor street trader in protest against police corruption and brutality in December 2010, the regime fell in a popular protest in January 2011 and President Ben Ali fled to Saudi Arabia. A new parliament was elected in October 2011, with the Islamist party gaining 37 percent of the votes.

Egypt

February 2011 saw the overthrow of President Hosni Mubarak in Egypt after 30 years in power, again due to popular protests concentrated in Cairo's Tahrir Square. The overthrow was followed by democratic elections which resulted in Mohammed Morsi, the leader of the Islamic Brotherhood movement, being elected President in 2012. Morsi was overthrown by the military in August 2013 after renewed protests.

Libya

Next door in Libya, dictator Muammar Qaddafi, who had run the country since deposing its king in 1969, was overthrown after a rebellion that began in February 2011 and was supported by a United Nations–backed military intervention. The rebellion led to his death in October 2011 and his replacement by a National Transitional Council.

Yemen

In Yemen, long-standing president Ali Abdullah Saleh faced protests beginning in January 2011. When he failed to follow through on a Gulf Cooperation Council (GCC) plan to hand over power in exchange for immunity, an assassination attempt in June 2011 left him injured and needing hospital treatment in Saudi Arabia. He eventually stepped down in favor of his vice president Mansur al-Hadi, who became President in January 2012. Nevertheless, Saleh continued to exercise influence on Yemeni politics.

Syria

Protests against police brutality and corruption in Damascus in February 2011 escalated into a "Day of Rage" in numerous cities in March and the occupation of several cities by opposition forces in April. The government of Basher al-Assad then responded by sending troops in to Hama and Herak, near Daraa in July and fighting gradually escalated into full-scale civil war by the end of the year. The conflict continues at the time of writing, more than two years later. Over a million refugees have fled to neighboring countries such as Turkey, Iraq, and Jordan.

Allies such as Iran and the Hezbollah movement in Lebanon support the Syrian government while the GCC countries support the Syrian rebels. The Syrian government was accused of using chemical weapons against its opponents in August 2013. The accusations led to dismantling of the weapons by United Nations inspectors under a deal brokered by Syria's sponsor, Russia.

Other Middle Eastern Countries

Jordan faced protests in 2011 and King Abdullah replaced several prime ministers as a result. In Bahrain, the Shiite majority protested the rule of the Sunni minority, leading to government countermeasures and intervention by the GCC. Finally in Iran, popular protests erupted in early 2011 against the theocratic regime, but died away due to lack of support from other countries and the efficiency of the Iranian security forces.

In spite of the riots and shootings you may have frequently seen in nightly newscasts in 2012 and 2013, the entire Middle East was not engulfed in flames. Large parts of the region remained at peace and in fact the United Arab Emirates (UAE), a member of the GCC, continued its role as safe haven, attracting large capital inflows from other areas of the region. At the same time, the flow of initial public offerings (IPOs) floated on the stock exchange in Dubai continued throughout the various crises playing out elsewhere. The six countries of the GCC are:

- Saudi Arabia
- Kuwait

- ✔ Bahrain
- ✔ The UAE
- ✔ Qatar
- ✔ Oman

With the exception of the protests in Bahrain in 2011 and some unrest in Saudi Arabia that led to a generous economic stimulus program and allowing women to vote in municipal elections in 2015, the GCC countries have not been greatly affected by the Arab Spring, largely due to their small wealthy populations. In fact, Qatar was awarded the soccer World Cup in 2022.

In a reverse twist, at the time of writing, Frontier Markets such as those in the Middle East (and other frontier regions) didn't feel any substantial impact as a direct result of the October 2013 partial shutdown of the American government. This illustrates a central principle of frontier investing: the lack of correlation between Frontier Markets and developed markets. Generally, Frontier Markets, including the Middle East, didn't feel the impact of the government shutdown because their economies generally run on domestic consumption rather than exports to developed nations. The single exception to that is oil, which had not been affected by the US shutdown at the time of writing.

Hollywood-Made Mistaken Impressions

Going out to the movies is a time-honored way to spend an evening, a date, or a family outing. That has been the tradition for decades and notwithstanding the advances of other entertainment choices, will no doubt continue being the tradition for decades to come.

A movie theater is a great place to relax, a great place to gather with friends, and a great place to spend a family evening. However, it is a very ineffective place for gathering information about foreign investment destinations.

Two recent films illustrate that fact in two different continents.

Each of the former Soviet bloc countries, including Kazakhstan, is currently at a different stop in its evolution along the road between tightly controlled Communist economy and more open market economy.

Borat got it wrong

The strongest, and in many cases the only impression that many Westerners have of Kazakhstan, one of the former Union of Soviet Socialist Republics (USSR) comes from a 2006 movie release entitled *Borat: Cultural Learnings of America for Make Benefit Glorious Nation of Kazakhstan.*

The film's narrative (such as it is) tells the story of Borat Sagdiyev, played by British actor and TV prankster Sacha Baron Cohen. He essays a sometimes crude, sometimes bizarre portrayal of a television reporter from Kazakhstan, who comes to the United States to produce a documentary about American society. He then decides to go to California in search of love with Pamela Anderson and encounters some hilarious aspects of American culture along the way.

The dismally unflattering view of Kazakhstan in the opening scenes (actually filmed in Romania) sets the tone for a film for which the phrase *low-brow* seems like unjustifiably high praise. Unfortunately, Western investors have few other points of reference for Kazakhstan and its suitability as an investment destination.

In fact, Kazakhstan started on the path to becoming a market economy in 1991 and currently ranks as a transitional economy, meaning that it continues evolving from tight government controls to a market economy.

Kazakhstan's future depends on its ability to expand revenues from its oil reserves and mineral resources and its ability to diversify into non-oil areas. It has very little connection with crude portrayal of the country in the film. It has an ambitious diversification program, with priorities on developing targeted sectors like transportation, pharmaceuticals, telecommunications, petrochemicals, and food processing.

It does have some legacy environmental problems and is attempting to deal with them, but with its extensive energy resources and large mineral reserves, Kazakhstan has large foreign exchange reserves. It enjoys a very positive trade balance, allowing it to address many of the same social and infrastructure problems of other members of the Former Soviet Union (FSU).

The shape that Kazakhstan is taking, therefore, promises far greater returns to investors (whether through mutual funds, exchange-traded funds, or equities) than one might calculate after watching the Borat film.

Blood diamonds are not the whole story

In Africa, the phrase *war-torn* still occasionally occurs in references to Sierra Leone, but for the most part, that phase ended over a decade ago.

In the early 2000s, Sierra Leone definitely qualified as a war-torn African nation, embroiled in a costly and bloody civil war. For some, the film 2006 film *Blood Diamond,* starring Leonardo DiCaprio as the tormented Danny Archer, surrounded by the war, may be the most enduring image, even seven years later.

The civil war partially revolved around the desire to control the diamond business and the sale of the notorious "blood diamonds." This led to the establishment of a certification system that benefited established diamond producers such as Namibia, South Africa, Australia, and Canada at the expense of poorer African countries like Angola and Sierra Leone.

In fact, the very bloody civil war ended in 2002 after many thousands of deaths and the forced relocation of roughly a third of the population. With the departure of United Nations peacekeepers in 2005, the country's military forces assumed responsibility for security and has worked for its stability. Significantly, the military forces remained neutral during the presidential contests of 2007 and 2012.

In fact, far from being war-torn, Sierra Leone demonstrates two important concepts in the study of Frontier Markets:

- ✔ Its low level of development gives it the rank of Exotic Frontier Market, meaning that if it evolves over time it will achieve frontier status and perhaps emerging status years later.
- ✔ It also demonstrates the importance of natural resources development.

Besides diamonds, Sierra Leone has high-quality iron ore deposits developed by companies listed on the London Alternative Investment Market. African Minerals has invested over US$2 billion over the last five years to develop the Tonkolili iron ore mine, with a forecast production of 20 million tonnes per annum. It also has state-controlled China Railway Minerals as a 12.5 percent shareholder. These developments would interest a serious Frontier Markets investor.

American oil companies Chevron Corporation and Anadarko Petroleum Corporation, as well as Australian exploration and development company Cape Lambert Resources Ltd. and Russia's Lukoil Oil Company, are also active there, creating a development environment that is a quantum leap away from the war-torn era.

Trading Places in the 19th century

There is a famous story that Nathan Rothschild of the well-known banking family made a (metaphorical) killing on the outcome of the Battle of Waterloo in 1815 when Napoleon's attempt to reconquer Europe was halted by the combined efforts of the British under the Duke of Wellington and the Prussians under Marshal Blucher. Supposedly, the Rothschild agents in Brussels released a carrier pigeon with the famous battle's result, which was received by Rothschild in London well before anyone else had the news.

Taking up his accustomed position in the Royal Exchange the next morning, Rothschild began selling British government stock (known as gilt-edged stock, because the British government had never defaulted for over a century, unlike other countries such as France and Spain). Thinking that Rothschild must have received news of a French victory, other investors began dumping their gilt holdings, driving down the price.

When it had fallen enough, Rothschild stepped in and began to buy, at much cheaper prices than would have been possible earlier. When news arrived of Wellington's victory, the price of gilts soared, and Rothschild's reputation for shrewd dealings was further enhanced. Imagine the final scenes of the film *Trading Places,* except for real!

As well as shaking off the war-torn image, if Sierra Leone eventually moves from the Exotic to the Frontier Market category, it would serve as a model for promising, but underdeveloped, African Frontier Markets that have low gross domestic product (GDP) per capita, very young populations, low levels of urbanization, low taxes as a percentage of GDP, and small or nonexistent stock markets.

All of this plays into the belief of some analysts that Africa can become the "new China" and move Sierra Leone even further away from the war-torn image that may alienate investors.

These facts, albeit some as yet unproven, provide a better platform for investment decision-making than Hollywood films!

Using Bad News to Turn a Profit

Investors can profit from bad news, assuming, that is, that they are confident that the reaction of the stock market to the bad news is overdone and that the company or country will recover. This ability to look beyond the headlines is even more difficult today, when the Internet, Twitter, and the 24-hour news cycle constantly provide a stream of information and commentary, whether it's relevant or not and regardless of whether it's correct.

In fact, studies have shown that the experts who are the most confident and dogmatic in their statements are usually the ones who get it wrong more often than not. In the words of philosopher Isaiah Berlin, they are *hedgehogs,* who know "one big thing" and hold onto their opinion regardless of contrary evidence.

The other type of expert Berlin defines as the *fox,* who knows many small things, and is much more flexible and responsive to new pieces of information. The problem is, the media finds hedgehogs make much better guests because a strongly held opinion comes across much better with audiences, even if the opinion subsequently turns out to be wrong! That's why economic commentators still have jobs even when many of their forecasts have proved incorrect.

As an investor, you have to have confidence in your decisions even when in the short-term, events seem to move against your thesis. That's one of the reasons why we recommend using an advisor who is available to discuss your reasons for making an investment and to remind you of them when things go against you.

It also helps to write down four or five reasons why you made the investment in the first place.

Then you can take them out when riots are erupting on the TV, or a well-regarded expert is dismissing the case for Emerging or Frontier Markets by claiming they are too risky, and see whether what's happening makes any difference to your long-term case.

Frontier Markets are attractive, in our view, because they have young populations with a rapidly growing workforce, a rising middle class, people moving from the countryside to the cities, and generally sound finances. Are any of these factors likely to be changed by what's on the TV screen or coming over the Internet?

The one major concern you may justifiably have is if a change in the political regime will lead to a more hostile attitude to capitalism and foreign investment. As noted in Chapter 6, if a country has a history of nationalizing foreign-controlled companies, is regarded as being exceptionally corrupt, or has a very wide income gap between rich and poor, then it probably doesn't stack up well as an attractive home for your money.

Using an actively managed Global Frontier Markets equity fund as your vehicle is the best way to go. The manager will be able to avoid those countries that have a bad record in areas such as property rights and fair treatment of their citizens and investors. Most frontier specialists don't have much exposure to Argentina, precisely because, despite its abundance of natural resources and well-educated population, that country has pursued disastrous economic policies for over half a century.

Similarly, although Egypt's stock market fell by more than 50 percent during the first flush of the Arab Spring in 2011, it rebounded by 40 percent in 2012. The overthrow of the elected Morsi government by the military in 2013 saw its market fall again, but some managers believe that this offers a good buying opportunity. Egypt, after all, has a large reasonably well-educated population, a long-established stock market, and some well managed and profitable companies. If the political situation becomes more settled, then the low valuations of Egyptian companies could make for a buying opportunity.

Likewise, the attack on the Westgate shopping center in Nairobi, Kenya, in September 2013 by Islamic militants from Somalia led to a sell-off in Kenyan stocks. Its tourist trade, already hurt by kidnappings of western tourists near the Somali border, will undoubtedly be further affected. Meanwhile, foreign multinationals continue to increase their investment in Kenya.

Investing in Frontier Markets requires a long-term view of at least five years for the excellent underlying fundamentals to provide results. With an experienced manager to run your Global Frontier Markets fund, you should regard bad news as an opportunity to buy some assets at a cheap price.

Chapter 10

Searching for Frontier Markets in Your Current Portfolio

*W*e obviously feel that it's a good idea for investors to have some exposure to Frontier Markets in their portfolios. After all, that's why we wrote this book! However, before you go out and put all your retirement savings into these markets, a move that we emphatically don't recommend, it makes sense to see whether you have any exposure to these markets already and if so to determine the extent of your exposure.

This means reviewing all your existing mutual funds and stocks as well as your pension plan to look for frontier holdings. Because Frontier Markets are a subset of Emerging Markets, you may find that you have some Emerging Markets holdings, either directly or through your pension fund, which may include a Frontier Markets allocation. This means you need to review what's in your company or organization pension plan.

We suggest you complement existing holdings with a specific Frontier Markets exposure through a Global Frontier Markets fund, which should not represent more than 5 percent to 10 percent of your total international equity holdings. This will be large enough to make a difference by reducing your portfolio's volatility and likely increasing its returns over time.

Why Your Current Exposure to Emerging and Frontier Markets Matters

When considering any target at any time in any pursuit it always helps to know how close you've come to your destination. In fact, it helps to identify your destination clearly at the outset. Don't confuse monitoring your position with drawing a map — that's a different process and a different set of skills. In the Frontier Markets investing context, we discuss the parts of the map in other chapters in this book.

You can parallel this part of the process with a more familiar target that many individuals have faced: It amounts to the difference between setting your weight loss target and checking for how much weight you have lost (how close you have come to your destination) and considering the map for getting to your destination (changing your diet, exercising more frequently, and so on).

In the case of the weight loss, checking the difference between present and desired weight is one part psychological encouragement and one part pragmatic checking to ensure that you haven't become stalemated along the way.

In this context, monitoring your current exposure to this type of investing serves the same purpose but has an additional purpose: It helps you determine whether and how much exposure to Emerging and Frontier Markets investments you have already acquired because you may not completely realize the situation.

Finding out where you're exposed

Elsewhere in the book, we suggest that you have between 5 percent and 10 percent of your total international holdings as exposure to Frontier Markets.

Don't sweat this calculation. You may not come up with a completely precise estimate. Arriving at a number between *XX* and *YY* doesn't really present problems. The numbers will change periodically anyway since the fund manager may make a transaction or even change the overall weighting. Moreover, a major rise or fall in one or more equity prices could also change the weighting.

Notwithstanding those quirks in the methods, please do the calculation before you make any new Emerging and Frontier Markets investment commitments. After all, you may be further along the road than you realize toward your ideal exposure. Alternatively, you may have the impression that you're heavily invested. Finally, your exposure might have increased or decreased without your knowledge if your company pension plan administrators made a policy change that led to a change in weighting.

To ascertain your current exposure, check the following:

- Your mutual fund exposure
- Your ETF exposure
- Your pension or retirement funds exposure
- Your holdings in companies domiciled in developed nations but with major activities in Emerging and Frontier Markets

Before going into specifics, we need to define what we mean by *exposure*. We mean that you are exposed to the opportunity for returns — and certainly the risk and volatility — of investment in these markets.

With the first three types of exposure above (mutual funds, ETFs, and pension or retirement funds), your dollars are invested in these markets through the fund's holdings in wells or banks in Africa or Kazakhstan or a cement company in Colombia.

With the fourth type — holdings in companies domiciled in developed nations — your dollars are invested in a company with activities in a developed nation and one or more Emerging or Frontier Markets. This produces an effect sometimes called *tailwinds,* referring to the revenues from these markets. The good news/bad news equation here is that your returns depend on both the health of the company's developed market revenues and its Emerging or Frontier Markets revenues. The cement company in Colombia can be termed a *pure play,* while a British brewery operating overseas cannot be termed a pure play.

By *pure play,* we mean that the revenues of the Colombian cement company flow totally from activities in Colombia while the revenues of the British beer company flow from a number of sources.

You may indirectly own companies domiciled in developed nations that have major activities in Emerging and Frontier Markets as holdings in your funds or you may own them as direct investments if you have bought individual shares. You may also own them in exchange-traded funds and your pension plan.

Getting help from an advisor

As we suggest frequently in this book, please work with your financial advisor to calculate your exposure to these markets. We do not suggest that this is an easy calculation and a little assistance wouldn't do you any harm.

We can guess that you may have started steeling yourself as you read these tips, perhaps thinking, "There they go again . . . those guys keep harping about the need for a financial advisor." We don't really harp on it — but we strongly urge you to consider having a knowledgeable advisor if you don't already have a good working relationship with an advisor or advisory firm. (The guy or girl at the gym with whom you discuss stocks during workouts doesn't count as an expert financial advisor.) As we state elsewhere, we (the authors) aren't financial advisors looking for clients. Nor do we get a commission for encouraging new clients to sign on with advisors. We don't get extra gifts at Christmastime in return for sending clients to them. More seriously, we have worked professionally with advisors for over five decades between us, so we understand the role they can play in your financial health.

We are not going to review here all the advantages and disadvantages of having a good advisor, nor are we going to set up a separate map to show you how to select an advisor. We can only urge you to make the most of this relationship if you have it or establish such a relationship if you do not currently have a solid and comfortable one.

Remember to put the proverbial horse before the cart. Become established with your advisor and allow the relationship to grow to the point where your advisor really knows you, your needs, and your risk tolerance before you broach the idea of Frontier Markets investing. We appreciate your enthusiasm, but going quickly from "Pleased to meet you" to "Now what do I do about Frontier Markets investing?" may be construed as going too far too fast.

Determining Your Exposure

Start the process of determining your exposure by examining your mutual fund holdings outside of your retirement portfolio. Check your portfolio statement for whether you already own units in an Emerging Markets or a Frontier Markets Fund.

When we suggest that you start by checking your portfolio statement we are not being sarcastic. How many people do you know who can recite their entire portfolio list of assets by heart without checking, and go on to include the value of each asset and the country or countries in which their assets are invested?

Mutual funds

As we explain in Chapter 15, we have a severely restrained enthusiasm for country funds and regional funds because this means a concentration of risk in one geographical area. Conversely, it also means that you may not share in the growth of another country or region.

If you own a global equity fund, check for the countries of holdings and for the possibility that the weightings could increase over time. You can do that by reading the paragraphs in the prospectus that suggest that the portfolio manager can hold up to a certain percentage of the total assets in Emerging and Frontier Markets investments. Look to see whether the manager has built up the holdings in a specific country or region to the maximum allowed or has substantially more room to increase them.

When you check your mutual funds, especially your Global Frontier Markets fund if you have one, look through the material to ascertain details such as minimum deposit of fresh dollars and withdrawal procedures. We discuss the various Global Frontier Markets funds that are available to North American investors in Chapter 16.

If you don't have a Global Frontier Fund, consider putting your frontier investment dollars into a mutual fund in this category. Using a Global Frontier Markets Fund as your main Frontier Markets investment enables you to make even more use than usual of one of the main advantages of these funds: diversification of your investment dollars across several companies and asset categories. Still, not all Global Frontier Funds are the same, so check your fund closely.

Exchange-traded funds

An exchange-traded fund (ETF) consists of a series of equities contained in a specific index that trades like stocks on a stock exchange. With minor exceptions such as small adjustments for the version of an ETF offered in a different country, the selections and weightings are determined by the index and the fund company has nearly zero discretion in selecting the contents and equity weightings of the fund.

The nature of Frontier Markets exchange-traded funds acts to reduce the diversification usually offered by these vehicles since at the time of writing, both of the two Global Frontier Market ETFs available, the iShares MSCI Frontier Markets 100 ETF (NYSE:FM) and the Guggenheim Frontier Markets DR Index ETF (NYSE:FRN) have heavy weights in one geographical area. For the iShares ETF, almost 60 percent of the index is concentrated in three Gulf Cooperation Council (GCC) markets, Kuwait, Qatar, and the United Arab Emirates (UAE). The Guggenheim ETF has over 80 percent in South American countries, namely Chile, Colombia, Argentina, and Peru.

Furthermore, both of these ETFs have heavy concentrations in financial institutions, with the iShares having over 55 percent of its assets in this sector and the Guggenheim ETF over 30 percent. That, in turn, increases your total risk since this approach may result in lower diversification than otherwise. While you're checking your overall exposure to Emerging and Frontier Markets, ask your advisor to outline the advantages and disadvantages of keeping or liquidating these funds.

If you liquidate one or more ETFs and put the proceeds into a Global Frontier Markets Fund, your dollar exposure to Emerging and Frontier Markets investments does not change substantially, but your risk exposure may change, depending on the contents of the global fund.

Pension or retirement funds exposure

The next step in examining your exposure involves a document that you may have put in your desk drawer some years ago and perhaps haven't read it since: the booklet given to you by your employer when you accepted the offer of employment. You may have received an updated version after several years and put it in the same drawer. If you have a company pension plan you may — or may not have some exposure to Emerging and Frontier Markets investments. Your company's pension administrators may have an advisor such as J.P. Morgan Asset Management providing professional advice on whether and how to initiate or increase its investments in these categories.

Typically, the outside team of advisors works with the person or people within an organization designated to supervise existing investment opportunities and to investigate new ones. During the approval process and in advance of a final decision, the company group may hold what could be called a *semi-finals* or *finals* meeting with two or more potential managers. The involvement of these groups reflects the degree of discretion placed by clients in the investment team and — where appropriate — pension consultants.

Getting your pension fund information from human resources

Make an appointment with the appropriate person in the human resources department for a careful explanation of the weightings of the different types of asset classes within your company's plan. Well-known pension plans such as those administered for the California Public Employees Retirement System (CalPers) and Yale University have Emerging Markets investments. At the end of June 2012, the second largest American public pension plan, the California State Teachers Retirement System (CALSTRS), had $3.7 billion of its $170 billion in assets invested in Emerging Markets shares or about 2.2 percent, of which only $100 million was in Frontier Markets.

The Harvard University Endowment Fund, the largest college endowment fund, had 11 percent of its $32 billion in assets invested in Emerging Markets shares in 2012, while the Yale Endowment, the second largest college fund with $19 billion in assets in June 2012, had 2 percent invested in Emerging Markets shares and another 3 percent invested in "opportunistic foreign positions." The expectations are that the holdings would be concentrated in those markets that offer the most compelling long-term opportunities, particularly with China, India, and Brazil making a total of 5 percent invested in Emerging Markets.

When you go for the chat with the human resources office about your pension plan, remember that you may never have done this previously. Take along a pad and paper as well as the company booklet, and don't hesitate to write up questions in advance. Ask the human resources person to walk you through the asset mix of the plan.

There is a good news/bad news equation to this part of your research. The good news is that if your plan has no Emerging or Frontier Markets component it simplifies this calculation. The bad news is that the pension decision-makers are missing future growth. Ascertain who makes pension decisions and how often they review the plan.

Before or after the meeting with your human resources office, ask your financial advisor for an estimate of what percentage of your total retirement the pension plan will eventually provide.

Bear in mind that the asset mix of a pension plan can change if and when the advisors make a compelling case to management. Besides the asset classes that the advisors consider most promising, they also factor into their thinking calculations such as the amount of liquidity required to satisfy benefits obligations.

Holdings in companies with major exposure

Your current exposure to these markets investing may include companies domiciled in North America, Europe, or Japan but with major activities in them. You may hear the expression *footprint,* referring to the area of a region in which the company operates or in how much of, for example, Africa they may sell their products.

Many of these companies are very familiar to Western consumers and investors and may feel comfortable and reassuring, but they only represent exposure to these markets to the extent that they derive a portion of their total revenues (the tailwinds) from them. So while familiarity is reassuring, remember that a part of your exposure in these cases is still to North American, European, or Japanese consumers.

Several examples of companies with familiar names and products will illustrate our point.

Unilever

UNILEVER PLC (NYSE:UN; LSE:ULVR), which is listed in New York and London, derives approximately 55 percent of its revenues from Emerging and Frontier Markets. It ranks as the third largest global food and consumer products company, making ice cream, packaged food, and personal care and cleaning products. In 2012, Unilever had revenues of $66 billion and net earnings of $6.4 billion. In September 2013, at its price of $40, the company had a market capitalization of $52 billion, and sold at a forecast P/E ratio of 17 times and a dividend yield of 3.5 percent.

Unilever's familiarity is twofold: Most knowledgeable investors will have encountered the listing and be familiar with its track record. Moreover, you've probably used a Unilever product recently. You may have used Dove soap, Hellmann's mayonnaise, Knorr soup, Lipton's tea, Vaseline products, or Persil laundry products. The company calculates it sells 190 billion packs of its products annually and that its products are used 2 billion times a day.

A large pillar of our belief in the future of these markets is the rising level of consumer expenditure by the growing middle class in these countries. Unilever and its products are well-placed to benefit from this trend, especially since many of them are small, affordable, and of the type that consumers increasingly purchase as income levels increase over time.

At the time of writing, Unilever has aggressive plans to continue rolling out existing products in its Emerging and Frontier Markets operations, including Magnum Ice Cream in the Philippines, Tresemme Shampoo in Indonesia and India, Lipton Tea in Turkey, and a re-launch of Lifebuoy hand wash in Russia. Meanwhile, it has been reducing its exposure to slower growth developed markets, just in 2013 alone selling its Skippy Peanut Butter division for $700 million and its Wish-Bone Salad Dressing business for $580 million.

Nestle

Another obvious beneficiary of rising middle class incomes is the world's largest food company. NESTLE SA. (OTC: NSRGY; SW:NESN), which is listed in Switzerland and has an over-the-counter ADR in the United States, had sales of $100 billion in 2012 and operating income of $15.3 billion, of which 27 percent was in Emerging and Frontier Markets. At its price of $57.50 in September 2013, it had a market capitalization of $202 billion and was selling for a forecast P/E ratio of 18 times and a dividend yield of 3.3 percent.

Maker of such well known consumer brands as Nescafe and Nespresso Coffee, Gerber Baby Food, Kit Kat candy bars, Maggi sauces, Perrier and San Pellegrino bottled water, and Purina, Nestle has been expanding its focus on health and welfare and the Emerging Markets. It purchased Wyeth's baby food business in 2012 for US$11.9 billion. Wyeth had 85 percent of its $2 billion in sales in Emerging Markets. Nestle spent US$490 million in 2013 to open two more factories in China, one for coffee extraction and the other for food products. Sales in greater China, including Hong Kong, Singapore, and Taiwan, doubled to US$5.5 billion in 2012. The CEO of its China operations noted that there were 350 million Chinese migrating from rural areas who would no longer grow their own food and ". . . who will come into the cit(ies). They will need to buy food."

Yum! Brands

Another multinational company that has aggressively taken advantage of the growth of the middle class in these markets is KFC, Taco Bell, and Pizza Hut operator YUM! BRANDS (NYSE:YUM). With more than 37,000 outlets, Yum is one of the largest global fast-food operators, with net earnings of $1.6 billion on sales of $13.5 billion in 2012, of which 75 percent was derived from Emerging and Frontier Markets and 44 percent from China alone. At its price of $73.25 in September 2013, it had a market capitalization of US$33 billion and sold a forecast PE ratio of 18 times and a dividend yield of 1.8 percent.

Yum suffered a setback in 2012, when excessive levels of antibiotics were found in some of the chicken supplied to its KFC chain in China, and sales in its restaurants in China were down sharply in the first half of 2013, leading the company to forecast a fall in its earnings for the year. However, growth for the company has continued with new restaurants opening in such markets as India, Indonesia, the Philippines, and Vietnam (85 percent of Yum's new restaurants are opened in Emerging and Frontier Markets). The company has forecast that sales in restaurants open for more than 12 months in China will be flat for 2013 as they recover in the second half. Yum planned to open 700 new restaurants in China for 2013, while sales in Latin America, the Middle East, and Africa were all expected to grow strongly.

SABMiller

In addition to food, the Emerging and Frontier Market consumer is also consuming more alcoholic beverages. SABMiller Plc (OTC:SBMRY:LSE SAB), the second largest global brewer lists its shares on the London Stock Exchange and in the United States as an American Depositary Receipt (ADR). In 2012 it derived over 75 percent of its revenues of US$34.5 billion and operating earnings of US$6.2 billion from these markets, partially due to the number of local brands it owns in these countries. These include the world's best-selling beer, Snow in China, Castle in South Africa, Aguila in Colombia, Tyskie in Poland, and Pilsner Urquel in the Czech Republic. At its price of $51.75 in September 2013, it had a market capitalization of $81.8 billion and sold for a forecast PE ratio of 20.1 times and a 3.1 percent dividend yield.

SABMiller also owns Miller Brewing in the United States, which it merged with MolsonCoors in 2009 to create a rival to Anheuser Busch and bought the largest Australian brewer, Foster's, in 2011 for US$10.9 billion. An investment in this company amounts to exposure both in developed nations such as the United Kingdom and Italy as well as Emerging Markets such as China and the Czech Republic and Frontier Markets such as Vietnam and Colombia.

Google, Samsung, Honda, and a host of other well-known companies fall into this category of companies domiciled in North America, Europe, South Korea, or Japan but with major activities in Emerging and Frontier Markets. In each case, they derive a portion of their revenues from developed markets and a portion from Emerging and Frontier Markets. None of these companies is a pure play.

Calculating How Much Is Too Much and How Much Is Not Enough

You may have noticed that in this book, we tend to avoid making flat statements about what you or any other investor should do, not do, adopt, or avoid. We have decades of experience in discussing financial concepts with professional advisors, fund company executives, and investors and clearly understand that every case is different. Even two individuals with roughly the same income, same investible assets, and the same risk tolerance may have other differences such as financial obligations that make them different.

Equally important is that each individual has a specific risk tolerance and each individual's situation changes with changes in the life cycle, such as age, marital status, and retirement horizon.

So how do we calculate how much is too much and how much is not enough?

As much as we believe in Frontier Markets, we also know that this is unfamiliar territory for many investors and we want you to sleep at night as well as increase your financial wealth and financial security.

For all of these reasons we are not going to suggest a firm figure for your total Frontier Markets exposure.

We suggest that you set a threshold of 5 percent to 10 percent of your international holdings as a baseline for your exposure to Frontier Markets. From there, and in full consultation with your professional advisor, you can adjust that threshold depending on your situation. Reviewing this threshold should become an integral part of the annual or semi-annual review of your investment portfolio.

Apart from the preceding considerations, you may raise your personal threshold over time even if your situation doesn't change. Perhaps if your own comfort level with Emerging and Frontier Markets increases, you and your advisor can discuss raising your exposure.

Increasing your exposure does not necessarily mean that you have to come up with new cash to inject in your portfolio. If you already have Emerging Markets investments, consider transferring some of the dollars in them to Frontier investments.

Look at it this way: Calculating how much is too much and how much is not enough is a complicated exercise that involves large parts of what you are, how you view the world, and where you see yourself going in the years to come.

Gambling with your future

Gambling with your future may sound like a flip expression or an alarmist way of getting your attention. Certainly, we do want your attention but we see our goal as providing useful information to help in your financial planning, not by alarming you but to help you look after your future. Face it, no one wants to depend on government handouts. Ask yourself how you would survive if you suddenly had to live today solely on government benefits. We can reasonably agree that that picture does not seem very reassuring.

So if you do not create a coherent financial plan with a financial advisor you are, in fact, gambling with your future.

And the gamble has increased in the last decade as we introduced a new phrase into financial lexicon. Less than ten years have passed since we first heard the phrase *longevity risk*. This risk results from a good news/bad news equation. The good news is that thanks to advances in medical science, nutrition, and lifestyle we all have longer life expectancies. The bad news is that we have to make our life savings last for more years than we might have realized, certainly longer than our parents might have considered necessary.

What this means is that the importance of a coherent financial plan actually increases with the onset of longevity risk. If we agree that we're going to live longer than our parents, and longer than we had originally realized, it follows that we have to stretch our resources over more years and most likely more medical expenses over the years. If you accept that truism, you need to go to the next step and have a plan drawn up in one or more meetings with your professional financial advisor.

More specifically, in this book, we suggest that setting aside some of the international portion of your total portfolio as Frontier Markets investments will provide growth over the long term.

Playing it too safe

You may wonder how you could possibly play it *too* safe. We can provide a simple explanation. Playing it too safe may have become part of the aftermath of the Financial Crisis of 2008 and 2009. Anecdotally, we know that some investors have not yet ventured back into the stock market or haven't made the necessary moves to repair portfolios damaged by the crisis or to update their portfolios. We know that they suffer a form of shellshock, in a sense frozen in place because of the shock of the crisis.

That state of mind has several possible consequences, none of them profitable:

- Faulty or ineffective investments continue taking up space or more accurately, dollars, in your portfolios.

- An unrealistic dependence on interest-bearing instruments, a poorly paying strategy in this low-interest rate environment. With inflation and taxes on interest, it is possible that this dependence can lead to a net loss.

- Opportunity cost or missing out on investment growth whether in Frontier Markets or other category.

- A lack of determination to put new dollars into the investment plan.

- Reduced dollars available for retirement lifestyle.

- Possibly reduced dollars available for lifestyle emergencies such as unforeseen medical expenses.

The net effect of all these consequences means that you have fewer dollars when you need them.

You can avoid the dangers of playing it too safe by having one or more honest conversations with your financial advisor about factors such as your risk tolerance, available dollars, ongoing cash requirements, and lifestyle priorities. After those conversations, you and your advisor can achieve a coherent asset allocation which ideally will embrace most or all investment categories, including Emerging and Frontier Markets.

Consider this: You've worked hard for your salary dollars and you owe it to yourself to make the most of the money that you can place in your retirement portfolio.

During the heady stock market days of 2007, some investors misunderstood their risk tolerance. When the market paid solid returns, these investors believed they had high risk tolerance. With the financial crisis, many of them realized they didn't have the risk tolerance they believed they had.

Chapter 11

Preparing for Your Participation in Frontier Markets

In This Chapter
▶ Looking at your investment timetable
▶ Deciding how to allocate your money
▶ Getting advice from a financial advisor

*G*oing into any frontier requires careful preparation with a greater level of detail than might seem appropriate for trips into more familiar territory. The newness and complexity of Frontier Markets means that preparing for your participation arguably requires more effort than preparing for participation in any other investment category. We believe that because they have a shorter history and greater complexity than any other investment category and we're still learning about it.

By comparison, you can prepare for your participation in fixed-income investments by calculating your cash and near-cash needs, allowing for a margin of error and emergencies. You would also take interest rate fluctuations into account, and where appropriate, factor in your risk tolerance, retirement horizon, and projected cash requirements. You may also decide to have a cash or near-cash pool ready in case the market delivers real investment bargains. Those and other tried-and-true considerations will help determine the weighting of fixed income in your asset allocation. If you encounter an emergency that forces you to dip into the fixed income assets, you can restore the weighting with fresh cash or by liquidating some of your assets in a mutual fund.

You can prepare for your participation in balanced funds by considering your risk tolerance and your projections for interest rates and where appropriate, by factoring in your retirement horizon and projected cash requirements.

However, investing in Frontier Markets still seems like new territory for most investors and financial advisors. For that reason, preparing for this move requires more preparation and more detailed work with your financial advisor.

You may have noticed that we continually circle back to your relationship with your financial advisor. Remember, Frontier Markets investing is fresh and complex territory. As with any new territory, you need an experienced guide. Perhaps when the rules of this category have crystallized over the next several years, you may have more room for doing it yourself. Right now, however, sign on with a good guide, spell out everything he or she needs to know, and then give the recommendations fair consideration.

If you can't accept the recommendations, don't file them in a drawer underneath other stuff. Instead, return to your financial advisor and discuss them and your objections. You may need to discuss your situation in greater detail than previously. Even the very best advisor can only work from the factors you've outlined in your conversations.

Using Your Previous Experience as an Emerging Markets Investor

You may be wondering why you need previous experience in order to invest in Frontier Markets. You have some cash available, you know that you can set it aside for five years or more, you feel comfortable with the risks and volatility, and you're ready to write the check. That's all that matters. Right?

Perhaps. However, we've found that investors with positive experiences investing in Emerging Markets tend to enter Frontier Market investing with a higher comfort level than those who do not have that kind of history. We're not suggesting that you *have* to be an experienced Emerging Markets investor — only that that kind of experience might increase your comfort level.

We view Frontier Markets as a subset of Emerging Markets, and many of the dynamics operate in a similar fashion. These include:

- ✔ Volatility
- ✔ The effect of political tumult
- ✔ The rising consumer class
- ✔ Increasing urbanization

In fact, Frontier Markets that continue evolving can eventually achieve the status of Emerging Markets. For example, in June 2013, MSCI Inc., the company that assembles the MSCI Emerging Markets Index and the MSCI Frontier Markets Index, upgraded Qatar and the United Arab Emirates from Frontier to Emerging status, effective in May 2014.

The reverse can also happen. At the same time, MSCI downgraded Morocco from Emerging to Frontier status, and Greece from developed status to Emerging status, effective November 2013. It also put Egypt under review for a possible downgrade from Emerging to Frontier status if the political situation in that country worsened. At time of writing that appears a serious possibility.

Taking into account the changes effective in May 2014, the countries listed in the MSCI Frontier Markets Index will include

- Argentina
- Bahrain
- Bangladesh
- Bulgaria
- Croatia
- Estonia
- Jordan
- Kazakhstan
- Kenya
- Kuwait
- Lebanon
- Lithuania
- Mauritius
- Morocco
- Nigeria
- Oman
- Pakistan
- Romania
- Serbia
- Slovenia

- ✔ Sri Lanka
- ✔ Tunisia
- ✔ Ukraine
- ✔ Vietnam

Getting a Grip on Your Timetable

The preceding section gives you a clear idea of the destination, so now let's check your personal timetable for getting there. Remember we're all still writing the rules of Frontier Markets investing.

This is an extremely personal calculation that varies from individual to individual and can certainly vary with changes in life cycle. Getting married can reduce one's risk tolerance while receiving a large inheritance can mean a hitherto-unforeseen amount of cash available for investment. The trick is to recognize these changes when they occur and proceed accordingly.

Whenever you encounter a serious life cycle change such as marriage or receiving an inheritance or becoming a parent, consider speaking to your advisor about whether it has any implications for your investment portfolio.

Every situation is different but here's a good general calculation. From your total investable assets, subtract:

- ✔ The amount of cash you will need for all conceivable day-to-day uses and emergencies such as large medical bills and job loss
- ✔ Your financial needs for the first two years of retirement, if you are approaching retirement age

Generally speaking and with many exceptions, the remainder is what you can invest in equities of various types, both domestic and international. From your international allocation, calculate 10 percent of the total. Using that figure, check your pension plans and other investments to ascertain whether you already have some frontier holdings in these holdings. You may have to discuss this with your employer's pension representative. Also check to see if any of your existing holdings of global funds are in Frontier Markets. Subtract those existing holdings; the balance is an estimate of how much you might consider investing in foreign markets.

A good rule of thumb is the younger you are, the higher that you can raise that figure while the older you are, the more you may need to lower it. You can also raise this threshold if you believe you have a high risk tolerance or lower it if you believe you have a lower risk tolerance. Assessing your risk tolerance requires a level of self-honesty that you may need to discuss with your financial advisor.

We know we are repeating ourselves, but we urge you to discuss all aspects of your investment strategy with your financial advisor. Trust us, we've met and worked with countless advisors during our careers and most professional advisors are people-oriented folks, just trying to do a good job for you.

Focusing on Your Long-Term Dollars

By long-term dollars we mean money that you believe you can set aside for at least five years and preferably longer. This doesn't mean you definitely won't be able to access these dollars in less than five years. We just recommend that you allow for the long-term. If the assets you in which invest these dollars mature in less time, so much the better. This way you save yourself from having to prematurely liquidate an asset when you may prefer to leave it intact. Many investors who needed cash during the Financial Crisis of 2008–2009 lived that painful experience.

We recommend that you use long-term dollars to invest in these markets for several reasons:

- ✔ Frontier Markets have lower liquidity than markets in developed nations.

- ✔ One of the factors driving our projections for Frontier Markets is the rise of the consumer class in these countries; this will take time to evolve and provide the kinds of returns we have suggested.

- ✔ In effect, investing in Frontier Markets amounts to an extension of the traditional buy-and-hold strategy that has actually fallen into disfavor in some areas of developed markets.

- ✔ This time period allows for recovery from dips caused by political tumult and unforeseen developments.

- ✔ The rules of Frontier Market investing are still being developed.

Limiting your total exposure

With some exceptions, limit your total exposure to 10 percent of your total international equity holdings, as discussed earlier. This suggestion refers only to pure holdings and does not include your holdings in developed nation multi-national equities that have large Frontier Market exposure, such as Coca Cola or Pfizer.

Don't invest short-term dollars in Frontier Markets mutual funds, exchange-traded funds, or individual equities; these investments need time to grow and appreciate. Your best bet, as we mention earlier, is to invest dollars that you believe you can leave untouched for five years or more.

Recognizing the risks of investing the money you need in the near future

Investing money that you may need in the near future amounts to swimming in deep water without a life jacket. If something goes wrong, you don't have adequate safety precautions in place.

Equity markets in any category can be volatile and change course suddenly and dramatically — a lesson we learned at serious cost during the Financial Crisis of 2008–2009. How many people do you know who had to raise cash by liquidating a mutual fund or stock holding that had suddenly depreciated even though they would have preferred to leave it intact and wait for a recovery?

Add to that the problems of liquidity associated with some Frontier Markets and the need to restrict frontier investing to dollars that you will not reasonably need for at least five years becomes more urgent than with most other investment categories.

With your financial advisor, calculate the amount of cash that you can reasonably leave intact for at least five years. That does not mean that you will not be able to liquidate your Frontier Funds in less than five years but it does mean that you've hedged your investment against having to cash in when you would otherwise leave it intact.

The other major risk of investing money that you might need in the short term in Frontier Markets is that, as we've noted elsewhere, these markets are volatile. Chances are, they will be experiencing one of the periodic sell-offs that happen in rapidly developing economies just when you realize you need your money! Given that they are illiquid and fairly small, the costs of a transaction in Frontier Markets can often be in excess of 3 to 4 percent, so quite apart from any capital losses you may have suffered, there will be a meaningful cost to selling. These are not markets where you can deal for $9.99 or less.

Parking your investments in the right place

Perhaps we shouldn't use the word "parking" here. We'd be more accurate if we refer to allocating your total assets in ways that reflect their intended uses. Retirement funds can be placed in longer-term assets but cash you may need for short-term uses or even the proverbial rainy day fund should be left in near-cash investments such as fixed income funds or laddered bank certificates.

Calculate the amount that is appropriate by determining all your current needs plus an amount you would need if you suddenly came to an abrupt and unscheduled parting of the ways with your employer.

When calculating how much you would need if you suddenly lost your job, you can adjust the amount up or down depending on employment trends in your profession and your area. If you work in a high-demand category, you can probably lower the number of months of expenses in your calculation. If you work in an area with a high unemployment problem or in a high unemployment profession, you probably should raise the number of months in your calculation. Like other considerations, this one varies from individual to individual. Six months is regarded by many advisors as a good starting point to be adjusted up or down depending upon your individual circumstances

Discussing Frontier Markets with a Financial Advisor

When you discuss Frontier Markets with your financial advisor, go for total honesty. You can only expect effective expert medical recommendations from your doctor when you spell out all your symptoms, allergies, and other medical issues. The doctor can only make recommendations based on the information available. Similarly, you can only expect effective expert financial recommendations from your financial advisor when you spell out all your hesitations about risk, concerns, problems, financial needs, and even your current view of these countries.

If you don't have complete faith in your doctor's recommendations you may choose to look around for a second opinion. Similarly, if you don't have a strong faith in your financial advisor's recommendations, and in his or her ability to deal with your most important financial concerns, you may need to look around for another advisor. After all, you're trusting your long-term financial health to this person. Do you leave the advisor's office feeling that you have effectively covered all of the bases?

By now you may have gotten tired of our emphasis on your relationship with your financial advisor. We consider this relationship important at all times and with all types of investments, but we believe that it's even more crucial when dealing with Frontier Markets investments because of the added risk, volatility, distance, and the possible lack of liquidity when compared to other asset classes.

Be patient with our constant reminders. Neither of us is a financial advisor, so we're not trying to recruit new clients or sell mutual funds here. However, we have both dealt with advisors professionally for several decades. We see a good relationship with a trusted advisor as a major part of being a successful investor.

In the post–financial crisis world, your advisor may tell you that his or her job is not just to make you rich but to prevent you from becoming poor.

At the same time, you have more have access to financial planning software and other tools (including this book) than you could have ever hoped to have in previous years. The software and tools make you more capable than ever at understanding the forces at work in the financial world and more aware of the options available.

In the Frontier Markets investing context, you may have formed impressions of these countries and markets before your discussions with your advisor. The financial processes may not be quite as confusing as otherwise, and you can feel on a more even footing with your advisor than might have been the case ten years ago.

Basically, both you and your advisor are looking for a kind of imaginary line in your relationship. On one side of that line, you trust your own counsel and on the other side of the line, you feel you need to accept the advisor's recommendation. To what extent do you want to lead the advisor and to what extent do you want the advisor to lead you? That may be one of the toughest financial planning questions you will ever have to encounter and it's another one of those factors that vary from individual to individual. Your advisor, if he or she is sensitive to you, is also looking for that line and where you have drawn it.

The line may shift a bit closer to the advisor when looking at Frontier Markets investments because these markets are still new and strange.

When an advisor proposes investments to you, his or her ability to frame the proposed investment within the context of your foreknowledge, needs, and concerns will go a long way to reassuring you. To get to that happy position, ensure that you have given your advisor all the necessary clues:

- ✔ All conceivable cash needs
- ✔ Your risk tolerance

- ✔ Your retirement horizon

- ✔ Your general view of Frontier Markets

- ✔ Any hesitations you may have about these markets

- ✔ Your previous experience — if any — with Emerging Markets

As much as we'd like to see you adopt our belief in Frontier Markets investing, first consider investing in Emerging Markets, which have a greater track record and will be at least somewhat more familiar to you. We don't suggest that you *must* take this route, but taking it may increase your comfort level.

Studying your asset allocation

Studying your asset allocation means asking yourself whether those colored pieces on the pie chart make sense to you. Ask yourself whether the allocation gives you a clear picture of the proposed division of your assets, the expected returns, and the risks to those returns.

Your financial advisor likely believes that his or her objective in creating an asset allocation plan is to reconcile your risk tolerance (and other factors) with the obvious aim of getting the best possible return for you over time.

Think of your asset allocation as one part art and one part science.

The art part occurs when your advisor assembles everything he or she needs to know about you in order to draw up the allocation. The science part occurs when he or she actually applies this knowledge to the actual construction of the allocation and the investment recommendations.

When studying the allocation, you can spot-check it for possible mistakes or misunderstandings that you can discuss with your advisor:

- ✔ Are you comfortable with the overall weighting of equities?

- ✔ Do you understand how your advisor arrived at the sizes of those pieces of the pie?

- ✔ Do you feel you could take more risks within the overall equities weighting (such as increasing your Frontier Markets exposure)? Or do the weightings feel comfortable?

- ✔ Is the cash and near-cash weighting sufficient to provide for all conceivable emergencies?

- ✔ In general, do you understand the goals and risk tolerance set within the allocation and are you comfortable with them?

- ✔ Does the allocation mirror your discussions with your advisor?

You play a large part in ensuring that your advisor constructs effective and useful allocations and recommendations. You can help by telling the advisor everything — and we certainly mean *everything* — connected to your financial situation and present and future needs. Your advisor may be knowledgeable, skilled, and well-meaning but probably not very experienced in mind reading or crystal ball gazing. Ensure that you've drawn a completely clear picture of your own situation and where appropriate, that of your family.

Facing the big divide: Stock and bonds

Understanding the big divide between stocks and bonds can be compared to understanding the difference between growth and stability. With the frequent caveat that every situation is different, the role of stocks (including individual equities, mutual funds, closed-end funds, and other types of funds) is to provide growth over time. In many cases, their role includes providing an income stream where the equities pay regular and substantial dividends.

By comparison, bonds provide a more predictable income but generally do not provide growth in a portfolio. The inclusion of bonds in a portfolio reduces the overall volatility of your portfolio since the bond portion is less exposed to equity market shocks.

The proportion of stocks to bonds in a portfolio represents a calculation based on several factors, including your risk tolerance, your retirement horizon, and your maximum possible cash needs over a given period. As always, this is an individual calculation. If you work in an industry that is currently being hit with massive layoffs and the proverbial rumors are going around your workplace, you probably want to increase the total weighting of bonds in your portfolio. If, on the other hand, you work for an institution that provides security of tenure, you can probably afford to lower the proportion of bonds to total assets.

Diversifying within the stock and bond categories

After you and your advisor have set the basic allocation of stocks to bonds, cash, and near-cash instruments, diversification within categories becomes the next major consideration. In this part of the financial planning process, you and your advisor discuss the proportion of total equities to be invested in domestic equities, Emerging Markets equities, and in this case, Frontier Markets equities. You have the same discussion about the bond category.

Embracing your risk tolerance

Your risk tolerance is very much a part of who *you* are and comprises a large part of your attitudes about investing and perhaps about life in general. It's important both to understand it and to embrace it.

Risk tolerance has two basic parts:

- ✔ Your psychological ability to deal with risk defines your mental capacity to absorb market shocks, keep smiling, and sleep at night.

- ✔ Your personal financial situation, including your financial obligations, defines your ability to absorb a sudden financial challenge such as a job loss.

Financial services professionals believe that many individuals misunderstood their own risk tolerance in the heady market days of 2007. During that period, we periodically heard the phrase "a rising tide lifts all boats," referring to the fact that the stock markets at the time seemed to be on a "high" and that most stocks rose with it.

Taking risks was easy when everything seemed to work perfectly and stocks continued going up. Then we had the Financial Crisis of 2008–2009, and many individuals decided they were not quite as capable of dealing with risks as they had assumed.

Embracing your risk tolerance means discussing these factors frankly with your financial advisor. To articulate your risk tolerance, some advisors use a classic question such as: "If your portfolio dropped by *xx* percent tomorrow would you feel forced to sell off or would you be able to ride it out?"

We've said it before and we'll say it again: Other than your spouse and family, there are two people with whom you really must be totally honest — your doctor and your financial advisor. To embrace your risk tolerance fully you first have to define it clearly and that means frank discussions with your advisor.

Revealing your home bias

Your home bias is your natural and understandable inclination to favor equities in your home turf for your investment dollars. After all, you feel comfortable in your familiar surroundings, and the names of the companies in a domestic fund are the companies that you work for or whose products you use regularly. You don't have to worry about those funny-sounding company names in far-off countries.

Understanding your home bias is a large part of determining your financial decision processes. If you feel that this bias is a part of your financial planning makeup, at the very least, review with your advisor the advantages to be gained by investing in foreign markets. Remember: No one is suggesting that you completely abandon investing in domestic equities. We simply recommend that you allocate a portion of your international investments to Frontier Markets.

There is nothing wrong with having a home bias. Start by recognizing its place in your personal financial makeup. It represents a part of your investment personality and as such is normal and understandable. As always, discuss it with your advisor and let him or her explain the alternatives, including frontier investments.

Part IV
Making Investment Selections

TIP

Top Three Global Frontier Fund Choices

- ✔ Harding Loevner Frontier Emerging Markets Fund (HLMOX).
- ✔ Wasatch Frontier Emerging Smaller Countries Fund (WAFMX).
- ✔ HSBC GIF Frontier Markets Fund (HSFAX).

Visit www.dummies.com/extras/frontiermarkets for more info on Frontier Market investing options.

In this part. . .

- ✔ Invest directly in Frontier Markets through American Depositary Receipts, Global Depositary Receipts, multinational corporations, and online trading

- ✔ Discover the advantages and disadvantages of bond funds.

- ✔ Determine the advantages and disadvantages of exchange-traded funds.

- ✔ Explore the advantages and disadvantages of regional and single-country funds.

- ✔ Take our preferred approach: global frontier funds.

- ✔ Examine the available global frontier funds and their performance.

- ✔ Monitor and review your portfolio.

- ✔ Adjust your investments to take life events into account.

Chapter 12

Investing Directly in Frontier Markets

*D*irect and indirect investing are two financial terms that have different definitions for different people in different contexts. In the way we use the terms here, we would define direct investing as putting investment dollars into a single asset, such as shares in a specific company like a bank or telecommunications company. In this context, the bank or telecom company is not necessarily located in a Frontier Market but has at least some exposure to one or more Frontier Markets. Direct investments in Frontier Markets or anywhere else can include:

✔ American Depositary Receipts (ADRs)

✔ Global Depositary Receipts (GDRs)

✔ Global Multinational Equities

In this chapter, we clear up the mysteries of direct versus indirect investing and offer several ways you can invest directly in Frontier Markets.

Distinguishing Direct from Indirect Investing

You may hear or read the phrase *foreign direct investment* or FDI. That refers to a sizable direct investment whether in a Frontier Market or elsewhere by a foreign corporation or entity, such as allocating the dollars to set up a subsidiary or other operation. That topic belongs in a different book. In this book, we use the phrase to refer to the way in which you make an investment of your personal dollars.

Direct investing indirectly works against diversification, at least to an extent. By definition, indirect investing, such as through a mutual fund, brings with it a degree of diversification proportionate to the number of regions, countries, and sectors. A direct investment only provides diversification to the extent that it varies sufficiently from other direct investments in a portfolio. Concentrating your investment dollars by owning a single investment in one country requires more work and time on the part of the advisor and client and increases the risks. We're not saying that you can't undertake direct investing, but rather that if you go that route, go with caution and do your homework.

By indirect investing, we mean investing through a financial vehicle that has investments in a list of countries, industrial sectors, and companies. These investments may include:

- ✔ Equity mutual funds of various types, including:

    - Global Frontier Funds

    - Regional funds

    - Country funds

    - Sector funds

- ✔ Bond mutual funds

- ✔ Exchange-traded funds

- ✔ Closed-end funds

- ✔ Pools created for pension funds, charitable institutions, or endowments

We certainly do not want to confuse you, but we need to make clear another distinction. Direct investments by their very nature cannot include indirect investments but indirect investments can include any or all direct investments.

For example, a global Frontier Fund might include ADRs, GDRs, and global multinational companies with large-scale exposure in one or more Frontier Markets.

Considering these distinctions, direct investing would rarely qualify as diversified investing unless the investor owns at least a dozen different securities while each type of indirect investing has a greater or lesser degree of diversification.

For example, as we explain in Chapter 15, a Global Frontier Fund generally has broad diversification across markets, sectors, and industries and with the exception of pools created for pension funds, charitable institutions, or endowments, has the greatest degree of diversification of the approaches discussed here.

By comparison, neither an American Depositary Receipt nor a Global Depositary Receipt (explained in detail in the section, "American Depositary Receipts and Global Depositary Receipts") provides diversification, but simply a shareholding in a single company. To use a universally recognizable expression, these approaches mean that you've placed all your frontier eggs in one basket. You've probably heard and read about the pros and cons of having all your investments in one investment vehicle since your earliest introduction to investing and no doubt have been discouraged from doing that. When you invest your Frontier Markets dollars solely through direct investments, you have, in fact, placed all your frontier eggs in a very small basket.

Eyeing the Ways You Can Invest Directly

We aren't suggesting that you cannot or must not invest directly. We merely want to make the distinctions clear so that you can make an informed choice with your Frontier Markets dollars.

Perhaps you have acquired a lot of previous investing experience and feel prepared to do serious homework. You may also feel prepared for the greater risk and volatility that comes with direct investing. These are considerations for you to discuss in advance with your financial advisor.

When you invest directly you put your investment dollars into one of several investment instruments listed previously.

This means that your investment stands or falls, and provides yield or leads to losses based on the fortunes (no pun intended) of one company. By comparison, an indirect investment such as a mutual fund consisting of several dozen holdings spreads the potential risks (and rewards) over those several dozen holdings.

That difference is the essential definition of diversification.

American Depositary Receipts and Global Depositary Receipts

Historical accounts often suggest that American Depositary Receipts (ADRs) began in 1927 as a means of allowing investors to own shares, denominated in American dollars, in foreign corporations. Each ADR, which is issued by a depositary bank, represents ownership of shares in the underlying company. The ADRs trade on an American exchange, usually the New York Stock Exchange (NYSE), but sometimes on NASDAQ or the over-the-counter (OTC) market.

The process works to the advantage of both sides of the transaction. The corporation selling the ADRs (shares) receives access to American investors on the American stock market. The investor enjoys access to corporations in distant countries. The fact that the equity is denominated in American dollars makes it simpler for domestic investors to purchase these investments through their own broker.

Global Depositary Receipts (GDRs) are similar to ADRs, in that they are denominated in American dollars, except that they are issued in Europe and traded on the London Stock Exchange (LSE), and sometimes on the Frankfurt or Luxemburg stock markets. Some observers believe that European reporting and disclosure requirements aren't as rigorous as those in the U.S. For instance, United Kingdom–quoted companies are only required to report twice a year rather than quarterly, as in the U.S. This reduces the cost of maintaining a GDR issue as opposed to an ADR issue for companies.

Although ADRs are denominated in American dollars, this doesn't remove an investor's exposure to foreign currencies. The underlying shares that have been packaged into an ADR are still denominated in Swiss francs, Euros, Japanese yen, or Brazilian reals, and the price of the security will be affected by the movement of the foreign currency against the dollar. Thus investors in ADRs will experience losses as the US dollar appreciates, and gains as it falls.

American authorities require the companies issuing the ADRs to comply with the same disclosure requirements and accounting rules as any other company that has a listing on an American exchange. In effect that means the company complies with the same requirements as if domiciled in the domestic market.

That requirement indirectly pressures companies with whom the foreign corporations compete for capital to meet similar standards, thereby easing some of your apprehensions about foreign investing.

Ways to explore investment options in Frontier Market ADRs and GDRs

Although there are around 30 Frontier Market ADRs listed at the time of writing in late 2013 that are just as easy to buy as a domestic US stock, anyone considering investing directly in them should pause before going ahead. You are about to put your stock-picking skills to work in markets which you know, or should be aware now that you've read some of this book, are volatile, illiquid, and pretty lightly regulated. As a famous film detective once asked, "Do you feel lucky?"

Secondly, the companies that have issued ADRs tend to come from only a few countries. Most of them are from South America, and a lot of them are from Argentina, which is the poster child for what can go wrong for investors in these markets. In fact, Argentina, which was as wealthy as France on a per capita basis a century ago, and wealthier than Sweden and Denmark, ended up being downgraded to Emerging Market status after its experience with hyperinflation in the 1970s and 1980s. In 2009, it suffered the further ignominy of being ejected from the MSCI Emerging Markets Index down to Frontier Market status due to its declining standards of economic management and the nationalization of private pension funds and the national airline.

The Guggenheim Frontier Markets exchange-traded fund (NYDSE:FRN), which we cover in Chapter 15, is intended to track the performance of the BNY Mellon New Frontier DR Index. The Index is comprised of ADRs and GDRs listed on the LSE, the NYSE, NYSE Arca, NYSE AMEX, and NASDAQ. The ETF will invest at least 80 percent of its assets in these ADRs and GDRs or the stocks underlying them.

Table 12-1 lists the countries within the ETF as June 30, 2013.

Table 12-1	Countries in the Guggenheim Frontier Markets exchange-traded fund
Country	*Percentage of Index*
Chile	50.5
Colombia	14.7
Argentina	9.7
Egypt	6.1
Kazakhstan	5.0
Peru	4.9

(continued)

Table 12-1 *(continued)*

Country	Percentage of Index
Nigeria	4.6
Lebanon	1.9
Isle of Man	1.3
Luxembourg	0.9

Interestingly, by far the largest country represented in the ETF — Chile, which accounts for over 50 percent of the index, is classified by Morgan Stanley Capital International (MSCI) as an Emerging Market, as are Colombia, Egypt, and Peru. While Colombia, Peru, and Egypt are included in some Frontier Markets indices, such as the MSCI Frontier Emerging Markets, over 55 percent of the ADRs in this Frontier Markets ETF come from countries that a major index provider does not regard as being frontier economies.

Among the ADRs that form the rest of the ADR portion in the top holdings of the ETF — Colombia, Argentina, Egypt, Kazakhstan, and Nigeria — the largest by market capitalization are:

- Colombian oil and gas play Ecopetrol
- Nigerian bank Guaranty Trust Bank plc
- Argentinean oil and gas stock YPF
- Egyptian bank Commercial International Bank
- Colombian financial Bancolombia
- Kazakh gas producer KazMunai Gas
- Egyptian listed mobile phone provider Orascom Telecom

In the following sections, we briefly examine these ADRs and try to get some feel for how well they've performed over the last few years and their current valuations.

Ecopetrol (NYSE:EC)

Ecopetrol is an integrated oil and gas company, owning oil fields, refineries, and pipelines in Colombia. It is the largest energy company in Colombia, producing around 70 percent of the country's oil and gas output and is 88.5 percent owned by the government of Colombia. Revenues have grown from $15.2 billion in 2009 to $38.6 billion in 2012, and it had net earnings of $8.3 billion ($4.08 per share) in 2012. Ecopetrol had a market capitalization of $94.5 billion at its price of $46 in September 2013, selling at a Price /Earnings Ratio of 12.8 times 2013's forecast earnings and a dividend yield of 5.9 percent.

Market analysts use a company's Price/Earnings ratio (P/E ratio) as a convenient method for working out how cheap or expensive a valuation a stock is selling at. It is calculated by simply dividing the company's share price by either last year's earnings per share (EPS) (known as the *historic* P/E ratio), or by its forecast earnings for the current year (*forward* P/E ratio). Thus Ecopetrol's forward P/E ratio for 2013 in September 2013 was Price $46 Earnings/forecast EPS $3.60 = 12.8 times P/E ratio.

Some companies find it difficult to consistently keep growing their earnings by more than 15 percent a year, unless they are very small or in a very rapidly growing industry, so P/E ratios above 20 times usually indicate that the company is getting expensive. P/E ratios below 10 times, on the other hand, are usually a sign that the company's stock is selling at what appears to be a cheap valuation. Of course, life is not as simple as this, because sometimes stocks will be cheap for a good reason (companies making buggy whips in 1900, makers of CDs in 2000). Meanwhile some stocks can remain expensive for many years if they consistently deliver good results (Cisco and Microsoft in the 1990s, Apple in the last decade). As always, investors need to do their homework and try to find out why a stock is selling at a particular valuation level.

ADR Cresud might be worth a look

Despite the country's fall from grace economically, Argentina's capital, Buenos Aires, remains one of the most delightful cities to visit, especially in the spring or fall (remembering that it's in the southern hemisphere). The legacy of its former wealth is visible in the splendid architecture in such wealthy suburbs as Riserva or Recoleta (where Evita's tomb is located) and its efficient, if dilapidated, subway system. Proving that even countries (or industries) in long-term decline can still provide profitable opportunities, Gavin recommended buying shares in Argentine ADR Cresud (Nasdaq:CRESY) in early 2010, after a visit to that country.

Cresud is one of the largest landowners in Argentina, growing soybeans and corn, raising cattle, and producing milk and dairy products. It also owns substantial agricultural properties in Brazil as well as a 65.5 percent stake in IRSA (NYSE:IRS). As Argentina's largest and most well-diversified real estate company, it owns major shopping centers and offices in Buenos Aires as well as three luxury hotels; it also develops apartments and residential subdivisions.

Cresud benefited from the Argentinean farming sector's recovery from drought in 2009, and also was able to sell some of its farms, which it does regularly to realize the value it has added through its improved farming methods. After the stock rose more than 50 percent in six months, a sale was recommended to lock in the profit, as inflation was picking up in Argentina and the government fired the head of the central bank when he protested about interference in the bank's affairs. Three years later, the share price at time of writing (late 2013) is at half what it was in late 2010, despite Cresud having grown its revenues substantially and listed its Brazilian subsidiary, BrasilAgro, as an ADR in 2013.

Ecopetrol has seen its stock price rise from US$17.50 in October 2008, at the height of the Financial Crisis, to US$63 in April 2012, as oil prices recovered and production expanded. Since then Ecopetrol stock has fallen 25 percent to the mid US$40s at the time of writing because oil prices have fallen below $100 per barrel. But its valuation is reasonable given its commanding position in the Colombian energy sector. Its US$98 billion market capitalization was equal to that of Brazilian state-controlled oil and gas company Petrobras, and slightly higher than the two Chinese state-controlled oil companies, China National Overseas Oil Corporation and Sinopec, which are valued at US$93 billion and US$90 billion, respectively. For comparison's sake, US oil major ConocoPhillips had a market capitalization of US$84.6 billion and British multinational energy giant BP US$133 billion.

Guaranty Trust Bank (LSE:GRTB)

Nigeria's largest bank by market capitalization (US$4.7 billion) had net earnings of US$550 million ($0.93 per share) in 2012, up 69 percent from the previous year. Its revenue rose 22 percent to $1.4 billion as loans grew 11 percent to US$4.9 billion and deposits 10 percent to US$7.4 billion. At its price of US$8 in September 2012, it was selling at a historic P/E Ratio of 8.4 times and a dividend yield of 1.9 percent.

In July 2013, Guaranty Trust Bank agreed to pay US$100 million for 70 percent of Kenya's Fina Bank, which had loans of US$184 million and deposits of US$285 million at the end of March 2013, and operated in Rwanda and Uganda. Guaranty Trust CEO Segun Agbaje said that the bank was targeting East African nations for ". . . their appreciable gross domestic product, growing investments, and ease of doing business."

Guaranty Trust has seen its share price rise over six times from US$1.25 in January 2009 at the height of the Financial Crisis to its present level of $8 at the time of writing. It had a one-year return of 28 percent to September 2013.

YPF (NYSE:YPF)

YPF is an integrated oil and gas company, owning oil fields, refineries, and pipelines in Argentina, where it is the largest energy company with a market capitalization of $7.1 billion. Its revenues grew from US$9.2 billion in 2009 to $14.8 billion in 2012 and its net earnings were US$862 million ($2.19 per share) in 2012. At its price of $18 in September 2013, it was selling at a forecast P/E ratio of 7.2 times 2013 earnings and had a dividend yield of 0.8 percent.

From 1999, it was majority-owned by Spanish integrated energy company Repsol, but Argentina's President Cristina Fernandez de Kirchner grew unhappy with YPF's supposed failure to invest sufficiently in growing Argentina's oil production. In April 2012, the government of Argentina announced it was nationalizing YPF by seizing Repsol's majority stake, fired the senior management, and installed its own executives. The price of YPF declined by one-third the day after the announcement, although it has risen by 44 percent over the year to September 2013.

Due to nationalization of Repsol's stake in YPF, the share price of YPF has fallen by almost two-thirds over the last five years, as it was trading near US$50 in late 2008, and recovered to that level in early 2011, when it issued US$1 billion of ADRs in New York.

Commercial International Bank Egypt (LSE:CBKD)

Commercial International Bank Egypt is the largest private-sector lender in Egypt (market capitalization of US$3.1 billion), with an estimated market share of 7.5 percent of the loan market with US$6.1 billion in loans outstanding and 8.6 percent and US$11.4 billion in deposits at the end of 2012. It had 161 branches and total assets of US$10.5 billion at the end of 2012 and net earnings of US$323 million (US$0.51 per share). At its price of US$5.25 in September 2013, it was selling at a P/E ratio of 10.3 times historic earnings and had a dividend yield of 3.5 percent.

Commercial International Bank was the first Egyptian company to issue GDRs in London in 1996, raising US$120 million by issuing 22 percent of its then share capital. American strategic investor Ripplewood acquired 19 percent of the bank in 2006 before disposing of its stake to Emerging Markets private equity group Actis in 2009.

Despite the political uncertainty created by the change in Arab regimes in the spring of 2011 and the recent replacement of the elected president in August 2013, Commercial International Bank has more than doubled since the height of the Financial Crisis of November 2008, although it had only risen by 4 percent in the 12 months up to September 2013.

Bancolombia (NYSE:CIB)

Bancolombia is the largest diversified commercial bank in Colombia, with a market capitalization of US$11.8 billion. It had assets of US$54.9 billion, loans of US$38.3 billion, and deposits of US$30.8 billion at the end of 2012. It had net earnings of US$953 million (US$4.47 per share) in 2012. At its price of US$56.25 in September 2013, it sold at a forecast P/E Ratio of 13.3 times and a dividend yield of 2.9 percent.

In February 2013, Bancolombia agreed to purchase HSBC's Panama operations for US$2.1 billion, three times book value. HSBC Panama had assets of US$7.6 billion, US$5.7 billion in loans, and US$5.8 billion in deposits at the end of 2012. This came two months after Bancolombia agreed to purchase a Guatemalan bank for $216 million. In March 2013, Bancolombia's shareholders approved the bank issuing up to US$2.4 billion in new preferred shares to fund the HSBC purchase.

Bancolombia shares appreciated over four times from US$17.50 to US$69 between the height of the Financial Crisis in February 2009 and its announcement of the HSBC Panama purchase and associated equity issue in March 2013. Over the last 12 months up to September 2013, the stock has fallen 5 percent.

KazMunai Gas Exploration and Production (LSE:KMG)

KazMunai Gas is one of the top three state-controlled Kazakh oil and gas exploration and production companies, with a market capitalization of US$5.7 billion. In 2012, it had revenues of US$5.2 billion and net earnings of US$1.1 billion ($2.54 per share). At its price of US$13.5 in September 2013, KazMunai Gas was selling at a P/E ratio of 5.3 times and due to paying a special dividend to help its state-owned parent company, a dividend yield of 13.2 percent.

KazMunai Gas listed on the Kazakh Stock Exchange and also listed GDRs on the London Stock Exchange in 2006, raising over $2 billion. In 2011, labor unrest at one of its two production centers led to a 7 percent fall in output and it seems unlikely that output will exceed previous highs reached in 2010 until 2016.

KazMunai Gas's share price has increased by 50 percent from its lows of US$9 in early 2009 to its present level of US$13.50 in September 2013, but had fallen by 19 percent in the last 12 months, partially due to lower oil prices and a slower recovery in production than anticipated by investors after the strike.

Orascom Telecom Holding (LSE:OTLD)

Orascom Telecom is the Egyptian-listed owner of the largest mobile phone networks in Algeria and Pakistan and the second largest in Bangladesh, as well as ownership of networks in Zimbabwe, Burundi, and the Central African Republic. It has a market capitalization of US$3.3 billion. In 2012, it had revenues of US$3.6 billion and a net loss of US$205 million, although its operating income for 2012 was US$1 billion and its cash generated totaled US$1.2 billion. At its price of US$3.10 in September 2013, it had a forecast P/E ratio of 17.1 times and did not pay a dividend.

Orascom's founding shareholder Naguib Sawiris sold a controlling 51.9 percent shareholding to Russian mobile phone company Vimpelcom in 2011. Also in 2011, Orascom sold its Tunisian mobile phone subsidiary for a US$700 million profit, which was used to reduce debt. In 2013, one of the major shareholders of Vimpelcom made an offer for Orascom Telecom at US$3.50 per share, but the independent directors rejected the offer, based on a third-party valuation that valued the company at US$4.31 per share.

Orascom Telecom's share price has declined from US$4.47 per share in September 2009 on the sale of its Tunisian subsidiary and negotiations with the Algerian government to sell a 51 percent stake in its Algerian subsidiary,

Djezzy, which accounted for over 50 percent of its revenues. In addition, devaluations of the Algerian and Pakistani currencies have led to exceptional charges on its revalued debt and reduced its revenues in US$ terms, although the stock has risen by 4 percent over the 12 months up to September 2013.

Exercising caution with ADRs and GDRs

As noted at the beginning of this review of ADRs and GDRs, an investor is essentially attempting to pick individual stocks in Frontier Markets, which are less liquid, less well-regulated, and less transparent than developed markets. So companies that issue ADRs and GDRs are saying they are willing to abide by North American or European auditing and reporting standards, which gives some comfort, but it does not mean that they aren't affected by the same factors that characterize any Emerging or Frontier Market.

Apart from the usual concerns of investors such as interest rates, foreign exchange, and commodity prices, the local government may be replaced (Egypt twice in two years), decide to nationalize a major foreign shareholder (Argentina), be affected by long drawn out strikes (Kazakhstan), or have the government change the regulations to favor its bargaining position (Algeria).

These issues are some of the curve balls that investing in less-developed markets can throw at you and unless you have a strong stomach or a long-term horizon, they are probably going to dampen your appetite for investing in Frontier Markets, however enticing the big picture looks. That's why we wouldn't advise buying individual ADRs and GDRs as a means of accessing these economies.

Global Multinational Equities

Global multinational equities are shares in large blue chip companies based (or domiciled) in developed markets but with substantial exposure in Frontier Markets. The main advantage to investing in these equities lies in their familiarity and stability and their long-established place in developed markets. The main disadvantage from the point of view of investors looking for a pure frontier investment is that they are not Frontier Markets *pure plays*. They are a mix of exposure to developed market and Emerging and Frontier Markets. Therefore, one stock can amount to a play on developed, Emerging, and Frontier Markets or a triple play of sorts. That can become quite complicated.

In Chapter 10, we look at some the global multinationals that have a major exposure to Emerging and Frontier Markets. We suggest that you read that chapter to get a feel for how the different factors affecting these triple plays end up playing out. To briefly summarize our findings, despite some multinationals like KFC and Pizza Hut owner Yum Brands, consumer products giants Nestle and Unilever, and drinks major Diageo having over 30 percent of their revenues and earnings coming from these developing economies, their stock prices tend to be more affected by what's happening in their domestic stock markets.

Online Trading

Online trading in the way we mean it here leaves all decisions in the hands of the investor who makes buy, sell, and hold decisions without the assistance of a financial advisor or broker. You can view online trading as an extension of the do-it-yourself approach to investing.

Successful online trading at the best of times means that you view it as a part-time job of sorts, since it requires large amounts of research time, undertaken without the help of a professional advisor.

You're probably thinking, "There they go again, talking about how I need the help of a financial advisor." You may be right in thinking that but trust us, we know what advisors do and how they can help you.

Start from the position that the complexities of online trading increase exponentially when dealing with Frontier Markets.

The upside

Online trading likely appeals to your do-it-yourself ambitions in the same way that shopping online might appeal to you. It provides speed, a wealth of choice, independent decision-making at any time of day or night, and usually a cost savings. It also appeals to your desire for independence and self-determination.

Going it alone has a wonderful sound for a certain kind of person in most areas of life and investing is no exception. Television commercials that appeal to your individualism as well as your independence of spirit only reinforce this idea. The commercials telegraph the notion that you are master of your destiny when with just a couple of clicks, you seemingly make large profits.

Some commercials for online trading sites will also appeal to the simplicity of trading, suggesting that you can just press a few buttons and wait for the money to come rolling in. Sounds nice, no?

The downside

Take the same careful reservations to online trading commercials that you take to real estate or car commercials. In fact, those investments might be smaller than investments made during online investing.

The commercials don't spell out the work and risks involved in online trading, even when dealing with equities in developed markets. Add to that the additional complexities and lack of familiarity inherent in Frontier Markets investing and the necessary work and risks increase exponentially.

The opposite side of this complicated coin is that you do not have access to a knowledgeable financial advisor while making the investment decisions.

Once you've made the decision you also don't have access to an advisor's expertise during volatile periods and might be tempted to sell an equity prematurely or hold on to it longer than appropriate.

An otherwise intelligent choice can become a severely eroded holding with a sudden development that even the most careful online trader could never have foreseen. The impulse to trade in the short term can result in severe losses in opportunity cost or in hard dollars.

If you want to try online trading, get some experience first with equities in developed nations. If you want to start online trading in frontier equities, restrict these dollars to an amount where the loss won't materially affect your financial position.

Chapter 13

Buying Bond Funds

Adding bonds to your asset mix is a great way to minimize volatility, in effect reducing the ups and downs of your investment portfolio balance. This applies whether the bonds are issued by the sovereign governments of developed countries, such as United States or Canada bonds, well-known corporations such as blue-chip banks or more speculative companies that have to pay a higher yield, or the governments and corporations of Emerging and Frontier Markets.

In this chapter, we look at the basics of bond investing and discuss how investors can best access this type of asset. We cover using bond mutual funds and exchange-traded funds (ETFs) to get exposure to Emerging and Frontier Market bonds, as opposed to buying individual bonds. It's very difficult to buy small amounts of bonds outside of the U.S. Treasury market, and if anything happens to an individual bond, such as a suspension of interest payments or even worse, bankruptcy by the issuer, investors can lose some or all of their money. That defeats the object of using the bonds as less volatile assets.

We examine the advantages and disadvantages of using bond funds and ETFs and then look at some of the largest and longest established Emerging Market bond funds.

Bond Basics

A *bond* is a debt obligation from an issuer, usually a government or corporation. These organizations issue bonds to raise money to build schools, highways and hospitals, and new factories or production lines. They're borrowing money from you, the bond investor. If you hold an individual bond until it matures, you'll receive the face value of the bond along with interest payments — as long as the borrower has not defaulted in the meantime.

The less likely the borrower is to default on payments, the less risky the bond; and the less risky the bond, the lower the interest rate the borrower is willing to pay you. Bond ratings agencies such as Standard & Poor's (S&P) and Moody's analyze and rate the financial security of the issuing government or corporation, giving investors guidance as to the likelihood of default. Although the ratings agencies can sometimes be slow to recognize adverse changes in the underlying fundamentals, they're a starting point.

Bonds issued by Emerging and Frontier Market countries and companies have usually been regarded as being among the more risky categories of bonds, with ratings below investment grade (lower than BBB- or B). But in recent years, their improving fundamentals have been recognized, with many countries being upgraded. While only 5 percent of the JP Morgan US$ Emerging Markets Bond Index was rated investment grade in the late 1990s, the percentage rose to 34 percent by 2002 and 57 percent by 2010.

Investing in Bond Funds

The best way for most investors to buy the bond portion of their portfolios is by purchasing bond mutual funds. This applies especially to those investors wanting to gain exposure to Emerging and Frontier bond markets. Because the best prices on bonds are usually found when buying in very large increments (think $1,000,000 per purchase), individuals benefit from participating in a pool of professionally managed funds invested in the bond market. Bond funds are especially sensitive to the fees of mutual funds because they typically don't see the high returns of stock funds, although given the additional economic and company research required when investing in Emerging and Frontier bond markets, fees on such funds tend to be higher than those of bond funds investing in developed markets.

An old market joke goes "What's the difference between a bond and a bond trader?" Answer: "A bond eventually matures." While we're not suggesting that the character of bond funds resembles the aggressive bond traders in their colorful jackets screaming at each other on the trading floor of the futures exchanges, they do share one important feature. Unlike an individual bond, *bond funds do not mature.* Therefore, the return that an investor receives from a bond fund consists only of the yield generated by the portfolio of bonds it contains (after the payment of fees) and any capital gains (less losses) that the manager of the fund has generated through the sales and purchases of bonds.

The advantages of bond funds

As noted earlier, the primary advantage that bond funds offer individual investors is *diversification.* Most investors won't have enough money to build a diversified bond portfolio themselves (other sources have suggested you need at least $50,000 to start), and avoid the volatility caused by fluctuating interest rates. When interest rates rise, bond prices fall; and when interest rates fall, bond prices rise. Longer term bonds are more sensitive to interest rate changes, but as a bond maturity date gets closer, it fluctuates less in price.

Standard deviation is a way of measuring the volatility of bonds. A standard deviation of 4 percent means that, historically, the returns of a given security class have ranged from 4 percent below the category average to 4 percent higher. The lower the standard deviation, the lower the volatility and market risk.

Shorter-term bonds have lower volatility and lower returns and long-term and high-yield bonds have greater volatility, as do Emerging Markets bonds, while delivering higher returns.

Investing via a bond fund allows an individual investor to hold many different bonds from a variety of different issuers and with different maturities. Thus an individual's exposure to risks such as interest rate risk, default risk, and liquidity risk is much reduced in exchange for paying the manager of the bond fund a small annual fee. Bond funds also allow individual investors to construct their own bond portfolio because there are a wide variety of different funds with different maturity profiles, different types of issuers, and different credit ratings.

Bond funds are divided into various categories, some of which reflect the maturity of the bonds contained in the fund, and some of which reflect the different sorts of issuers. Thus there are short-, medium-, and long-term domestic bond funds, and high yield, international, and emerging market bond funds. The definitions are relatively straightforward:

- *Short-term* bonds have maturity dates of five years or less.
- *Intermediate-term* bonds have maturities of five to ten years.
- *Long-term* bonds have stated maturities that are longer than ten years.
- *High-yield bonds* are usually rated below investment grade, which means they have to pay a higher rate to attract investors.

✔ *Emerging and Frontier Markets* bonds were usually rated below investment grade, and therefore also paid higher yields, but in the last decade many countries have been upgraded to be classified as investment grade.

An ideal allocation for a long time horizon would be a blend of short-term and intermediate-term bonds with some high-yield and/or Emerging Market bonds, which deliver the same historical return as investment grade long-term bonds and with lower volatility. Furthermore, except in the most extreme circumstances, such as the Financial Crisis of 2008–2009, high-yield and Emerging Market bonds are not highly correlated with investment grade bonds, so including a small percentage of them in a diversified bond portfolio reduces its overall volatility.

It is possible to purchase bond funds entirely devoted to short-term bonds issued by one state or province, those investing only in long-term inflation-protected or Real Return bonds (bonds whose interest rate fluctuates with the Consumer Price Index), or those that invest only in bonds issued by a single country. However, bond investors with a longer time horizon can benefit from exposure to all parts of the bond market because they don't have to be as defensive against hard times in the investment cycle, and purchasing diversified funds with the appropriate maturity dates with low management fees should produce the desired outcome.

The disadvantages of bond funds

While having many advantages for the individual investor, bond funds do have some less attractive features.

The fees are high

Given the lower returns that they generate compared to stock funds, the level of fees is especially important when considering investing in bond funds.

While the level of fees should always be considered when choosing a mutual fund, it is especially important for bond funds. With the low level of absolute bond yields at present, even a 10 basis point (0.10 percent) difference in fees can reduce an investor's return by a meaningful amount. For example, if an intermediate-term bond fund was yielding 1.5 percent from its portfolio, a management fee of 0.30 percent would be equal to 20 percent of the return, as opposed to a fund with a 0.20 percent fee, which is only equal to 13.3 percent of the return.

WARNING!

Government bonds and interest rates

The very low yields on government bonds at the time of writing (2013–2014) mean that it is especially important to have a low allocation to long-term investment grade bonds, whether corporate or government. With 10-year government bond yields in many developed countries such as the United States, Canada, Germany, and the United Kingdom near 60-year lows between 1.5 percent and 2.5 percent, the risk of capital losses on long-term bonds should interest rates begin to rise is very high. The low yield provided by the bonds is below the inflation rate. This means that holders of these bonds are not receiving a "real" after-inflation return, while being exposed to the risk of capital loss. Although yields on short-term and intermediate-term bonds are even lower, as we noted, their vulnerability to rising interest rates is much lower.

They never mature

Bond funds never mature, so there is always the risk of capital loss if an investor needs to sell the fund at an inopportune time. This is not a risk faced by holders of individual bonds, where, as long as they retain their bond until maturity, they are guaranteed to get their money back, in nominal terms anyway.

They aren't as liquid as stocks. For passively managed bond funds, known as bond index funds, which attempt to replicate the return from the bond market by passively investing in the same range of bonds as an index, bonds aren't as liquid as stocks. Trading costs can be higher and matching the index can be more difficult.

More important however, is the fact that the largest components of a bond index are the governments and companies that are borrowing the most money! While this may make sense for a stock index, where the most successful companies become bigger over time, the opposite is true for bond issuers. Those countries and companies that need to borrow the most money have underlying budget issues that will need to be addressed eventually.

The Top Bond Funds for Emerging and Frontier Market Exposure

At the time of writing, there are no pure Frontier Market debt funds available to North American investors. While there are numerous Emerging Market debt funds, some of which have substantial exposure to the Frontier Markets, the earlier stage of economic development in these markets means that they have not, in general, issued large amounts of debt.

This, in turn, means that there are not enough bonds available to allow professional fund managers to construct diversified portfolios solely devoted to frontier economies. Ironically, one of the only Frontier Markets that does have a lot of debt outstanding is Argentina, which carried out what was then the biggest default in history in 2001–2002 when it stopped paying interest on approximately $90 billion of debt. Investors who accepted the terms of a restructuring that was agreed in 2010 effectively lost two-thirds of their original capital, as well as eight years of interest payments, making it easy to understand why investors today are reluctant to purchase Argentinian debt.

iShares JP Morgan US$ Emerging Markets Bond Index Exchange-Traded Fund

Specs
Launch Date: December 17, 2007

Assets under management (August 2013): $4.1 billion

Performance (August 2013)
1 Year: -3.3%
3 Years (p.a.): +4.5%
5 Years (p.a.): +7.5%

Management expense ratio (MER): 0.6%

Top 5 Countries (30th April 2013):
Russia: 6.8%
Turkey: 6.6%

Mexico: 6.4%
Philippines: 6.2%
Indonesia: 6.0%

Top 5 Holdings (as of August 9, 2013):
Philippines Rep 7.75% 2031 2.2%
Rep of Turkey 7% 2020 1.8%
Russian Federation 7.5% 2030 1.7%
Lithuanian Tr Bond 2020 1.6%
Colombia Rep 6.125% 2041 1.5%

Running Yield (August 2013): 4.6%

Outlook

The largest passive index vehicle investing in emerging market debt is the iShares JP Morgan US$ Emerging Markets Bond Index exchange-traded fund (ETF), which tracks the return of actively traded debt instruments in emerging market countries.

With over $4 billion in assets under management and a management expense ratio of 0.6 percent, the fund had a yield to maturity of 5.1 percent in June 2013. Eligible securities must be denominated in US dollars, issued by sovereign entities (for example, countries or institutions guaranteed by them), have a face value of US$1 billion outstanding, and more than two years to maturity. The index has holdings from 39 countries and the top five countries, in order, Russia, Turkey, Mexico, Brazil, and the Philippines, represent 32 percent of the index.

Its duration of 7.5 years means that when interest rates move by 1 percent, the price of the ETF would move by 7.5 percent, making it a fairly volatile investment. This was illustrated in May and June of 2013, when worries over the end of Quantitative Easing (QE) by the US Federal Reserve saw its price fall more than 7 percent as US 10-year Treasury bond yields rose by 1 percent.

Moody's rates 65 percent of the countries in the fund as investment grade. While there are some countries in the index such as Venezuela (5 percent weight) that are at risk of downgrades from the ratings agencies, Morningstar notes that the index has historically proven to be a good diversifier for a fixed income portfolio, with a correlation of only 0.31 with the Barclays US Bond Index over the three years to 2013.

Two investments that have a correlation of 1.0 with each other are perfectly correlated; in other words, they move together in lockstep (or perfect harmony). Negative correlations mean that the two securities move in opposite directions, while low correlations mean there is no relationship between them. Therefore adding some Emerging Markets bonds to a traditional investment-grade bond portfolio makes the whole portfolio less volatile because the two elements do not move in the same direction or at the same speed, even though one of them may be quite volatile.

TCW Emerging Markets Income Fund (TGEIX)

Specs

Launch Date: Prior to 1998

Assets under management: $6.2 billion

Performance (August 2013)
1 Year: +0.9%
3 Years (p.a.): 7.5%
5 Years (p.a.): 12.0%

Management expense ratio: 0.84%

Top 5 Countries (30 April 2013):
Russia: 16.2%
Brazil: 13.5%
Mexico: 9.6%
Venezuela: 4.6%
Turkey 4.1%

Top 5 Holdings (as of June 30, 2013):
Sec Tesouro Nacl 10% 2023 2.7%
Petroleos de Venezuela 8.5% 2017 2.1%
Rep. of Venezuela 7.75% 2019 1.9%
Vereinigte Mexikanische 7.75% 2042 1.5%
Rep. of Turkey 3.25% 2023 1.5%

Running Yield (August 2013): 6.3%

Quantitative easing: It's not a Pilates move

Quantitative easing is effectively money printing by a central bank, in this case the United States Federal Reserve, which agrees to buy all new bonds issued by its government or government-guaranteed institutions such as the mortgage banks, Fannie Mae and Freddie Mac. Introduced in 2008–2009 to offset the effects of the Financial Crisis, the program has continued for the last four years, keeping interest rates low not merely for short-term borrowings, but also for longer-term bonds.

Outlook

The TCW Emerging Income Fund is one of the largest and longest established Emerging Markets bond funds in the U.S. With large positions in corporate debt (debt issued by companies — over 60 percent at June 30, 2013) and in local currency sovereign and corporate debt (debt issued in the local currency of the issuer, such as Brazilian reals or Russian rubles, rather than US dollars), this fund has outperformed other emerging market debt funds over the last few years, as local interest rates have fallen and more companies have issued bonds due to their improving credit ratings.

It is one of only two Emerging Market debt funds to be ranked 5-star by fund rating company Morningstar, but the fund is vulnerable to periods when the dollar rises against Emerging Market currencies and credit conditions tighten, such as occurred in the first half of 2013. It has a duration of 5.97 years and has been quite volatile over the last four years, with its non-investment grade holdings totaling 56 percent at mid-year 2013.

MFS Emerging Market Debt A (MEDAX)

Specs

Launch Date: March 17, 1998

Assets under management (August 2013): $6.7 billion

Performance (August 2013)
1 Year: -1.5%
3 Years (p.a.): +5.6%
5 Years (p.a.): +8.6%

Management expense ratio: 1.11%

Top 5 Countries (30th June 2013):
Russia: 11.6%
Mexico: 9.1%
Venezuela: 8.6%
Turkey 7.7%
Brazil: 7.0%

Top 5 Holdings (as of June 30, 2013):
Russian Fed. 7.5% 2030 2.4%
United Mexican States 3.625% 2022 2.3%
United Mexican States 5.125% 2020 1.8%
Rep. of Venezuela 7.75% 2019 1.5%
US Treasury 1.75% 2022 1.5%

Running Yield: 4.09%

Outlook

The MFS Emerging Debt Fund has grown rapidly over the last few years to become one of the largest funds in this sector. Its holdings were 55 percent investment grade and 98 percent in US dollar–denominated bonds issued largely by sovereign and quasi-sovereign (government-backed) issuers at end June 2013. It also had about 15 percent in Emerging Market corporate debt at that date.

Although its duration is 6.71 years, its low foreign currency exposure has helped to make it less volatile than many of its peers and it is ranked 4-star by Morningstar. While its large size and concentration on sovereign US-dollar denominated debt means that its asset allocation resembles the JP Morgan Emerging Market Bond Index, it has small (less than 1%) positions in some Frontier Markets such as Nigeria and Ivory Coast.

Fidelity New Markets Income (FNMIX)

Specs

Launch Date: April 5, 1993

Assets under management: $5.3 billion

Performance (August 2013)
1 Year: -1.0%
3 Years (p.a.): +6.8%
5 Years (p.a.): +9.6%

Management expense ratio: 0.84%

Top 5 Holdings (June 30, 2013):
Venezuela: 10.9%
USA: 10.3%
Mexico: 7.4%
Russia: 7.3%
Netherlands: 5.2%

Top 5 Holdings (June 30, 2013):
Russian Fed. 7.5% 2030 3.2%
Petroleos de Venezuela 8.5% 2017 2.8%
Petroleos de Venezuela 4.9% 2014 1.7%
Petrobras Gl. Fin.FRN 2019 1.6%
Slovenia Rep. 5.5% 2022 1.5%

Running Yield: 4.6%

Outlook

The Fidelity New Markets Income Fund is one of the largest and oldest of the Emerging Markets debt funds, with a policy of having at least two-thirds of its assets in US dollar–denominated sovereign and quasi-sovereign debt issues. In the middle of 2013, the fund had 11 percent in corporate debt and 7 percent in local currency bonds, but its managers have been willing to take on sovereign credit risk, as shown by its high weight in Venezuela (11 percent against 9 percent in the JP Morgan Emerging Market Debt Index).

With 48 percent in investment-grade debt, its high U.S. dollar weighting, and its duration of 5.43 years, the fund has been less volatile than many of its peers, although it will tend to lag when the dollar weakens against Emerging Market currencies. Its high weight in major Frontier Markets such as Venezuela and Argentina and its out-of-index bets on such Frontier Markets as Slovenia mean that it can under-perform during periods when credit concerns are rising.

Columbia Emerging Markets Bond (REBAX)

Specs
Launch Date: February 16, 2006

Asset under management (August 2013): $909 million

Performance (August 2013)
1 Year: -0.7%
3 Years (p.a.): +6.7%
5 Years p.a.): +9.7%

Management expense ratio: 1.16%

Top 5 Countries (30th June 2013):
Russia: 15.8%
Venezuela: 9.2%
Indonesia: 9.0%
Mexico: 8.3%
Brazil: 6.3%

Top 5 Holdings (31st March 2013):
Uruguay Rep. 4.375% 2028 3.0%
Bolivarian Rep. Venezuela 9% 2023 2.9%
Rep.Oriental del Uruguay 4.25% 2027 2.9%
Petroleos de Venezuela 9% 2021 2%
United Mexican States 7.5% 2027 2%

Running Yield: 5.1%

Outlook

With over 20 percent in local currency bonds and 9 percent in corporate Emerging Market debt at mid-2013, the Columbia Emerging Markets Bond Fund has been willing to take positions outside the JP Morgan Emerging Markets Bond Index to add value for its investors, which has produced a top quartile performance over the last few years.

Its portfolio is over 60 percent investment-grade credit, so that although its 6.12 years duration and its local currency exposure have made it more volatile than the average fund, it has not been as volatile as might have been expected. The lower volatility contributed to its 4-star Morningstar rating.

Chapter 14

Buying Exchange-Traded Funds (ETFs)

....

....

*E*xchange-traded funds, popularly known as ETFs, have been around for almost 25 years in the United States and Canada but their popularity has grown more rapidly over the last few years than previously. An **ETF** represents a basket of stocks or bonds that you can purchase just like a share of stock. However, with a single investment in an ETF, you own a piece of lots of different stocks or bonds — in some cases several hundred, because there are some ETFs that track broad indices such as the Standard & Poor's (S&P) 500 Index. Unlike index mutual funds, which also aim to track indices containing many different companies, ETFs trade on a stock exchange, so you can buy and sell them just like you buy and sell stocks.

In this chapter, we examine the basics of ETF investing and discuss the advantages of using them to gain access to Frontier Markets. We also look at some of the disadvantages of investing in ETFs, which are particularly important in an illiquid and rapidly developing asset class like Frontier Markets. Finally, we look at the top ETFs for Frontier Market investing.

ETF Basics

An ETF consists of a basket of stocks or bonds that tracks the performance of an index and trades on a stock exchange. ETF providers use several different methods to construct these funds, the simplest of which involves buying all the stocks or bonds that make up the underlying index. ETF providers can also attempt to replicate the index by buying futures contracts based on the index, a quicker method with lower costs. When some of the stocks or bonds that make up the index are illiquid or represent only a small percentage of the index capitalization, the providers may decide not to purchase them, as long as the remaining stocks or bonds in the index comprise the vast majority of the ETF and account for almost all of its performance.

The oldest and most popular ETFs track very broad, well-known indices such as the S&P 500 Index and the S&P/TSX Composite Index. However, a wide variety of methodologies has emerged for creating new indices in narrower markets such as small capitalization stocks and individual market sectors such as financial, energy, or gold stocks. For international stocks, ETFs have also expanded from tracking broad indices such as the MSCI Europe, Australasia, and Far East (EAFE) Index, which covers all developed stock markets outside the U.S., to Emerging and Frontier Markets and individual countries.

Because ETFs trade on a stock exchange, trading and price quotes are available throughout the day, unlike for mutual funds which are priced once a day after the conclusion of trading. Although the aim of the ETF is to closely follow the tracked index, because the price of the basket of stocks comprising it is based on supply and demand, it may be higher (trade at a premium) or lower (trade at a discount) than the actual value of the securities held in the fund.

Since ETFs trade on stock exchanges, investors have to pay commissions each time they buy or sell their shares. This is an additional cost not included in the management fees charged by the ETF provider. Extra fees mean that ETFs aren't well suited for regular investment programs, such as when you have amounts deducted from your paycheck or bank account on a monthly or bimonthly basis for 401(k) or RRSP contributions.

Advantages of Investing via ETFs

Exchange-traded funds have grown rapidly in popularity over the last decade as investors have come to appreciate their advantages with lower costs the most often-cited example.

Low costs

Low management fees is one of the principal features that has contributed to their success in the last few years. Fund managers don't actively manage ETFs in an attempt to beat the performance of the index because an ETF merely tracks the performance of the underlying index. That amounts to what we often call *passive investing*. Thus these funds don't have to pay large salaries to superstar fund managers and their associated analysts and researchers. Therefore, their management costs are much lower and due to economies of scale the larger an ETF becomes, the lower its fees as a percentage of its assets.

The largest ETFs tracking broad indices in the United States, such as the S&P 500 or the NASDAQ, have management fees of less than 0.15 percent per annum (p.a.). This is well below most actively managed mutual funds, which charge over 1 percent p.a. As a result, about 75 percent of all actively managed funds can't outperform their market index. Of course, passively managed funds and ETFs will never outperform their index because they always aim to produce the performance of the index they're tracking, less their management fees. However, because their fees are so low, many investors are happy to receive the performance of the market minus a small amount, rather than attempt to guess which of the more expensive actively managed funds will be among the 25 percent that do manage to beat the index.

When investing in Emerging and Frontier Markets, the cost advantage of ETFs is not so clear cut. This occurs because the management fees for ETFs in these markets are much higher than ETFs tracking long-established broad market indices such as the S&P 500. The markets themselves are much less liquid and the expenses such as commissions, custodian fees, foreign exchange charges, and government taxes such as stamp duty make it a lot more expensive to manage even passive portfolios than in developed markets like the U.S. and Canada. The management fee for the longest-established Emerging Markets ETF, the iShares MSCI Emerging Markets ETF (NYSE:EEM), is 0.69 percent and the fee for the iShares MSCI Frontier 100 ETF is an even higher 0.79 percent. In these cases, ETFs can still be regarded as costing less than mutual funds over all, but are nothing like the low cost of a domestic ETF.

Successfully delivering market returns

The other major reason that an investor buys an ETF rather than an actively managed fund is confidence of receiving the performance of the index, less the fees. In a perfect world, the only difference between the performance of an ETF and the underlying index it tracks should be its fees.

Anything else is known as a *tracking error* — there may be a small difference in performance after fees due to the timing of inflows and outflows for the ETF. Those ETF providers using sampling may also discover that the stocks or bonds they choose to include don't match the performance of the index as closely as they hoped. When considering which ETF to select, you should seek out reports that show the performance of the ETF over various time periods against its index. With an effectively run ETF, the only difference should be its fees.

In a decade (2000–2009) when investors suffered two of the worst *bear markets* (usually defined as a fall in the stock market index of more than 20 percent) since World War II, the returns from ETFs that track the broad market indices in developed countries have not been impressive, but they have at least matched those delivered by the indices. In other words, investors have shown they'd rather have the certainty of slightly under-performing the indices through an ETF than guessing which active manager would be able to beat the indices. This was especially relevant because between two-thirds and three-quarters of actively managed funds underperformed the indices, largely because their higher management fees ate up any outperformance their managers generated.

Ease of acquisition

Buying an ETF requires an investor to open an account with a stockbroker but the spread of low cost brokers who can be accessed electronically means that this not a major handicap. With most no-advice brokerages offering trades for under $10 a deal and the majority of investors choosing to hold their share certificates in electronic form with custodians, opening a brokerage account has become as easy as ordering books or electronics over the Internet. ETFs are listed on stock exchanges, so you can track the performance of your holdings on your smartphone or computer on a minute-by-minute basis, if you so choose (although we wouldn't advise you to do so!). Furthermore, with the explosion of new ETFs tracking everything from junior gold mining stocks to heating oil to Vietnamese companies, an investor can construct a very diversified portfolio comprised of several dozen ETFs. However, most advisors don't recommend this strategy, feeling that all most people need are the major building blocks that make up any portfolio.

These building blocks are:

- A diversified bond ETF
- A broad, diversified domestic equity ETF, such as one tracking the S&P 500 or S&P/TSX Composite Index
- A diversified international ETF, investing in developed markets, such as the MSCI EAFE Index
- A diversified Emerging Markets equity ETF, such as one tracking the MSCI Emerging Markets Index

Some publications, such as *MoneySense* magazine in Canada, run what they describe as "couch potato portfolios," ones that contain the major building blocks, and recommend automatically rebalancing the portfolio once a year to return it to its original allocation. This approach allows you to "set it and forget it," while the rebalancing means that you're automatically selling down the part of the portfolio that has risen and buying that which has fallen, thus selling high and buying low. Using this method also means that you don't trade too much, a situation that helps preserve the returns from the portfolio.

The Disadvantages of ETFs

ETFs are a low cost, liquid, and transparent method of tracking the performance of an underlying stock market index, which accounts for their rapid growth in assets over the last decade. However, they have several disadvantages, apart from the obvious fact that fees mean that an ETF can never outperform the index.

Unequal weighting in stock indices

The major disadvantage of most ETFs is that the index they track is market capitalization-weighted. This means that the larger a company's stock market value becomes, the bigger weight it has in the index. This also means that companies whose market value falls may be dropped from the index leading to funds that track that index having to sell that stock. Therefore, indices can end up having a very high weighting in one or two stocks, which defeats the purpose of buying an index, namely diversification. In 2000, the S&P/TSX Composite Index had telecommunications stock Nortel Networks as its largest weight, comprising almost 35 percent of the index. Subsequently, Nortel fell 95 percent in value over the next two years and eventually filed for bankruptcy.

For Frontier Markets ETFs, unequal weighting is a major problem because stock markets in these economies are concentrated, illiquid, and undeveloped. The issues of overconcentration in a few countries and stocks are so great at present that they almost defeat the purpose of using ETFs to gain exposure. The MSCI Frontier Markets Index is comprised of the 141 largest companies in the 25 countries that make up the index, adjusted for their *free float* (the percentage of their stock market capitalization that is freely available to outside investors). These companies had an average market capitalization of $3 billion at the time of writing (2013).

Because the small but wealthy states that make up the Gulf Cooperation Council (GCC) in the Persian Gulf have the largest and most developed stock markets in the Frontier category at the time of writing (end 2013), they represent an astonishing 57 percent of the MSCI Frontier Markets Index. Kuwait, on its own, accounts for more than 30 percent of the index's market capitalization, with the National Bank of Kuwait representing 6.4 percent of the index. The other 20 countries, which include such populous and economically important countries as Argentina, Bangladesh, Kazakhstan, Kenya, Nigeria, Pakistan, Ukraine, and Vietnam, account for only 43 percent.

The MSCI Frontier Markets 100 Index ETF (NYSE:FM) was launched in 2012 to provide a representative and more easily replicated alternative to the broader index and includes 100 of the largest and most liquid companies in the parent index. The problem of overconcentration is almost as great, however, with the top 10 holdings making up just over 40 percent of the ETF, and GCC members Kuwait, Qatar, and the United Arab Emirates (UAE) comprising 57 percent of the fund on their own. The next largest countries are Nigeria (13.3 percent) and Pakistan (4.4 percent). The effect of that is that nearly 75 percent of the fund is in only five countries, of which three are very small, wealthy states. This is probably not what most investors would expect if they bought a fund investing in the Frontier Markets.

The problem worsens with single-country ETFs, which, as their name suggests, invest in only one country, rather than globally or regionally. Two ETFs for Pakistan and Bangladesh, launched in 2012 by Deutsche Bank, had 24 percent and 60 percent of their assets, respectively, represented by their top five holdings.

Frontier countries have rapidly developing stock markets, so they tend to have lots of Initial Public Offerings (IPOs), as companies list on the stock exchange to raise capital for expansion. This means that the composition of the index changes a lot in a relatively short period, and ETFs, seeking to track the index, need to buy shares in the new listings. As anyone who has applied for shares in an IPO knows, you do not always get your desired number of shares but the index reflects the capitalization of the new listing from the first day. This means that the ETF's tracking error will increase, as will the need to sell down its existing holdings to reflect their reduced weight in the index.

Reclassification

The final disadvantage of ETFs investing in rapidly developing markets is that the index can change as countries are promoted or relegated from one category to another. Thus Argentina went from being classified as a developed country to being classified as an Emerging Market due to its dreadful economic performance in the 1970s and 1980s, and was then further demoted to Frontier Market status in 2009. This meant ETFs tracking the MSCI Emerging Markets Index had to sell all their Argentinian holdings. Similarly, MSCI announced that Morocco would be reclassified as a Frontier Market rather than an Emerging Market.

Going the other direction, Qatar and the United Arab Emirates (UAE) are due to be promoted from Frontier to Emerging Market status in May 2014. This means 27.6 percent of the MSCI Frontier Markets 100 Index will be reclassified at a stroke, necessitating ETFs such as those investing in Frontier Markets selling their entire positions in these stock markets. They will then need to reinvest the proceeds in countries whose markets are much less liquid over a short period of time.

Therefore, while market capitalization-weighted ETFs are a low-cost, transparent, and liquid means of gaining market exposure in developed markets such as North America, Japan, and Western Europe, we would caution investors against simply going out and buying them as an easy or inexpensive way to gain exposure to Frontier Markets. These markets will likely continue to appreciate, giving investors good absolute returns, but we believe there are better and more effective ways of gaining exposure. This crucial difference underpins the authors' preference for global funds with well-designed investment mandates.

The Top Global Frontier Markets ETFs

Although ETFs are often the most suitable method of investing in major developed stock markets such as the United States, Japan, and Europe due to their low cost, liquidity, transparency, and ability to deliver the returns of the stock market index they track (less their low management expenses), this is not the case in Frontier Markets.

The two major global Frontier Markets ETFs, the iShares MSCI Frontier Markets 100 Index and the Guggenheim Frontier Markets Index ETF, have major issues that make them unsuitable for investors wanting to gain exposure to global Frontier Markets. The iShares MSCI ETF is heavily concentrated in the Middle East, with over 60 percent of its assets in the small, wealthy GCC countries of Kuwait, Qatar, and the United Arab Emirates. Furthermore, Qatar and the UAE will become classified as Emerging Markets from May 2014, meaning the ETF will have to sell down its exposure to those countries. The Guggenheim ETF has over 80 percent of its assets in Latin American countries, with 50 percent in Chile, now classified as an Emerging Market.

Thus neither of the two global Frontier Markets ETFs gives much weight to the large rapidly growing economies of Asia and Africa that are probably the most attractive Frontier Market countries in terms of economic outlook, and both of them are heavily concentrated in a particular region. Their management expense ratios (MERs) are also quite high in absolute terms (0.7–0.8 percent). The regional and single-country ETFs also have high MERs and the regional funds often have high weights in a single country.

iShares MSCI Frontier Markets 100 ETF (NYSE:FM)

Launch date: September 9, 2012

Market Capitalization (at time of writing): $261.4 million

No. of Holdings: 102

Performance since launch: +20.9%

Management Expense Ratio (MER): 0.79%

Top 5 Countries (at time of writing):
Kuwait: 26.5%
Qatar: 18.6%
United Arab Emirates: 13.7%
Nigeria: 12.5%
Pakistan: 4.7%
Total: 77%

Top 5 Holdings (as of June 20, 2013):
National Bank of Kuwait 7%
Mobile Telecommunications Co. 5.6%
Kuwait Finance House 4.2%
Emaar Properties PJSC 4%
Qatar National Bank 3.6%

Dividend Yield (at time of writing): 4.1%

Price/Earnings: 16.4

Price/Book: 2.7

The iShares Frontier 100 ETF is new (launched in September 2012), and dominated by the small wealthy countries of Kuwait, Qatar, the UAE, and Oman, which comprise over 60 percent of the MSCI Frontier Markets Index. This geographic concentration in relatively wealthy and developed economies that have large market capitalizations means that investors in this ETF get only limited exposure to Frontier Markets in other regions. The large Asian and African Frontier Markets such as Pakistan, Nigeria, Bangladesh, Vietnam, and Kenya are the most demographically vibrant and attractive countries among Frontier Markets. Furthermore, MSCI Inc., the provider of this index, announced in its annual review in June 2013 that Qatar and the UAE, which comprise 32% of this ETF, will be moved into the Emerging Markets category in May 2014. Meanwhile, it downgraded Morocco from the Emerging Market to the Frontier Market category in November 2013. That means that this ETF will need to sell almost one-third of its assets in a short period to conform to these changes — an awkward development when stock choices are determined by the composition of the index and not by a manager's judgment.

We would not recommend that investors purchase this ETF until after these changes have taken place. Even then, over one-quarter of the index that this ETF tracks will be invested in the small, wealthy economy of Kuwait, which is probably not what most investors would want when they think about investing in Frontier Markets.

Guggenheim Frontier Markets ETF (NYSE:FRN)

Launch Date: June 12, 2008

Market Capitalization (at time of writing): $89.3 million

No. of Holdings: 32

Performance (at time of writing):
1 Year: –13.2%
3 Years (p.a.): –6.7%
5 Years (p.a.): –4.6%

Management Expense Ratio: 0.7%

Top 5 Countries (as at time of writing):
Chile: 48.4%
Colombia: 13.2%
Argentina: 10%
Egypt: 7.1%
Kazakhstan: 6%

Top 5 Holdings (at May 31, 2013):
Ecopetrol SA ADR 8.7%
Enersis SA ADR 8.2%
Cencosud SA ADR 7.1%
Latam Airlines Group SA ADR 7%
Empresa Nacional de Electricidad SA ADR 6.7%

Dividend Yield (at time of writing): 3.8%

Price/Earnings: 11.9

Price/Book: 1.8

The Guggenheim Frontier ETF is the longest-established ETF investing in Frontier Markets and invests at least 80 percent of its assets in stocks in the BNY Mellon New Frontier DR Index. That consists of liquid American Depositary Receipts (ADRs) and Global Depositary Receipts (GDRs) listed on the London and New York Stock and Nasdaq Exchanges. As a result, it has a heavy weight in Latin America with almost 50 percent of its assets in Chile and another 25 percent in Argentina, Colombia, and Peru. Because Chile is considered by most index providers to be an Emerging Market rather than a Frontier Market, and Colombia and Peru are often classified as "Frontier Emerging" markets rather than pure Frontier Markets, this ETF can't be considered as a particularly effective means of gaining Frontier Markets exposure. Also, like the iShares Frontier 100 ETF, it doesn't give investors the exposure to the Asian and African Frontier Markets that are the most attractive from a demographic and economic development viewpoint.

We would not recommend that investors purchase this ETF over a broader global Frontier Market fund unless they want to gain exposure specifically to Latin America, rather than broader global frontier exposure. Investors should be aware that since this ETF has almost half of its portfolio in Chile, it is not an especially effective means of gaining exposure to purely Frontier Markets.

The Top Regional Frontier Markets ETFs

Regional Frontier Market ETFs are ETFs that invest in just one geographical region, such as Africa, Eastern Europe or the Middle East and North Africa (MENA). They have the same issues as global Frontier Market ETFs, in that they tend to be concentrated in only a few countries within the region and often will be dominated by a few large companies. While they may be a suitable investment for those investors who only want exposure to a specific region, investors should bear in mind that there is a chance that the region they choose will not do as well as other areas and the ETF is not designed to allow a wider range of countries to be included. The same argument applies even more to single-country ETFs.

The Market Vectors Africa ETF, because it caps country weights at 25 percent, is probably the best way to gain exposure to Africa, which has been one of the fastest-growing regions in the world over the last decade, but it has lost –3 percent a year over the five years since it has been launched, showing that strong growth in GDP does not always translate into strong stock performance.

Market Vectors Africa Index ETF (NYSE:AFK)

Launch date: July 22, 2008

Market Capitalization (August 2013): $99.9 million

No. of holdings: 52

Performance (at time of writing):
1 Year: +6.1%
3 Years (p.a.): +0.9%
5 Years (p.a.): –3%

Management Expense Ratio: 0.78%

Top 5 Countries (as of 31 December 2012):
South Africa: 25.6%
Nigeria: 21.5%
U.K.: 19.6%
Egypt: 16.6%
Morocco: 10.1%

Top 5 Holdings (as of June 28, 2013):
Orascom Construction Industries SAE 7.9%
Commercial International Bank (Egypt) SAE 6.5%
Orascom Telcom Holdings SAE GDR 4%
Guaranty Trust Bank PLC 3.5%
Subsea 7 SA 3.5%

Dividend Yield (at time of writing): 3.7%

Price/Earnings: 11.1

Price/Book: 1.46

This ETF tracks the Dow Jones Africa Titans 50 Index, which, while it includes South Africa, an Emerging Market, caps each country at a maximum weight of 25 percent, and each holding at a maximum of 8 percent. Stocks from Egypt, Kenya, Morocco, and Nigeria are eligible if they have a market capitalization of at least US$200 million and an average trading volume of US$1 million per day over the previous year. It also allows the inclusion of non-Africa-listed stocks, provided they generate the majority of their revenue from Africa. Hence the United Kingdom comprises almost 20 percent of this ETF.

We recommend that investors looking to invest purely in Africa consider this ETF, as it has a long enough track record, large enough assets under management, and a reasonable MER for a Frontier Market ETF. However, investors should note that it has not made any money for them over five years, showing that strong GDP growth doesn't always translate into strong stock market performance.

There is also the SPDR S&P Emerging Middle East and Africa ETF (NYSE:GAF), which was launched in 2007 and had US$73.8 million in assets at time of writing. However, as it has over 90 percent of its assets in South African, and only 3.5 percent in Egyptian and 3 percent in Moroccan stocks, it doesn't provide meaningful exposure to Frontier Markets in Africa, instead being effectively a South African fund.

Similarly, the SPDR S&P Emerging Asia Pacific ETF (NYSE:GMF) has 36.8 percent in China and Hong Kong, 25.2 percent in Taiwan, 15.5 percent in India, and between 6 percent and 7 percent each in Thailand, Indonesia, and Malaysia, all of which are included in either the MSCI World Index (which largely focuses on developed-nation markets) or the MSCI Emerging Markets Index.

Therefore, this ETF amounts to essentially an Emerging Market fund. Similarly, the SPDR S&P Emerging Europe ETF (NYSE: GUR), which has 58.5 percent in Russia and 22.6 percent in Turkey, also amounts to an Emerging Market fund. Neither of them provides a suitable vehicle for investing in Frontier Markets in these regions.

The iShares MSCI Emerging Market Latin America ETF (NYSE:EEML) also has the vast majority of its assets in established Emerging Markets, with Brazil representing 57.8 percent and Mexico 25.9 percent of the total. This one also does not provide a good way to get exposure to Latin American Frontier Markets.

Market Vectors Gulf States Index ETF (NYSE:MES)

Launch date: July 22, 2008

Market Capitalization (August 2013): $15.4 million

No. of Holdings: 40

Performance (at time of writing):
1 Year: +36.1%
3 Years (p.a.): +11.5%
5 Years (p.a.): –6.6%

Management Expense Ratio: 0.99%

Top 5 Countries (as at 31 December 2012):
Kuwait: 38.2%
Qatar: 27.2%
UAE: 26.8%
Oman: 3.2%
Bahrain: 2.8%

Top 5 Holdings (as of July 31 2013):
Emaar Properties PJSC 6.6%
National Bank of Kuwait SAK 5.9%
National Bank of Abu Dhabi PJSC 5.3%
Mobile Telecommunications Company KSC 4.9%
First Gulf Bank PJSC 4.8%

Dividend Yield (at time of writing): 2.4%

Price/Earnings: 12.2

Price/Book: 1.46

This ETF provides a suitable vehicle for investors looking to invest in the Gulf region although despite its five-year track record, it has only US$15 million in assets, meaning its expense ratio is high for an ETF at almost 1 percent. It has performed well recently as the GCC countries have been regarded as a "safe haven" during the uncertainty caused by the events of the Arab Spring in North Africa and Syria from 2011 onwards.

Powershares MENA Frontier Countries ETF (NYSE:PMNA)

Launch Date: July 11, 2008

Market Capitalization (August 2013): $15.2 million

No. of Holdings: 37

Performance (at time of writing):
1 Year: +13.6%
3 Years (p.a.): +1.1%
5 Years (p.a.): –11.4%

Management Expense Ratio: 0.7%

Top 5 Countries (as at time of writing):
UAE: 25.8%
Kuwait: 25.3%
Egypt: 21.1%
Qatar: 20.4%
Oman: 4.4%

Top 5 Holdings (at April 30, 2013):
National Bank of Abu Dhabi PJSC 8.5%
Emaar Properties PJSC 8.4%
National Bank of Kuwait SAK 7.9%
Mobile Telecommunications Co. 7.7%
Orascom Construction Industries 7.3%

Dividend Yield (at time of writing): 1.7%

Price/Earnings: 10.3

Price/Book: 1.42

The Powershares MENA ETF, as its name suggests, includes not only the GCC countries but also Egypt and Morocco in North Africa. Egypt makes up over 20 percent of the ETF and is responsible for its under-performance against the Market Vectors Gulf States ETF. That followed a fall of 50 percent in Egypt's stock market during the turmoil caused by the overthrow of President Mubarak during the Arab Spring, although it rebounded 40 percent in 2012.

With Morocco being reclassified as a Frontier Market in November 2013 and Egypt under review by MSCI Inc. for a possible downgrade to Frontier status, this ETF has a high weighting in Frontier Markets in the MENA region. Morocco and Egypt are both countries with large populations, hence sizeable domestic markets with some natural resources (oil and gold in Egypt, fertilizers in Morocco) and relatively well educated populations. These are factors that history suggests contribute to rapid economic progress when combined with a supportive government. The outcome of the political upheavals in Egypt after the overthrow of Mohammed Morsi's democratically elected government by the military in late 2013 is unclear at present, but both countries have been successful investments in the last decade.

The Top Single-Country Frontier Markets ETFs

Finally, we round out this chapter by covering single-country Frontier Markets ETFs. Vietnam is the only country included in the MSCI Frontier Markets Index with its own ETF. Five other countries are included in the MSCI Frontier Emerging Markets Index and are the so-called "crossover markets." These are Colombia, Egypt, Morocco, Peru, and the Philippines. These smaller Emerging Markets are so much larger than the Frontier Markets that they comprise 53 percent of the MSCI Frontier Emerging Markets Index. Morocco became a Frontier Market in November 2013 and Egypt is under review for a similar downgrade so the Middle East and North Africa will still be the largest weight in the MSCI Frontier Index even after Qatar and the UAE are promoted to Emerging Market status in May 2014.

We do not recommend investing in single-country Frontier Market ETFs or mutual funds. We believe the most effective way of gaining exposure to the Frontier Markets is a well-managed global Frontier Markets Fund. However, for investors who wish to buy a regional fund, such as an African or MENA fund, at least there are several countries with different levels of economic and political development in such a fund. With a single-country fund, a serious catastrophe, such as political upheaval as in Egypt, or economic problems, as occurred in Vietnam a few years ago, means that the only action open to the investor is liquidation at a loss. Therefore, we cover the single-country ETFs only briefly and for the sake of providing a comprehensive treatment of the options available to you.

Market Vectors Colombia ETF (NYSE:COLX) and Global X FTSE Colombia 20 ETF (NYSE:GXG)

The Global X FTSE Colombia 20 ETF is much larger (US$153 million at time of writing) and was launched in 2009, and has a three-year track record (+2.7% p.a.). The Market Vectors Colombia ETF was launched in 2011 but only has US$3.7 million in assets, although its MER is similar to the Global X ETF (0.75% vs. 0.78%). They have similar stocks among their top holdings, including Ecopetrol, BanColombia, Pacific Rubiales, and Grupo de Inversiones Suramericana. Colombia is regarded by many analysts as one of the most promising Frontier Emerging markets, as it recovers from its years of civil unrest and problems caused by the illegal drugs industry in the 1980s and early 1990s.

Market Vectors Egypt ETF (NYSE:EGPT)

The Market Vectors Egypt ETF was launched in 2010, just in time to run straight into the turmoil arising from the Arab Spring in 2011. It still had US$46.3 million in assets at the time of writing despite having lost –11.3 percent p.a. over the last three years and a relatively high Management Expense Ratio at 0.98 percent. Interestingly, it has a yield of 8.3 percent, showing that with danger comes opportunity, to use the definition of the Chinese symbol meaning crisis. Its top five holdings include familiar names such as Orascom Telcom and Orascom Construction as well as Commercial International Bank (Egypt) and Egypt Kuwait Holding Company. We would term this fund as only for the very brave or foolhardy at present.

iShares

MSCI All Peru Capped Index Fund (NYSE:EPU)

Launched in 2009, the iShares MSCI All Peru ETF has US$291.2 million in assets (August 2013) and a MER of 0.51 percent. It had returned +1.4 percent p.a. over the last three years although was down –13.1 percent in the year to August 2013 and yields 4 percent. Its top five holdings reflect the commodity-based nature of the Peruvian economy with almost 50 percent of the ETF in basic materials and Southern Copper and Buenaventura Mining Co comprising 20 percent. Other major holdings include Credicorp, Alicorp, and Grana y Montera. Peru has grown steadily over the last decade, despite the last presidential elections returning former left-winger Alan Garcia in 2011 to power. However, he maintained his predecessor's pro-growth policies.

iShares MSCI Philippines Investable Index ETF (NYSE:EPHE)

Launched in 2010, the iShares MSCI Philippines Index ETF has US$365.4 million in assets (August 2013) and a MER of 0.61 percent. It had returned +17.8 percent in the year to August 2013 and yields 0.92 percent. Its top five holdings have a greater exposure to rising consumer incomes than many Frontier Markets ETFs and funds, with 35 percent in consumer and utility stocks, including SM Investments, Ayala Corp, and Philippine Long Distance Telecom as well as BDO Unibank and Ayala Land. The Philippines has enjoyed almost a decade of consistent pro-growth economic policies, and been ranked among the most promising frontier and Emerging Markets by many analysts.

Market Vectors Vietnam ETF (NYSE:VNM)

Launched in 2009, the Market Vectors Vietnam ETF has US$360.9 million in assets at time of writing and a Management Expense Ratio of 0.74 percent. Its performance reflects the economic problems caused by overly rapid expansion of the banking industry in 2010–2011, and it lost –7.9 percent p.a. over the three years to August 2013, although it has risen 3.9 percent in the last year and yields 2 percent. Its top five holdings include JS Commercial Bank for Foreign Trade, Vingroup, Bao Viet, PetroVietnam Fertilizer & Chemical, and Pha Lai Thermal Power. Vietnam, despite still being officially Communist, has followed pro-growth, capitalist-style policies since its *Doi Moi* opening 20 years ago, and was chosen as the most attractive Frontier Market by a poll reported in *Bloomberg* magazine in early 2013.

Chapter 15

Moving into Regional and Country Funds

You do have an alternative to investing in individual Frontier Market stocks via American Depositary Receipts (ADRs) or Global Depositary Receipts (GDRs) or the global multinational equities that we discuss in Chapter 12. You can buy a diversified regional or individual country fund. In this chapter, we examine the main features of these funds, how they work, and their advantages and disadvantages.

The Basics of Regional Funds and Single-Country Funds

You may have read in other chapters of this book our discussion of why going it alone in Frontier Markets is usually a bad idea, so it may not surprise you that we believe a well-managed regional Frontier Markets fund offers a good way to gain access to these markets. They do, however, have one major drawback: They only cover one region to the exclusion of other regions.

Regional funds

Regional Frontier Market funds are diversified equity funds that invest in a particular geographic region. At the time of writing, you can invest in them in three main regions:

- Africa
- Eastern Europe
- Middle East and North Africa (MENA)

Given the limited number of Latin American countries classified as Frontier rather than Emerging Markets, or that are large enough to make investing practical, no one has launched a Latin American Frontier Markets fund at time of writing. However, as we discuss in Chapter 14, the Guggenheim Frontier Markets DR Index ETF has over 80 percent of its assets in South American markets.

But since over 50 percent of the ETF is invested in Chile, an Emerging Market, you would not have much exposure to Frontier Markets in this region if you invest in that fund.

Similarly, at time of writing, no company offers an Asian Frontier Market fund, although several companies have individual country funds for Vietnam, which we examine later in this chapter.

As of late 2013, fund companies offer 19 African Frontier Market funds to European investors along with 13 Middle East and North Africa (MENA) funds and 3 Eastern European funds. American investors have a much smaller choice, with 2 African funds, and 1 each in the Eastern European and MENA categories. This may reflect European investors' much greater familiarity with Africa and the Middle East, partially due to their geographical proximity and partially due to their historical links as the former colonial rulers of most of these countries.

Single-country funds

As the term implies, single-country funds invest in equities and occasionally debt instruments from only one country. Obviously, the country or its economy needs to be above a certain size, otherwise the investment opportunities would be too limited to make buying stock worthwhile. Thus, there are no funds specializing in Laos or Uganda, although both countries have very promising prospects.

However, several funds invest in Vietnam, which had a population of 92.5 million and a stock market capitalization of US$38 billion at the end of 2012. Other Frontier Markets with individual country funds include Ukraine, Iraq, and Qatar.

To show what happens when a country becomes a popular investment destination: Among Emerging Markets, there are 28 US-registered China or China regional mutual funds and 3 NYSE-listed closed-end China funds. There are 11 US-registered India mutual funds and 2 India NYSE-listed closed-end funds.

An old stock market saying goes: "There only three sure bets in life: death, taxes, and that all closed-end funds will go to a discount." This is one of those old stock market sayings that is actually true, which is why you should never buy a closed-end fund at a premium to its net asset value (NAV). Why would you pay $1.05 for $1? — especially when, if you can resist the temptation to rush into the next "hot" play, you will have the chance to buy it at a discount in a year or two.

Over two dozen listed closed-end funds invested in Emerging Markets were available in the U.S. at the end of 2013. These included not only the three Chinese and two Indian funds mentioned previously but also two other funds each invested in Thailand, Mexico, Korea, Taiwan, and an Asian regional fund. There were also individual funds for Chile, Indonesia, Malaysia, Singapore, Turkey, and Russia, and Eastern Europe. With the sole exception of the Chile fund, all of these traded at discount to their NAV of between 5 percent and 15 percent at the time of writing.

Open-ended versus closed-ended funds

As many investors know, a conventional mutual fund is an open-ended investment, meaning that the manager can create or redeem any number of shares in the fund on a daily basis, depending on demand for the fund's country or sector.

Therefore, it always trades at its net asset value, calculated by dividing the value of its investments by the number of shares.

By comparison, a closed-end fund has a limited number of shares and is listed on a stock exchange where it trades just like an ordinary company. If there is rising demand for country or sector closed-end funds, the shares will trade at a premium to the underlying investments.

If there is falling demand then the shares will trade at a discount. In that scenario, investors will be able to purchase one dollar of assets for 95 or 90 cents.

Closed-end funds are almost always launched when a country or sector is wildly popular, such as technology stocks in the late 1990s or Emerging Markets like China and India in the early 1990s. They initially traded at a premium as those investors who couldn't buy enough shares in the initial public offering (IPO) of the fund chased the shares higher. Then reality set in, the country or sector had some disappointments, the NAV fell, and the shares went from a premium to a discount.

Examining Regional Funds

Regional funds are, by definition, a less risky way to gain access to volatile markets such as Emerging and Frontier Markets than single-country funds. When you invest in a number of different countries in a region, the political and economic risks you face are reduced substantially as some countries may be resource producers and others importers, some democracies and others dictatorships or autocratic.

We stress this point elsewhere, particularly in Chapter 9, but it's vital to reiterate that what happens in one country in a region doesn't automatically affect other countries in that region. In fact, some countries may even benefit from turmoil or political upheaval in other countries in the same region. As a case in point: the flow of money out of Egypt and Syria and into safe havens in the wealthy and stable Gulf Cooperation Council (GCC) members such as the UAE and Qatar that occurred during the crises in 2013.

Within Africa, events such as the terrorist attack by presumed Islamic militants on the Westgate Shopping Mall in Kenya in late 2013 have nothing to do with tribal uncertainties in the oil rich Delta region of Nigeria. Neither of them has any direct relationship with the labor unrest in South Africa. Making investment decisions on the basis of the nightly news headlines amounts to an inefficient way to build a sustainable long-term Frontier Markets portfolio.

An experienced fund manager running a regional fund will overweight those countries and companies with attractive long-term prospects, and underweight those with a high degree of political or economic risk. This reiterates the case we may for active management (as opposed to passive management) elsewhere in this book.

South Africa demonstrates another reason why using market capitalization weighted-ETFs to access Frontier Markets is not the best approach. Any African ETF that does not have a restriction on how much it can invest in one country would end up with an overwhelming percentage in South Africa, a country whose population is shrinking and which has the highest level of income inequality in the world.

Three simple rules of thumb for Frontier Markets investors:

- ✔ **Single-country funds** are potentially the most volatile and carry the highest risks.

- ✔ **Regional funds** are less risky due to investing in a number of different countries, but will still be pretty volatile.

✔ **Global Frontier Market funds** are the least volatile fund category and have the lowest level of political and economic risk. This is because they can invest in any of the Frontier Markets around the world, reducing the chance that an entire region may fall out of favor or succumb to worsening economics.

The advantages

A regional fund generally has to invest at least 80 percent of its assets in the geographic region specified in the fund's prospectus. Within the region, however, the fund manager has the freedom to invest as much or as little as appears appropriate in the listed companies in the different countries within that region. They can also invest in ADRs and GDRs issued by companies from that region or companies listed in other developed or Emerging Markets that derive the majority or a substantial proportion of their revenues and earnings from that region.

In general, managers of regional funds tend to have a higher percentage of their investments in the countries with larger and more liquid stock markets. This is only common sense; larger companies generally tend to have higher revenues and be more profitable as they benefit from economies of scale. Having larger market capitalizations means it's much easier to invest substantial amounts of money in them, and just as importantly, the manager can sell them fairly quickly if anything changes for the worse, without substantially forcing down the share price.

African regional funds tend to have larger weightings in South Africa and Nigeria, which are the largest and most populous African economies with the biggest stock markets. Nigeria has 175 million inhabitants and South Africa 49 million and their stock markets stood at US$40 billion and U$1 trillion, respectively, at the end of 2012. Although Kenya's population is almost the same as South Africa's (44 million vs. 49 million), its stock market stood at only US$10 billion at the end of 2012, a quarter of the size of Nigeria's and a mere 1 percent of South Africa's total. This makes country-to-country comparisons difficult.

Similarly in Eastern Europe, Russia dominates the holdings in regional funds with 147 million people and a stock market capitalization of US$845 billion at the end of 2012. It towers over Ukraine, Romania, and Croatia, with 45 million, 22 million, and 4.5 million inhabitants, respectively. More to the point, their stock markets are only worth US$25 billion, US$30 billion, and US$22 billion, respectively — added together still less than 10 percent of Russia's total.

In the MENA countries, the largest stock market, that of Saudi Arabia, is worth over US$350 billion, but does not allow foreign investors to buy shares directly. Iran, which has a market worth over US$100 billion and a population of 80 million, cannot be bought by foreign investors due to American and European sanctions because of its nuclear development program.

That means that the largest country weights in MENA funds tend to be in Turkey (US$200 billion stock market and 80 million population) but the fate of Egypt, which had 85 million inhabitants and a stock market capitalization of US$51 billion in 2013, is instructive. Before the Arab Spring of 2011, Egypt's stock market was worth almost US$90 billion, and usually formed the largest or second largest country weight in MENA funds.

That drop illustrates our point. At the time of writing (Autumn 2013), Egypt's stock market had fallen 40 percent after the removal of its first elected government in the summer of 2013 and the second change of regime in two years. Most MENA funds now have less than a 5 percent weight in Egypt, although a few managers have suggested that the sell-off represents a buying opportunity.

One of the major advantages of using a regional fund to gain exposure to Frontier Markets is that the manager is not required to have the same weight as the index in different countries. That difference allows him or her to reduce or avoid countries with unfavorable developments. The manager may also hold positions in countries that are considered attractive but are not in the index, such as Saudi Arabia in MENA funds. Foreign investors can access Saudi Arabia by purchasing participation certificates issued by investment banks that give them exposure to the performance of companies listed in that country.

Investors can also purchase ADRs and GDRs issued by companies domiciled in these countries but trading in New York or London, which in some cases may not be listed on the local stock market, or have lower liquidity, meaning the ADRs and GDRs trade at a premium to the local stock.

The manager of a regional fund can also purchase shares of companies listed and based in developed or emerging countries that derive a high percentage of their revenues and profits from the countries in that region. For example, British personal care and infant nutrition company PZ Cussons gets one-third of its sales and profits in Nigeria and Ghana and another 20 percent in Indonesia, Thailand, and Vietnam, and is often found in African regional funds.

In this fashion, actively managed regional funds can, and usually have, outperformed the underlying index for the region, whether the funds are in Africa, MENA, or Eastern Europe.

As a Frontier Markets investor, a regional fund is a good choice if you are really enthusiastic about the prospects for a particular region or a country in that region. The wider range of countries and types of stocks that can be bought helps reduce the volatility of the fund and allows the manager to add value and outperform the index, on the evidence of the last few years' performance of regional funds.

The disadvantages

Given the excellent track record of actively managed regional funds when compared against the appropriate index, they are certainly worth considering as one of the ways to gain access to Frontier Markets. However, we need to stress some disadvantages.

The first is that, however promising the outlook of the region may appear, and however strong the performance of the funds may have been over the last few years, as it says in the mutual fund prospectuses and advertisements, ". . . past performance is no guarantee of future results." Although you may be convinced that the outlook for Africa is very positive, and note that six of the ten fastest-growing economies in the world over the last decade have been in sub-Saharan Africa, there is always the possibility that things could go wrong.

Given the lamentable track records of African governments in economic and political management since the colonial powers granted independence in the 1950s and 1960s, investors can welcome the recent improvement in governance in the last decade. The improvements account for much of the strong economic growth experienced in the continent. However, there are still examples of failed countries, such as Somalia, and continuing insurgencies in the Democratic Republic of the Congo.

Putting all your eggs in one basket, or all your Frontier Market investments in one continent, amounts to leaving yourself hostage to fortune. Even the best active fund manager could not produce good absolute returns if there's a recurrence of nationalization, expropriation, and dictatorship in a number of countries.

In Latin America, the example of Hugo Chavez's populist policies in Venezuela in the last decade encouraged the leaders of Argentina and Bolivia to pursue similar tactics, including widespread nationalization. The Arab Spring spread from its start in Tunisia in late 2010 to the overthrows of the long-established regimes in Libya and Egypt in 2011 and the start of the civil war in Syria in 2013.

This leads to the other major concern over using regional funds. Investing in unfamiliar Frontier Mmarkets makes it difficult to control one's emotions, especially given that the investor has probably never visited the countries in question and has little idea of their history or background or even of their geography.

Therefore, when a story appears on the TV news about terrorist attacks in Kenya or the escalating conflict in Syria, some might lump all the countries in that region together and conclude that the entire region is going up in flames and has become too risky.

As we have pointed out numerous times, particularly in Chapter 9, it is a mistake to be overly influenced by news headlines. Today's Internet-driven, 24-hour-news world means that it's all too easy to get lots of news about the countries or regions to which you are exposed. Given the tendency of news to feature the bad stuff, most of what is available will not be comfortable to contemplate.

To reiterate a central point in our analysis, the Frontier Markets are developing economies with young, relatively poor populations, political systems at an early stage of development, and lacking much of the infrastructure that we take for granted in the developed world. These national characteristics can lead to political unrest, disputed elections, bankruptcies, defaults, and the occasional coup. Add to that the toll of natural disasters such as drought, floods, fires, hurricanes, and typhoons and the total picture can become intimidating.

These are not reasons to flee the Frontier Markets, any more than the Fukushima earthquake and tsunami in Japan, riots over austerity in Greece and Italy, high speed train crashes in Germany, or Lehman Brothers and 9/11 in the United States are reasons to abandon the developed markets.

In fact, the sell-off caused by such high profile but ultimately short-term events may provide buying opportunities for experienced fund managers who have seen it all before. Anyone who experienced the Asian meltdown in 1997 and 1998 saw stock markets falling 50 percent to 60 percent and currencies collapsing, with the result that some countries' stock markets, such as Indonesia, Thailand, and the Philippines, lost 90 percent of their value in U.S. dollar terms. Yet within a few years, the economies had recovered, the stock markets had doubled or tripled, and over the next decade, Emerging Markets, including those in Asia, strongly outperformed the developed markets.

However, it is very difficult to remember these comforting statistics when CNN or the BBC continually shows riots, military action, and toppling regimes. The lenses through which most western news organizations focus on certain regions are usually not very subtle and outlooks apparently need to be expressed in a couple of sound bites.

Thus Africa is usually presented as poor, backward, and war torn, even when, as in countries such as Sierra Leone, the conflict ended a dozen years ago. The pictures that stick in the average observer's mind would be those of Somali pirates, the Rwandan genocide, and the attack on the Kenyan shopping center, mixed with appreciation of the continent's wealth of natural beauty and wildlife and respect for Nelson Mandela's achievements.

In the Middle East and North Africa, the images are of Islamic terrorism, the Arab Spring and the Syrian civil war, the excesses generated by massive oil wealth, the Iraq war, and the glittering cities of the Gulf. Although there is a good deal of truth in these images, many other factors aren't included or even known. That means that the entire region may suffer from investor dislike or neglect as people decide to put their money some place where everything seems a lot simpler and, most important, more familiar.

Investors must remember that regions can go in and out of favor with the big institutions that drive most of the money flows in Emerging and Frontier Markets. While you may still believe in the prospects for the Middle East and North Africa, if the professionals have decided it's not worth trying to figure out whether Egypt will stabilize, when the civil war in Syria will end, or what may happen with Iran's nuclear development program, they won't wait around.

They will sell and go elsewhere. In a regional fund, at least the manager has other investment destinations, such as Turkey and the GCC states, but the absolute performance of the fund won't be great and certainly not enough to compensate you for all the volatility you have to endure. As an investor, you have to be very certain that your long-term view is right. Most investors find it very difficult to hang in there when the going gets tough.

Regional Frontier Markets funds available to North American investors

One of the problems with investing in regional Frontier Markets funds is that there aren't many of them around. In fact, as far as regional funds are concerned, looking at those available to American investors, there are only four mutual funds.

Nile Pan Africa Fund (NAFAX)

Launched in 2010, the fund has US$34.5 million in assets and a Management Expense Ratio (MER) of 2.5 percent. Since its launch, Nile Pan Africa Fund has delivered an annualized return of 8.7 percent a year through the end of September 2013 and 8.9 percent over the last 12 months after expenses. Its five largest holdings consist of one Government of

Ghana bond, the Nigerian food and consumer products giant UAC, and three South African stocks with wide exposure to the domestic consumer in sub-Saharan Africa — electricity sub-station and building materials producer Consolidated Infrastructure Group, private schools group Curro Holdings, and Famous Brands.

Famous Brands is the leading local fast food operator in South Africa and other countries in southern Africa, with 2,175 outlets. In September 2013, it announced its purchase of a 49 percent stake in UAC's Mr. Bigg's fast food restaurant chain for an undisclosed amount. This gives Famous Brands 165 restaurants in Nigeria to add to its existing 172 restaurants outside South Africa, the majority of which were located in Botswana, Namibia, Zambia, and Mauritius.

Commonwealth Africa Fund (CAFRX)

This tiny (US$2 million in assets) fund has only been open for two years, launching in July 2011. Its small size also means that its two largest holdings are African ETFs, the Market Vectors Africa Index ETF and the iShares MSCI South Africa ETF, which comprise 12.4 percent and 11.9 percent of its assets, respectively. Other top holdings are South African stocks, insurance group Discovery, shipping and ports operator Grindrod, and state-controlled oil company Sasol. Over the 12 months ending September 2013 it has fallen –2.4 percent.

The Nile Pan Africa Fund is bigger, has a longer track record, and has performed better. That makes it the obvious choice for American investors looking for African exposure.

US Global Emerging Europe Fund (EUROX)

Started in 1997, this fund had net assets of US$124.6 million at the end of August 2013, had an MER of 2.2 percent, and had returned 9.4 percent annually since its inception to the end of July 2013. Over the ten years to the end of July 2013, it had returned 10.3 percent annually compared against 7.6 percent for the S&P 500 Index.

Its regional breakdown was as follows:

Country	Percentage
Russia	37.2
Turkey	24.3
Austria	5.9
Poland	5.1
Hungary	2.8

While its ten largest holdings contain familiar names such as Russian energy giants Gazprom and Lukoil, as well as Sberbank, its largest holding is Russia's biggest retailer, Magnit, and it also owns successful private sector Russian gas producer Novatek, Austria's Erste Bank, Turkish auto stock Tofas Turk, and mobile telephone play Turkcell.

The US Global Emerging Europe Fund is also large, well-diversified, and has outperformed the S&P 500 over the last decade after expenses. Investors willing to buy Russian stocks should consider this fund.

T Rowe Price Africa and Middle East Fund (TRAMX)

Started in 2007, this fund had US$185.5 million in assets at the end of September 2013, had an MER of 1.5 percent, and had returned –13 percent annually over the period since its inception to April 2013. More recently, it had returned 22.6 percent in the 12 months ending September 2013 and 7.4 percent annually over the three years ending in September 2013.

Its regional country breakdown was as follows:

Country	Percentage
Saudi Arabia	29
South Africa	28
UAE	12
Nigeria	10
Qatar	8

Amongst its largest holdings, through indirect vehicles, are Saudi financials Al Rahji Bank and Samba Financial as well as Saudi Basic Industries, South African-listed Pay-TV provider Naspers and retailer Shoprite, telecom operators MTN and Etihad Etisalat (Saudi), and Qatar National Bank and Emaar Properties in the United Arab Emirates.

With almost US$200 million in assets and an MER under 2 percent (very low for a Frontier Markets fund) and with Saudi Arabia being its largest holding, the T Rowe Price Africa and Middle East Fund is a good choice for those investors who want a non-South African dominated regional fund. However, although its recent performance is respectable, losing 13 percent annually since its inception in 2007, this is a reminder that Frontier and Emerging Markets can be very volatile and lose investors a lot of money if they buy at the wrong time.

Single-Country Funds

Single-country funds invest in only one country. There are only a limited number of developing markets that have their own country funds. Some are simply too small to justify creating a fund, however attractive their economies.

Examples include the Baltic states of Estonia, Latvia, and Lithuania, the members of the Gulf Co-operation Council like Kuwait, Qatar, and the United Arab Emirates, and the southern African resource-producing states of Botswana, Namibia, and Zambia.

To make it worthwhile to create a fund focused on a single country, it needs a decent-sized population and domestic economy so that its progress won't be too dependent upon exports or producing a couple of commodities. It's probably no surprise that Vietnam, with its 93 million population and a stock market worth US$38 billion at the end of 2012, has several country funds, or that Ukraine and Iraq with 44 million and 32 million inhabitants, respectively, also have their own investment funds.

Buying a single-country Frontier Fund is not a straightforward investment if you are an investor based in North America. You either have to use an ETF, which we describe in Chapter 14, or you have to buy London-listed or traded funds or be wealthy enough to qualify as a hedge fund investor.

When you add in the disadvantages of having all your eggs in one basket (sorry, you knew we were going to use that phrase, didn't you?) in volatile and illiquid markets, this route really becomes more trouble than it's worth.

Also, the returns from Frontier Markets are not always that exciting. The longest established Vietnam fund, the Vietnam Enterprise Investment Fund, launched in 1995, has only returned 5.9 percent a year over almost 20 years. And Vietnam's economy has grown by a factor of four or five times over that same period, showing that strong GDP growth doesn't necessarily translate into good stock market returns.

The advantages

Obviously, the major advantage of investing in a single-country fund is its concentrated exposure to the market that you feel offers the best chance of good returns. If you are really convinced that Vietnam is going to become the next China or Brazil, a fund that only invests in that country may be a logical choice.

It helps if the country of your choice is big enough to develop a major domestic market for consumer goods and capital investment. If the country's population is over 30 million it will be same as that of Canada, and larger than the Netherlands, Belgium, Sweden, Switzerland, and Australia.

Table 15-1 lists the largest Frontier Markets countries by populations (2012).

Table 15-1	Largest Frontier Markets by Population
Country	*Population in Millions*
Pakistan	194
Nigeria	175
Bangladesh	164
Vietnam	93
Egypt	85
Iran	80
Myanmar	55
Tanzania	48
Colombia	46
Ukraine	45
Kenya	44
Argentina	43
Iraq	32
Peru	30
Venezuela	29
Saudi Arabia	27
Ghana	25
Romania	22
Sri Lanka	22
Kazakhstan	18

It also helps if the country has a fully functioning stock market, even if the size is fairly small. That Frontier Markets such as Iraq, Ghana, and Tanzania had capitalizations of only US$4 billion, US$3 billion, and US$1.5 billion, respectively, at the end of 2011 is less important than the fact that they have stock markets that are open and functioning.

Table 15-2 lists the largest frontier stock markets by capitalization (end December 2012, except where noted).

Table 15-2	Largest Frontier Markets by Market Cap (in Billions of Dollars)
Country	*Market Cap (Billions of Dollars)*
Saudi Arabia	339 (2011)
Colombia	201
Peru	153
UAE	121 (2011)
Iran	107 (2011)
Kuwait	101 (2011)
Qatar	94 (2011)
Egypt	48 (2011)
Argentina	44
Nigeria	39 (2011)
Vietnam	38
Kazakhstan	36
Pakistan	34
Romania	30
Ukraine	26
Bangladesh	24
Croatia	21
Sri Lanka	18

The next step is to check which countries have both large populations and reasonably sized stock markets. These criteria are not completely mandatory. Don't feel that you shouldn't examine a country with a large population whose stock market is still fairly small. It's much easier to grow the stock market than the population.

Combining the population and the stock market size together, the top countries worth examining would be:

1. Colombia

2. Iran

3. Nigeria

4. Egypt

5. Pakistan

6. Vietnam

7. Peru

8. Saudi Arabia

9. Bangladesh

10. Argentina

11. Ukraine

12. Kazakhstan

13. Romania

14. Sri Lanka

Of course, because it's fairly crude, this ranking comes up with some obvious issues for investors. American, Canadian, and European investors are prohibited from investing in Iran due to sanctions over its nuclear development program and Saudi Arabia, at the time of writing, doesn't permit direct investment by foreigners.

Egypt has been experiencing political turmoil and Argentina has defaulted on its debt and nationalized various industries within the past dozen years. You would also need to look at the measures of corruption perceptions, income disparity, and human development, which we discuss in more detail in Chapter 6.

Of these countries, Colombia, Egypt, Pakistan, Vietnam, Peru, Bangladesh, and Ukraine have either single-country funds or ETFs that provide access to them.

The disadvantages

The big disadvantage of investing in just one country is that there is nowhere to hide if you get it wrong. If your confidence in the outlook of a particular economy is misplaced (or too early), then you may suffer substantial losses.

Even with a good active manager running a country fund and able to mitigate the damage by concentrating the portfolio in companies with strong balance sheets and good prospects, a general downturn can still affect its results.

However, ironically, in a strong bear market in Emerging or Frontier Markets, the share prices of good quality companies may lose value as much or more than those of their weaker brethren.

Often, they are the only stocks that you can sell when everything is falling. Investors know that the local subsidiary of Unilever or Nestle will still be around and doing business when the dust settles. Furthermore, they can rely on the financial figures reported by these companies or the largest banks and utility companies. That's not always the case for smaller or more recently established local businesses.

In a regional fund, the manager can switch assets into countries that are doing better than others, or better still, in a global fund, the manager can move out a region where most of its countries are suffering. However, in a single-country fund, you're stuck, unless you decide to sell your units. In that case, you're probably locking in your losses near the worst point; all the bad news is already reflected in the price. If it is a closed-end fund, the share price is almost certainly trading at a discount to its net asset value, so you're hit with a double whammy.

Single-country funds for Frontier Markets

A limited number of single-country funds are available for investors. There are four investing in Vietnam, and one each in Ukraine and Iraq. All of them are closed-end, except for the Vietnam Emerging Equity Fund and the Euphrates Iraq Fund, which is open to high net worth investors.

Vietnam Enterprise Opportunities Fund Ltd (VEIL)

Launched in July 1995, VEIL is listed on the Irish Stock Exchange and had assets of US$470 million at the end of September 2013. The oldest and largest of the Vietnam funds, its long-term track record (since its inception) of returning 5.9 percent annually after 2 percent management fees and a performance fee of 20 percent of returns above 8 percent a year is not especially impressive.

Its five largest holdings are Vinamilk, the country's largest food and beverage producer, which makes up 33 percent of the fund, against 14 percent of the Vietnam (VN) Index, diversified financial Masan Group, Asia Commercial Bank, real estate investment and manufacturing company REE, and steel group Hoa Phat. Together these five holdings make up almost 70 percent of the fund, making VEIL a concentrated portfolio.

Over the last five years to the end of September 2013, its Net Asset Value has declined by –2 percent a year against –2.2 percent for the VN Index. However, to show you what can happen with closed-end funds, its share price has almost halved over the same period as Vietnam has fallen out of favor with international investors. Over three years up to September 2013, its NAV has risen by 33 percent annually versus the VN Index's 12 percent, but its share price has lagged, rising only 9 percent a year.

Vietnam Growth Fund Ltd (VGF)

Managed by the same team as VEIL at Dragon Capital, based in Ho Chi Minh City (formerly Saigon), the fund had assets of US$260 million at the end of September 2013. Launched in October 2004, its return since inception of 7.8 percent annually is somewhat higher than its sister fund, reflecting the better performance of the Vietnamese market over the last decade. Like VEIL, it has the same 2 percent management fee with a performance fee of 20 percent of returns above 8 percent a year.

VGF's five largest holdings are Vinamilk, making up 42 percent of the fund, Masan Group, fertilizer group Phu My, REE, and Hoa Phat. In the five years up to the end of September 2013, its NAV had risen 11.6 percent a year against a decline of –2.3 percent for the VN Index, although its share price had declined by –9.4 percent a year. Over the two years up to end September 2013, its NAV had risen by 25.4 percent annually against 16 percent for the index and its share price had risen 15.7 percent.

PXP Vietnam Opportunities Fund (VNF)

Launched in December 2003 and listed on the London Stock Exchange since 2010, VNH had $63 million in assets at end March 2013. Its five largest holdings at that date were Vinamilk at 29 percent, Sacombank, REE, Hoa Phat, and computer and systems company FPT. Since its inception, it has returned 119 percent up to the end of September 2013 against 109 percent for the VN Index and over the five years to that date had a return of 8.2 percent against –31 percent for the index after its 2 percent management fee.

PXP Vietnam Emerging Equity Fund (VEEF)

An open-end Cayman Islands-domiciled mutual fund, VEEF was established in 2005 and had US$29 million in assets at the end of August 2013. Its five largest holdings were Vinamilk at 19.5 percent, Hoa Phat, Sacombank, FPT, and real estate group HAG. It limits individual holdings to no more than 20 percent of the fund. It had returned –28.9 percent annually over seven years against –27 percent for the VN Index, but 1.5 percent annually against –4.1 percent for the index over three years after its 2 percent management fee and performance fee of 20 percent of returns above 8 percent a year.

Ukraine Opportunity Trust plc (UKRO)

Launched in November 2005, UKRO is a closed-end fund primarily invested in private equities in the Ukraine, which comprised 70.5 percent of its US$20.3 million of assets at end June 2013. Restaurant group Foodmaster represents 40 percent of its assets, real estate investor Korsando 25.7 percent, and pharmacy chain Chalsen 7.7 percent. Listed but illiquid Platinum Bank and agricultural processor Crativ make up the remaining top five holdings, which together amount to 93 percent of the fund. Over five years up to the end of September 2013, it has returned –16.2 percent annually although over the three years to that date, it has risen 3.4 percent a year.

Euphrates Iraq Fund

A US-based hedge fund, the Euphrates Iraq Fund launched in 2010 and had US$62 million in assets at the end of August 2013. It has returned approximately 30 percent since inception. Among its largest holdings are the No. 2 private bank of Baghdad, 7.5 percent of Pepsi distributor Baghdad Soft Drinks, and Al-Mamoura Real Estate.

Chapter 16

Putting Your Dollars in Global Frontier Funds

*I*n other chapters of this book where we discuss ways that investors can access Frontier Markets, we discourage the use of single-country frontier funds or regional Frontier Market funds due to their high level of volatility and the likelihood of a country or region suffering a period of poor performance.

Likewise, we pointed out that global multinational companies, whether US-based or listed in the U.S. through ADRs or U.K.-based or listed in the U.K. through GDRs, can give good exposure to Emerging and Frontier Markets and produce excellent returns.

However, their stock prices tend to move in line with (be correlated to) their own local stock markets rather than what's happening in the Frontier Markets. That makes them more of a developed market play than an Emerging or Frontier Markets play, regardless of how much direct exposure they have to these markets. They may also have a single company risk when some unexpected development causes its stock price to sell off.

We looked at Frontier Market exchange-traded funds (ETFs) and concluded that the two available Global Frontier Market ETFs had very high weightings in just one region, making them more of a regional play than a truly global vehicle. As with regional Frontier Market ETFs, they suffer from the same problems as actively managed regional and single-country funds. They have the added disadvantage that they are invested in the largest companies, a component that may not necessarily be the most profitable investment.

In this chapter, we discuss our belief that the best way for investors to gain exposure to the Frontier Markets is to invest in an actively managed Global Frontier Markets Fund. While they have higher Management Expense Ratios (MERs) than ETFs, almost all of them have outperformed the ETFs over the two to three years since their inception, because the fund managers have been able to add value by under- and overweighting various regions. They have also invested in countries such as Saudi Arabia that are not in the indices.

What an Investment Mandate Involves

When you're considering a mutual fund or closed-end fund, you should always look at its investment objectives, set out in the prospectus and in the fund fact sheets often provided by the fund company.

For example, the Templeton Frontier Markets Fund states that the fund:

> . . . seeks long-term capital appreciation by normally investing at least 80 percent of its net assets in securities of companies located in "Frontier Market countries" which, in general, are a subset of those currently considered developing by the World Bank, the International Finance Corporation, the United Nations or the countries' authorities, or countries with a stock market capitalization of less than 3 percent of the MSCI World Index.

That description leads to these observations:

- **The fund is looking for long-term capital appreciation.** Although investors' definitions of "long-term" differ, most agree that a long-term investment is one that should be held for at least five years.

- **The fund is aiming for capital appreciation.** You shouldn't invest in this fund if your main objective is income, although it does pay an annual dividend.

- **The fund will normally invest at least 80 percent of its net assets in securities issued by companies located in "Frontier Market countries."** The fund doesn't have to only invest in companies that are listed in frontier stock markets. Four of its top ten holdings are listed on the London Stock exchange, but they are based in frontier economies. Also, note the use of the word "normally." This allows the manager to hold more than 20 percent in cash if he or she becomes concerned by the outlook for frontier economies.

✔ **The fund description classifies Frontier Markets, so an investor can identify them.** They're a "subset" of those considered to be developing by such authorities as the World Bank or United Nations. Alternatively, they are countries with a market capitalization of less than 3 percent of the MSCI World Index. So, an investor will know they're small and at an early stage of economic development.

As with all investment products, ideally a fund should "do what it says on the label." If a fund is supposed to be investing in Emerging Markets, high-yield bonds, or short-term cash instruments, then mutual fund regulators require that at least 80 percent of the fund should be in securities which match that description.

The other 20 percent allows the managers enough leeway that he or she does not have to keep the fund 99.9 percent invested at all times. The fund may attract lots of new inflows, so the manager may have cash building up which he or she does not want to invest in an illiquid market, thus forcing prices up unnecessarily.

Alternatively, as noted, the manager may want to raise cash out of concern about the level of the stock market or the outlook for the investment destinations. Nonetheless, investors are entitled to expect that if a fund says it's investing in a sector or region, it will normally have most of its assets invested there.

How Global Funds Differ, Even Within a Category

One of the more interesting factors when looking at global funds is the differences in their asset allocations. The manager has the freedom to go anywhere around the world of Frontier Markets, so he or she may end up with a regional breakdown quite different from other funds in the same category. By comparison, managers of regional funds are somewhat limited in the countries in which they can invest, although of course they can choose to under- or overweight specific countries just like managers of global funds.

Looking at the major Global Frontier Market Funds available to North American investors, the principal difference is between those that use the MSCI Frontier Markets Index and those using the wider MSCI Frontier Emerging Markets Index.

The MSCI Frontier Markets Index

The principal fund using the MSCI Frontier Markets Index is the biggest and oldest Frontier Markets fund, the Templeton Frontier Markets Fund. It grew to over US$1.3 billion by June 2013 and Templeton closed it to new investors. The other fund that uses the MSCI Frontier Markets Index is a European registered fund run by Danish bank Bankinvest.

The MSCI Frontier Markets Index is a market capitalization-weighted index consisting of the approximately 160 of the largest companies by market capitalization in the 25 countries that MSCI has designated as Frontier Markets. We go into more detail about the index and its composition in Chapter 3, but here are the countries in the MSCI:

- **Americas**
  - Argentina
- **Africa**
  - Kenya
  - Mauritius
  - Nigeria
  - Tunisia
- **Asia**
  - Bangladesh
  - Pakistan
  - Sri Lanka
  - Vietnam
- **Europe and CIS (Commonwealth of Independent States)**
  - Bulgaria
  - Croatia
  - Estonia
  - Lithuania
  - Kazakhstan
  - Romania
  - Serbia
  - Slovenia
  - Ukraine

✔ **Middle East**

- Bahrain

- Jordan

- Kuwait

- Lebanon

- Oman

- Qatar

- United Arab Emirates (UAE)

The major problem with the MSCI Frontier Markets Index is that it is very heavily concentrated in the Middle East countries because they have the largest stock markets. Kuwait on its own accounts for over 25 percent of the Index and Qatar and the United Arab Emirates together comprise almost 30 percent, meaning almost 60 percent of the index is made up of three small, very wealthy Gulf states. This is probably not what most investors think they're investing in when they buy a Frontier Markets fund!

The MSCI Frontier Emerging Markets Index

The other Frontier Markets funds available in North America all use some version of the broader MSCI Frontier Emerging Markets Index. The difference between the two indices is that this broader index includes five of the smaller and less-developed Emerging Markets.

Emerging Markets included in MSCI Frontier Emerging Markets Index are:

✔ Colombia

✔ Egypt

✔ Morocco

✔ Peru

✔ The Philippines

Proving that indices are not fixed in stone, MSCI announced in May 2013 that Morocco was being downgraded from Emerging to Frontier Market status in November 2013 and that Egypt was under review for a possible downgrade. It also announced that Qatar and the UAE would be upgraded to Emerging Market status in May 2014, moving almost 30 percent of the MSCI Frontier Markets Index to Emerging Markets status at one time.

The MSCI Frontier Emerging Markets Index is also a market capitalization-weighted index, meaning that the bigger a company's market capitalization, the higher its weight in the index, although it is adjusted for how much of the company's shares are freely available.

Some issues arise with the MSCI Frontier Markets Index heavy weighting in the Middle East. Because the five Emerging Markets are so much bigger than the Frontier Markets, they make up 53 percent of the MSCI Frontier Emerging Markets Index, with the Gulf Co-Operation Council (GCC) countries of Kuwait, Qatar, the UAE, Bahrain, and Oman now making up 27 percent. Every other Frontier Market, including such large and populous countries as Pakistan, Nigeria, Bangladesh, Vietnam, Argentina, and Kenya, make up only 20 percent.

One of the Frontier Markets Funds, the HSBC GIF Frontier Markets Fund, uses the MSCI Frontier Emerging Markets Capped Index. This is a proprietary index maintained by MSCI for HSBC that aims to solve the problems inherent in the heavy weights given to both the five "crossover" markets and the GCC countries.

The five crossover Emerging Markets' total weight in the index is set at 25 percent, and every other country at no more than 10 percent of the capped index. When the total of the five crossover Emerging Markets rises above 30 percent of the index, it is reset back to 25 percent, and when any country's weight exceeds 12 percent, it is automatically reset back to 10 percent.

As a result, the five crossover Emerging Markets have a weight of 25 percent in the MSCI Frontier Emerging Markets Capped Index, the five Gulf Cooperation Council countries comprise 31 percent, and the remaining 20 Frontier Markets, including the large Asian and African ones we mentioned earlier, make up 44 percent. That is much more than representative of the size of their economies.

Of course, active fund managers do not need to follow the index, however well or badly it's constructed, and as result, virtually all of them have managed to beat the Frontier Markets indexes over the last few years. They're able to underweight or overweight countries based on their own analyses about the countries' outlooks, and can include countries such as Saudi Arabia that are not included in the index.

The Templeton Frontier Markets Fund has major underweights in Kuwait, Qatar, and the UAE, with the Middle East representing 31 percent of its assets, and holds positions in Saudi companies like Saudi Basic Industries, and several Egyptian stocks. Neither Saudi Arabia nor Egypt is included in the MSCI Frontier Markets Index.

Examining Your Global Frontier Fund Options

Investors have three solid Global Frontier Fund choices in the Harding Loevner Frontier Emerging Markets Fund, the Wasatch Frontier Emerging Smaller Countries Fund, and the HSBC GIF Frontier Markets Fund, all of which have reasonable expense ratios and decent track records for the short periods that they have been in operation in their present forms. Any of them would be a perfectly suitable vehicle for investors who have decided to make the first step into Frontier Markets.

It seems a little paradoxical that having launched their Frontier Markets Fund as a retail vehicle trading as a closed-end fund on the NYSE, Morgan Stanley should not provide a retail version of the fund now that it's become an open-end mutual fund. It's also a pity that Templeton has temporarily closed its long running and successful Frontier Markets Fund to new investors.

Templeton Frontier Markets Fund (TFMAX)

Inception: October 14, 2008

Assets under Management (AUM) as of September 30, 2013: $1.4 billion

Number of Holdings: 93

Management Expense Ratio (MER): 2.15 percent after waiver

Return to September 30, 2013:

> 1 Year: 15.4 percent
>
> 3 years: 5.9 percent per annum
>
> Since inception: 13.2 percent per annum

Closed to new investors since June 30, 2013

The fund was launched by Templeton in 2008 and managed by Dr. Mark Mobius and his colleagues Alan Lam, Dennis Lim, and Tom Wu. This is the same team that manages the long-established Templeton Emerging Markets Fund (TEMAX). The Templeton Frontier Markets Fund is the oldest and largest Frontier Market Global fund available to North American investors and has US$1.4 billion in assets under administration effective at the end of September 2013. There is also a Canadian-registered fund, launched in 2011, which feeds into the American version of the fund.

Unfortunately for new investors, Templeton closed both the American and Canadian versions of the fund at the end of June 2013, and its European-registered sibling as well. The company felt that it could not continue investing the sums of money flowing into the funds. It did allow existing holders to continue making deposits, a strategy known within the mutual fund industry as a *soft closing*.

Between the American, Canadian, and European versions of the fund, Templeton had over US$3.6 billion invested in Frontier Markets. Their small size and lack of liquidity made it very difficult for the managers to continue investing in the same companies held in the funds without owning too much of the free float of shares available.

If Templeton experiences significant outflows from the various versions of the fund, the managers would almost certainly have some difficulty in quickly selling more than a limited percentage of their holdings. For example, the various versions own $118 million worth of United Kingdom-listed oil company Dragon Oil plc, which operates two oil fields in Turkmenistan. Dragon Oil's market capitalization is US$480 million, meaning that the Templeton Funds own 24.5 percent of the whole company.

Even though the company is listed in London and has a share price of PDS 6 (approximately US$9.6 at the exchange rate at time of writing), and an average weekly volume of 1.23 million shares in 2013, it would take Templeton ten weeks to sell its entire position in Dragon Oil, even assuming that no other shareholders are selling at the same time.

Templeton is thus acting very responsibly in soft closing the fund, which has a 5-star ranking in Morningstar's Emerging Markets category. As of June 30, 2013, the fund's holdings had a Price/Earnings Ratio of 9.6 times the previous 12 months' earnings and a Price to Book Value Ratio of 1.6 times, as opposed to the Index's P/E ratio of 15.9 times and P/B of 2.6 times. Both measures show the companies in the portfolio to be cheap compared to the average company in the Index, a circumstance that in the past, has contributed to above average returns.

As far as performance is concerned, the Templeton Frontier Markets Fund has outperformed the MSCI Frontier Markets Index substantially over the five years since its inception, producing an annual return of 13.2 percent per annum against the index return of –1.6 percent per annum.

The managers achieved this by underweighting the Middle East, where it has only 31.8 percent against 62.6 percent in the index, and overweighting in Africa, Eastern Europe, and Asia.

In their sector breakdown, the managers overweight telecommunications, energy, and materials stocks at 48.5 percent of the total, versus the index's concentration in banks and financials at 55.9 percent.

Here are the fund's top ten holdings in order of size.

Company	Country	Percentage
Ooredoo	Qatar	4.5
OMV Petrom	Romania	3.9
Industries Qatar	Qatar	3.9
Dragon Oil	UAE	3.5
KazMunaiGas Exploration	Kazakhstan	3.2
First Gulf Bank	UAE	2.9
MTN Group	S Africa	2.8
FBN Holdings	Nigeria	2.6
Zenith Bank	Nigeria	2.6
Saudi Basic Industries	Saudi Arabia	2.4
Total		32.3

Templeton Frontier Markets Fund would be an excellent choice for an investor wanting a large, well-established fund with a good track record of absolute and relative performance. However, its closure to new investors in June 2013 makes it unavailable at the time of writing. Should it reopen, it should be included in any Frontier Market investor's portfolio.

Harding Loevner Frontier Emerging Markets Fund (HLMOX)

Inception: Institutional version May 27, 2008, Retail version December 31, 2010

Assets under Management as of September 30, 2013: $131.5 million

Number of holdings: 78

MER: 2.25 percent after waiver

Returns to September 30, 2013:

  1 Year: 19.3 percentage

  Since inception: 2.2 percent per annum

The institutional version of the Harding Loevner Frontier Emerging Markets Fund is actually the oldest Global Frontier Fund in North America but the retail version, managed by the same team of Rusty Johnson and Pradipta Chakrabortty, did not follow until 2½ years after the opening of first version.

Smaller than the Templeton Fund, its major distinguishing characteristic is that it uses the MSCI Frontier Emerging Markets Index as its benchmark. That allows it to invest in the five smaller crossover Emerging Markets of Colombia, Egypt, Morocco, Peru, and the Philippines.

Together these five Emerging Markets comprise 53 percent of the index, meaning that the Middle East has a much lower weighting at 31.4 percent against the MSCI Frontier Market's 62.6 percent. Meanwhile, Latin America, Asia, and Africa account for 27.4 percent, 21.1 percent, and 15.5 percent each of the Frontier Emerging Markets Index.

The fund's asset mix has major underweights in the Middle East (21.4 percent) and Latin America (16 percent), but overweights in Asia (28.9 percent) and Africa (23.3 percent).

Therefore, the Harding Loevner Fund is much more exposed to the younger populations in less-developed countries with large domestic markets than the Index. That makes it a good choice for investors wanting exposure to Asia and Africa.

The portfolio has a P/E Ratio of 12.5 times against the index's 13.5 times, a Price/cash flow of 8.6 times against the index's 7.8 times, and a P/B of 1.2 times against 1.8 times for the index. Thus, the Harding Loevner Fund is somewhat cheaper on two out of three measures against the MSCI Frontier Emerging Markets Index, although the difference is not as great as for the Templeton Frontier Markets Fund.

The retail fund has outperformed the index over the almost-three years of its operation, returning 2.2 percent per annum against 0.8 percent per annum. Over the almost 5½ years up to September 30, 2013, since the launch of the institutional version, it has returned –2.9 percent per annum against –5.3 percent per annum for the index and 4.4 percent per annum over the five years up to September 30, 2013, against 0.04 percent per annum for the index.

This outperformance has been achieved by overweighting consumer staples and discretionary stocks, industrials, healthcare, and materials (51.9 percent in total) and underweighting financials, telecommunications, and energy.

The fund's top ten holdings in order of size are shown here.

Company	Country	Percentage
Jarir Marketing	Saudi Arabia	3.8
Universal Robina	Philippines	3.6
Engro	Pakistan	3.4
Alicorp	Peru	3.3
FBN Holdings	Nigeria	3.2
Bank of the Philippines	Philippines	3.1
Industries Qatar	Qatar	3.0
Etihad Etisalat	Saudi Arabia	2.9
John Keells	Sri Lanka	2.7
Cementos Argos	Colombia	2.5
Total		31.5

The Harding Loevner Frontier Emerging Markets Fund is a relatively small fund with a short track record, but the outperformance by the longer established institutional class with the same managers means this is a suitable choice for investors looking for a fund with a wider mandate that includes the smaller Emerging Markets. It also has the advantage of giving investors meaningful exposure to the larger and faster-growing Asian and African Frontier Markets.

Wasatch Frontier Emerging Smaller Countries Fund (WAFMX)

Inception: January 31, 2012

Assets under Management at November 30, 2012: $874 million

Number of Holdings: 119

MER: 2.25 percent after waiver

Returns to 30th September 2013:

> 1 Year: 25.6 percent
>
> Since inception: 27.3 percent

The Wasatch Frontier Emerging Small Countries has the shortest track record of the available global frontier funds, only being launched at the end of January 2012. However, it has rapidly grown to become the largest fund still open to investors, reaching almost $900 million within two years. Managed since inception by Laura Geritz, whose investment commentary is always informative and insightful, the fund uses the wider MSCI Frontier Emerging Markets Index as its benchmark, similar to the Harding Loevner fund.

The fund has outperformed both this benchmark and the MSCI Frontier Markets Index by a wide margin over the 20 months since inception to end September 2013, returning 27.3 percent against 10.3 percent and 17.3 percent, respectively, for the two indices.

The fund has a massive overweight in consumer stocks against the index, with 50.8 percent in consumer staples and another 7.2 percent in consumer discretionary stocks. This has contributed to its outperformance with the remaining sectors in the top five being financials at 13.6 percent, cash at 8.9 percent, and industrials at 5.2 percent.

Similarly, its geographical allocations look nothing like the indices, with Africa as its largest weight at 42.7 percent, Asia at 28.6 percent, the Middle East at only 18.7 percent, and Latin America at 5.9 percent. Nigeria and Kenya are the two largest countries, at 16.6 percent and 11.8 percent, Saudi Arabia at 7.2 percent, Sri Lanka at 6.9 percent, Pakistan and the UAE at 6.1 percent, and Vietnam at 5.3 percent.

The fund's Top ten holdings at 30th September 2013 were:

Company	Country	Percentage
Vietnam Dairy Products (Vinamilk)	Vietnam	4.3
East African Breweries	Kenya	3.8
Nestle Nigeria	Nigeria	3,5
Safaricom	Kenya	3.2
Nigerian Breweries	Nigeria	3.0
Brasseries Maroc	Morocco	2.7
Zenith Bank	Nigeria	2.2
Kuwait Foods Americana	Kuwait	2.1
Commercial Bank of Ceylon	Sri Lanka	1.9
Lucky Cement	Pakistan	1.8

While the Wasatch fund has only been in existence for less than two years at the time of writing (December 2013), it has grown very rapidly and performed well as it provides investors with the means to access the emerging middle class consumer in the fast growing markets of Africa and Asia, the areas which we feel are the best exposure to the growth of the Frontier Markets. With 58 percent of the fund in consumer stocks and another 14 percent in financials which are also benefiting from rising incomes and increasing urbanization, and over 70 percent in Africa and Asia, the Wasatch fund is the most concentrated way to gain exposure to these attractive areas. To this appraisal, however, we would add the proviso that such an approach is likely to prove volatile if there is a setback in these markets.

HSBC GIF Frontier Markets Fund (HSFAX)

Inception: September 6, 2011

Assets under Management as of September 30, 2013: $79.3 million

Number of Holdings: 71

MER: 2.2 percent after waiver

Returns to September 30, 2013:

> 1 Year: 22.4 percent
>
> Since inception: 14.7 percent per annum

While the HSBC GIF Frontier Markets Fund has only a two-year track record, its predecessor was launched in 2008. Managed since 2011 by Andrew Brudenell and assisted since 2012 by Chris Turner, the fund uses the capped version of the MSCI Frontier Emerging Markets Index as its benchmark. The index caps the percentage of the five Emerging Markets of Colombia, Egypt, Morocco, Peru, and the Philippines at 25 percent and all other countries at 10 percent each.

The five Emerging Markets thus have a 25 percent weight in the Index, the Middle East countries 31 percent, and the remaining Frontier Markets 44 percent. The Fund had a slightly higher P/E Ratio at 9.9 times versus the index at 9.2 times at the end of April 2013, but a higher dividend yield at 4.4 percent against 3.7 percent.

The fund has outperformed both the capped MSCI Frontier Emerging Markets Index and the original MSCI Frontier Markets Index by 5 percent annually in the two years of its operation. Since inception, it has returned 14.7 percent per annum against 9.5 percent for the capped Index and 9.7 percent for the Frontier Markets Index.

The Fund's asset mix shows major overweights in Asia (19.6 percent) and Africa (12.2 percent) and an underweight in Latin America (7.6 percent), while within its Middle East exposure (48.6 percent) it has a large (8.7 percent) weight in Saudi Arabia and overweights in the United Arab

Emirates (14.5 percent) and Qatar (13.9 percent). It also has overweights in Asian countries with 9.9 percent in Pakistan and 4.1 percent in Vietnam and an underweight in the Philippines (3.3 percent).

Its sector weights are not notably out of line with the index with financials constituting the largest segment at 45.3 percent, followed by industrials at 14.3 percent and energy at 9.9 percent. However, it tends to have some medium-sized companies as its largest holdings rather than the expected large capitalization names. Thus the financials among its top ten holdings at the end of September 2013 were Qatar National Bank, Bank of Georgia, Samba Financial, Bank Muscat, and United Bank, a Pakistani stock.

Here are the fund's Top ten holdings as of September 30, 2013.

Company	Country	Percentage
Emaar Properties	UAE	4.2
Qatar National Bank	Qatar	3.5
Bank of Georgia	Georgia	3.2
Ooredoo	Qatar	2.9
Industries Qatar	Qatar	2.8
Samba Financial	Saudi Arabia	2.7
Credicorp	Peru	2.6
Bank Muscat	Oman	2.5
United Bank	Pakistan	2.5
First Gulf Bank	UAE	2.5
Total		29.4

HSBC GIF Frontier Markets Fund is a small fund with a short track record but that has outperformed both the MSCI Frontier Emerging Markets Capped Index and the MSCI Frontier Markets Index since inception two years ago. It has a higher dividend yield than the index and focuses on medium-sized companies rather than the usual large capitalization Frontier Markets stocks, although the managers are not afraid to take sizeable out-of-index positions. It would be a suitable choice for investors who want a less volatile fund with exposure to companies not found in other Frontier Markets funds.

Morgan Stanley Institutional Frontier Emerging Markets Portfolio (MFMIX)

Inception: August 27, 2008, as a closed-end fund and converted to an open-end fund in September 2012

Assets under Management as of September 30, 2013: $167.1 million

MER: 2.38 percent

Returns to September 30, 2013:

> 1 Year: 29.4 percent
>
> 3 Years: 8.1 percent per annum
>
> 5 years: 3.1 percent per annum

The Morgan Stanley Institutional Frontier Emerging Markets Portfolio is the largest and longest-established Frontier Markets fund after Templeton's closure to new investors. The same manager, Tim Drinkall, has run it since inception and has an excellent long-term track record.

In fact, it would be the preferred choice for investors in North America except for one problem. When the fund was converted from a closed-end fund listed on the New York Stock Exchange in 2012, because it had been persistently trading at a discount, it was made into an institutional open-end mutual fund.

The minimum investment required? A cool US$5 million! Yes that's right; unless you're an institution or happen to have a spare US$5 million on hand, you can't buy this fund. What's that? You don't have a spare $5 million. Then you're out of luck.

Annoyingly, Morgan Stanley has launched a retail version of this fund, but it's in Europe. So unless you are legally entitled to purchase a European registered open-end fund you can't access this version either. Given the length and out-performance of the index demonstrated by its track record, that is a pity.

Its top holdings are pretty similar to those of the other Frontier Market Funds discussed here, including Emaar Properties, Qatar National Bank, Ooredoo, FBN Holdings, Zenith Bank, and First Gulf Bank. That proves that all frontier managers look in pretty similar places.

Chapter 17

Assessing and Adjusting Your Frontier Investments

*B*y the time you get to this chapter, you may have already taken our advice and started investing in Frontier Markets. Now we need to make sure that everything works in the way that we've promised and that you experience as few surprises as possible.

The first step that you need to take is to monitor your portfolios, whether they are investments that you hold directly yourself or indirectly through your pension fund. You need to make note of how much (if any) is invested in Frontier Markets.

Then we recommend reviewing your investments on a regular basis, hopefully with your financial advisor, to ensure that you rebalance your holdings back to the original allocation if they have moved too far away from it. At the same time, we point out that it makes sense to adjust your weightings if your life circumstances change.

Over the years, we have heard several "rules" about portfolio reviews. Most of these rules focus on time thresholds, such as quarterly, semi-annually, or even annually. In this chapter, we show you a better way to determine the schedule for portfolio reviews, and we outline some strategies for evaluating your Frontier Market investments.

Setting a Schedule for an Ongoing Review

In any area of life, reviews serve two purposes: to check an individual's initial grasp of important facts and to act as memory refreshers to reinforce that grasp later on. When you were in school, the classroom instructor or professor may have carried out classroom reviews just before an examination. A well-executed review refreshed your knowledge and pointed up areas that needed more work, enabling you to fill in the gaps before the examination.

A thorough investment portfolio review serves similar purposes. Start with the asset allocation that you've worked out with your financial advisor. A competent financial advisor would have carefully interviewed you about your finances, ongoing financial commitments, risk tolerance, expectations, life plans, and almost everything else that has any impact on your financial status and well-being.

After the interview, the advisor would have worked out an asset allocation that suggests how much of your total investment portfolio should be in areas such as:

- Cash
- Fixed income investments, possibly including *laddered* certificates, which provide a series of staggered expiry dates, and bonds and similar investments
- Balanced funds
- Domestic funds
- Global funds, including a frontier weighting

Your advisor likely explained his or her rationale to you for the allocation and satisfied you that it made sense in your life situation *at that time*. Once you and the advisor agreed on the allocation — or general framework for your investment portfolio, you both settled on specific assets and the advisor may have recommended specific balanced, domestic, and global funds.

A regular review is always important for three standard reasons:

- Assets in your portfolio may have performed differently than anticipated, in some cases even better than anticipated; if your advisor had suggested that your domestic funds account for 40 percent of your total assets and these funds benefited from a stock market rally and have come to account for 50 percent of the total, your advisor may recommend trimming those funds back to 40 percent.

✔ Your risk tolerance may have changed; perhaps you've done some serious thinking since the last review and have concluded that you are more risk averse — or even more capable of dealing with risk than you had originally believed; self-introspection has a definite place to play effective portfolio construction.

✔ Your life circumstances may change (more about that later) and those changes may have changed your financial needs.

Under these circumstances, many advisors would recommend a review and rebalancing once annually at a minimum. This does not necessarily mean that you will rebalance the portfolio each time. It may just mean affirming that rebalancing has not become necessary.

However, if you add Frontier Markets investments into the equation, or if any of the preceding factors change substantially, you and your advisor may decide to have this conversation twice annually.

Some financial advisors have a different approach. They prefer to undertake portfolio rebalancing whenever one of the asset categories reaches a specific threshold. In one scenario, the asset allocation may call for Frontier investments at 5 percent. If that grows to exceed 6 percent (which amounts to 20 percent beyond the target) the rebalancing may take place before the actual review.

However it takes place, ensure that you and your advisor have a clear understanding of how often the two of you (or the three of you if you are married) should have this conversation.

There is no one absolutely right or wrong rebalancing strategy. What is most important is that you and your advisor have a clear understanding of the circumstances under which a rebalancing becomes appropriate.

Rebalancing to maintain your asset allocation

Rebalancing to maintain your asset allocation means restoring it back to the weightings that you and your advisor had agreed upon in your earlier meetings. Since those meetings, one or more of several events may have triggered the need for rebalancing:

- ✔ **Outperformance of an asset category, such as domestic funds as above.** In that case the actual weighting of domestic funds now exceeds the original allocation and needs to be restored to the original 40 percent.

- ✔ **Underperformance of an asset category.** In this scenario, an asset has not yielded a strong enough return for its category and now accounts for (in this example) 30 percent instead of 40 percent.

- ✔ **An unforeseen emergency such as a large medical expenditure that eroded your cash and fixed income allocation.** In this case, you'll need to inject new cash or liquidate a portion of an asset — perhaps some units of one of your funds — in order to make up the difference.

- ✔ **A change in your perceived risk tolerance.** Before the Financial Crisis of 2008–2009, while stock markets were generally rising, many individuals overestimated their tolerance for risk only to find that they could not mentally deal with the tumult, uncertainty, and long recovery that accompanied the crisis. The "sleep-at-night" factor often comes into clearer focus over time as the individual looks at the ups and downs of monthly statements.

    Make no mistake — the sleep-at-night factor is even more important than the projected return.

- ✔ **A change in employment status such as a new job at a higher salary or sudden job loss requiring unforeseen use of cash reserves.** This situation may require liquidating all or part of an asset in order to restore the cash and fixed-income allocation that you and your advisor had originally discussed.

    The amount of liquid and near-liquid funds that you'll need in the event of job loss varies by industry and local employment conditions but in these uncertain times, allow for at least six months' expenses; also bear in mind that you may actually have added expenses no longer covered by your employer, such as insurance and daycare.

- ✔ **A change in life priorities.** In this scenario, you may have decided (though we would not recommend it) to trade off some of your investment plans against a once-in-a-lifetime cruise around the world and you have to write a large check to cover the expenses, not to mention a new cruise wardrobe, travel insurance, and all the other purchases that go with the trip.

- ✔ **A life change that affects financial commitments (more about this later).** This is a case that may also require liquidating all or part of an asset in order to restore the cash and fixed-income allocation.

Suppose, for purposes of this discussion, that you and your advisor agree that the original asset allocations still work for you. In this case, re-balancing means restoring it to the original weightings and in most of the preceding scenarios that involves restoring the cash and fixed-income components.

Responding to life events that change your goals and risk tolerance

Any one of these life events can change your investment goals and risk tolerance and mean less investible capital, likely a lowering of risk tolerance, and often a change in your asset allocation:

- Marriage.
- The decision to buy a house and how you're going to finance the down payment and monthly expenses that will most likely exceed what you are currently paying.
- Divorce and a need to come up with a large settlement, not to mention those nasty legal bills.
- Birth of a child.
- Job loss.
- Taking on responsibility for elder care of your parent or parents.
- A change in education plans by your offspring.
- Job loss by one or more of your adult children who then moves back home; with that the expenses that went down when they moved out suddenly increase again.
- Early retirement, whether you make this decision voluntarily or the move is thrust upon you by an ungrateful employer late on a Friday afternoon.
- Your boss did not fire you but you decided to fire your boss and buy that coffee franchise that you've been considering. (Remember that the first two years [at least] will be a bit rocky.)

You can prepare for some of these events in advance. Job loss and elder care responsibilities can occur suddenly, perhaps even blindsiding you, but a decision about marriage or buying a new home usually takes place well before the fact. As soon as you have made the decision, start talking to your financial advisor. Give him or her a chance to review your finances and formulate coherent recommendations. In some cases, the decision may be more voluntary than others. Before you decide on early retirement, again, consult your financial advisor.

Life changes are not always bad news. You may also get some good news in this category. Some changes will mean more investible capital, perhaps even an increase in risk tolerance and therefore a change in your asset allocation:

- ✔ A large inheritance
- ✔ A new job at a higher salary
- ✔ Downsizing from a large house to a smaller residence
- ✔ Children completing their education and going out on their own

These factors are not mutually exclusive. Downsizing from a large house to a smaller residence may free up a large amount of hitherto frozen cash that was locked up in the larger house, but it may then be used to give offspring their start.

Whenever life throws you a curve, or even some unexpected good news, deal with the bad news or celebrate the good news and then check to see whether it has any real impact on your financial planning.

Keeping Your Perspective While Assessing Your Performance

Keeping your perspective is the same as keeping yourself focused on the long-term. Every little emergency does not necessarily change the game plan. Hopefully many of the changes — such as a sudden need for cash — can be absorbed within your established asset allocation. Change is not always necessary. The trick is to know when you have to change the asset allocation and when you are already covered.

Studying the recent performance of global equity funds

Making generalizations about global equity funds can be as dangerous as making generalizations about domestic funds. Check the prospectus of a fund for its frontier weighting. Within that distinction, check whether (for example) the developed European component has performed better or worse than the Emerging Market component.

Given that the MSCI Emerging Markets Index has almost doubled over the last decade in US$ terms, while the European and Japanese indices are only back to where they were before the Financial Crisis of 2008–2009, it is probable that those global equity funds with a larger Emerging Markets exposure will have outperformed those with holdings in only developed markets.

Does each component have a reasonable track record, perhaps interrupted by recent events? Do these events — such as a war or other political tumult — have the potential for long-term impact? Alternatively, check whether the negative impact might be short-lived — such as a hard-fought bitter election.

Keeping your perspective in this case may not necessarily mean running for cover. It may mean riding out the storm. Remember, we have stressed that the dollars that you put into frontier investments should be dollars that you will not reasonably need for a period of at least five years or more.

However, if the fund isn't performing well and improvement doesn't appear promising, check the costs (if any) of liquidating the holding. This becomes a kind of cost-benefit analysis: the cost of escaping versus the cost of patience while you wait for the fund to recover.

We've said this in other chapters but we repeat it here for emphasis: One secret to effective investing in any category is the quality of information upon which you base your decision. Do your own research with materials from reputable publishers. Another secret is a close working relationship with a trusted financial advisor who will help you avoid most of the *don'ts.* One key to working effectively with your advisor — as with your family doctor or any other professional — is to tell him or her everything needed for an expert recommendation.

Examining the recent performance of developed nation equities

When examining the performance of developed nation equities, look past the numbers and look at the reasons for differences in performance — in this case, the presence or absence of Emerging or Frontier Market revenues. In an example current at the time we wrote this book, Las Vegas Sands (NYSE:LVS), a popular — and very volatile casino stock derives a large part of its revenues from overseas casinos, especially in the former Portuguese territory of Macau. Meanwhile, Caesar's (Q:CZR) has turned in a negative performance and appears set to retreat from Macau, partially due to licensing difficulties there.

Avoid generalizations. In this example, it would be easy to generalize about casino stocks but they are not all the same, any more than all restaurant stocks or auto manufacturer stocks are the same. In this specific case, look for the influence of Frontier Markets revenues.

Considering what stages of development and low liquidity mean to you

One of the reasons why we emphasize using your long-term dollars for your Frontier Markets investments is that frontier countries have less sophisticated market mechanisms. Each of the former Soviet bloc countries is in a different point on the road from controlled Communist economy to a market economy.

Compared to other members of the Former Soviet Union (FSU), Kazakhstan has a promising future, largely due to oil revenues. At the time of writing, roughly 130 equities trade on the Kazakhstan Stock Exchange but they break down into two main categories: those which form part of the KASE index, which are fairly liquid, and those with lower liquidity. The KASE contains these equities considered more liquid than the other equities.

At the time of writing, the major stocks in the KASE Index consisted of:

- Bank CenterCredit JSC, a financial institution with a capitalization of US$241 million

- Kazakhmys PLC, one of the leading global copper miners, cross listed on the London Stock Exchange (LSE) with a capitalization of $6,776 million

- Halyk Savings Bank of Kazakhstan JSC, with a capitalization of $2,537 million

- Kazkommertsbank JSC, with a capitalization of $975 million

- Kaztelekom JSC, the leading telecoms operator with a market capitalization of $1.2 billion

- KazMunaiGas EP JSC, one of the three largest Kazakh energy companies with GDRs listed on the LSE, which raised $2 billion in its IPO in 2006 and has a market capitalization of $8,112 billion

- KazTransOil (ticker KZTO), the largest oil pipeline network under the People's IPO programme

- K'Cell (KCELL), a subsidiary of Nordic telecommunications operator TeliaSonera, with over 11 million subscribers, which raised $525 million in an IPO in December 2012

At the time of writing, these stocks have more of a free float and therefore more liquidity than the other listed companies on the same exchange.

Keeping low correlation in mind

Within the context of investing, correlation refers to the relationship between two assets and the extent to which they move together at any given time. When two assets move in lockstep with each other, they are said to have a correlation of 1.0. When their correlation is completely random, they are said to have a zero correlation. When they move in opposite directions, they are said to have a negative correlation.

When two assets have a low correlation with each other (such as the equities of two different countries), their performance is very different. Returns on one asset were increasing while returns on another asset were declining.

This relationship has several benefits:

- Good performance in one asset will offset poor performance in another one.
- The factors causing poor performance in one asset have not caused similar damage to the other asset.
- Even though the individual countries or stocks may be very volatile themselves, because they move in different directions, the volatility of the overall portfolio is actually reduced.

Keeping low correlation in mind means remembering that Frontier Markets do not move in correlation with each other, with Emerging Markets, or with developed nation markets. That is not to say that the markets of each country are not affected by what is happening elsewhere; they don't live in a vacuum either. Certainly, the markets of frontier countries such as Kazakhstan suffered with the Euro-zone crisis of 2010–2012, but they didn't drop to the same extent.

This means making individual judgments on individual markets. To borrow an example from the world of Emerging Markets: The well-known BRICs — Brazil, Russia, India, and China — are attracting differing appraisals of their future at the time of writing. Brazil appears set to regain some of its momentum as it approaches hosting the soccer World Cup in 2014 and the Summer Olympic Games in 2016.

At the same time, despite its extensive natural resources and geopolitical ambitions, Russia suffers from a negative birth rate, a declining population, and capital flight and is often termed as *broke*. China, the second largest economy in the world on a purchasing power parity (PPP) basis, suffers from overinvestment in property and capital assets, a rapidly aging population, and an extensive "shadow banking" system with high levels of bad debts. Observers believe it should be able to orchestrate a soft landing, where growth slows to 5 percent to 7 percent per annum, but some think it could be headed for a very hard landing, when growth falls to only 1 percent to 3 percent, with the associated risk of political unrest.

Consider each country as a separate case and look for global funds in which the country holdings generally match your thinking.

Here's one last thing to consider: Although we are generally restricting our focus in this book to Frontier Markets, we can't suggest that they operate in a vacuum separate from Emerging Markets. For example, at the time of writing, China's falling consumption of resources means reduced commodity purchases from some Frontier Markets.

Part V

The Part of Tens

Enjoy an additional Part of Tens chapter online at www.dummies.com/extras/frontiermarkets.

In this part. . .

- ✔ Explore the most promising Frontier Markets.

- ✔ Examine the investment opportunities of the companies with the most Frontier and Emerging Markets exposure.

- ✔ Decide whether to invest in or avoid the riskiest Frontier Markets.

- ✔ Learn from the mistakes of others when investing in Frontier Markets.

Chapter 18

The Ten Most Promising Frontier Markets

*W*hen headed into a new frontier, it helps to have as clear a view as possible of the terrain. That in turn helps to increase the individual's comfort level. This chapter presents ten options to help narrow your choices in Frontier Markets investing.

This new investment category obviously has some countries that look more promising than others. If you have read other chapters in this book, you probably won't be surprised by some of the names you see in the ten most promising and five riskiest Frontier Markets.

Vietnam

With its large population, well-developed stock market, low level of urbanization, extensive natural resources, and large domestic market, Vietnam includes most of the components that an investor should check for when considering promising Frontier Markets.

Population	GDP per Capita	Market Cap.	Corruption	Income Inequality
92.3 mill.	$3,500 p.a.	$38.2 bill.	123/174	75/136 (2008)

Since its opening to capitalism, or *Doi Moi,* in 1990, Vietnam has enjoyed almost 25 years of fast gross domestic product growth, admittedly with some booms and busts in the meantime.

A large, fast growing labor force with a median age of 29, exports that exceeded US$114 billion in 2012, mobile telephone penetration of 137 percent in the same year, and an urbanization rate (percentage of the total population that lives in cities) of only 30 percent make Vietnam well positioned to become the next major Asian export success story. It has the added advantage of a large domestic market.

It also acts as an outsource supplier. Chinese exporters in Guangdong province are moving their factories to northern Vietnam next door, as rising Chinese labor rates make low-end industries such as garments, footwear, and cheap electronics uncompetitive at home.

Possible weaknesses include a tendency to expand too rapidly, leading to periodic credit crises and bursts of inflation. As recently as 2011, inflation ran at 18 percent although at time of writing had fallen to 6 percent. The banking industry remains largely state controlled. Vietnam officially remains a Communist state, with the usual problems suggested by that status, including the lack of an independent judiciary and state-directed lending to favored industries.

Overall, though, Vietnam should be one of the more successful Frontier Markets, and it would be no surprise to see it graduate to full Emerging Market status within the next decade.

Colombia

Already considered an Emerging Market by many observers and included in the MSCI Emerging Markets Index, Colombia has a large population and a well developed stock market. It also has extensive natural resources, a large domestic market, as well as numerous companies listed as ADRs on the American stock exchanges.

Population	GDP per Capita	Market Cap.	Corruption	Income Inequality
45.7 mill.	$10,700 p.a.	$201.3 bill.	94/174	17/136

Since the end of the armed conflict with the Fuerzas Armadas Revolucionarios de Colombia (FARC) guerillas and the taming of the drug gangs at the end of the 1990s, Colombia has progressed rapidly over the last 15 years.

With a relatively young population (median age 28.6), exports of US$60 billion in 2012, mobile telephone penetration of 101 percent, and well-developed oil and gas and coal sectors, Colombia has become one of the most promising Latin American markets.

Although its high level of urbanization at 75 percent means that it will not benefit from rural migration to the cities in the same way as less-developed countries, it still has 18 percent of its population working in agriculture, the second highest amongst the largest South American countries. It has also signed Free Trade Agreements (FTAs) with the United States, Canada, and the European Union. These agreements have opened up large foreign markets for the country's exports.

Its high level of income inequality, 10 percent unemployment, the remnants of the FARC guerilla movement, its often stormy relationship with its trouble-some neighbor Venezuela, and high exposure to energy commodity prices are all factors to take into consideration in investment decisions.

Nonetheless, Colombia will undoubtedly be one of the fastest growing and best governed Latin American states over the next decade.

Ghana

Although one of the smaller countries on our list in terms of its population and economy, Ghana has been one of the fastest growing and best-governed frontier countries and not only in Africa.

Ghana also has important economic fundamentals. It has a reasonably sized population, a well-developed stock market, extensive natural resources, and a functioning and vibrant democracy.

Population	GDP per Capita	Market Cap.	Corruption	Income Inequality
25.2 mill.	$3,300 p.a.	$3.3 bill.	64/174	63/136 (2008)

Since the government of Flight Lieutenant Jerry Rawlings took power in the early 1980s, it has been one of the best-governed African nations with a vibrant if occasionally noisy democracy. With an extremely young population (median age 20.7 years) and rapid population growth, the domestic market looks well-positioned to enjoy a strong period of growth. This will comple-ment the strong growth in its commodity production over the last decade, initially gold and more recently oil and gas. As a result, Ghana has enjoyed strong GDP growth, slowing to 8.2 percent in 2012 from 14.4 percent in 2011. Its welcoming attitude toward Foreign Direct Investment, with a realistic atti-tude to the sharing of the resulting economic benefit, has enabled it to attract a disproportionately large share of inward funds.

Its smaller population and relatively high level of urbanization at 51 percent mean that it is unlikely to enjoy as rapid a rate of growth going forward as other African countries. At the same time, its proximity to several troubled West African states such as Liberia and Sierra Leone has involved it in peacekeeping and colored perceptions of the region.

Ghana remains one of the most attractive Frontier Markets and probably the best positioned of the African economies to graduate to full Emerging Market status in the next few years.

The Philippines

One of the largest of the Frontier Emerging economies in terms of population, market capitalization, and size of its economy, the Philippines has enjoyed a renaissance in its improved domestic government and strong inward investment over the last decade.

The Philippines has a large, youthful, and well-educated population, a well-developed stock market that is one of the largest in emerging Asia, and a large domestic market, as well as a functioning and vibrant democracy.

Population	GDP per Capita	Market Cap.	Corruption	Income Inequality
105.2 mill.	$4,500 p.a.	$266.3 bill.	105/174	42/136 (2009)

With the peaceful removal of Joseph Estrada as president in 2001, the Philippines under his successor Gloria Macapagal Arroyo enjoyed a decade of stable government and strong GDP growth. With a median age of 23.2 years, an urbanization rate of 49 percent, and mobile telephone penetration of 95 percent, the Philippines is well-positioned to benefit from further movement from rural areas into the cities, the growth of its status as an outsourcing destination, and further inflows of Foreign Direct Investment. Remittances from the large overseas Filipino community are a major source of inward fund flows and help balance fluctuations in the domestic economy.

While the legacy of past misgovernment and corruption still shows in its poor infrastructure and the lengthy approval process for necessary improvements, it has had a notable acceleration of construction and capital projects in the recent years. The recent devastation wrought by Typhoon Haiyan in November 2013 with over 6,000 casualties and several million left homeless is a reminder that the country is comprised of volcanic islands in the middle of a hurricane zone. The country has a high exposure to the commodity markets due to a large portion of its US$46 billion in exports being composed of minerals and agricultural products although there has been substantial growth in exports of garments and low-end electronics.

The Philippines has become one of the most attractive developing Asian markets over the last decade and should continue its strong progress for the next few years.

Nigeria

One of the largest Frontier Markets in terms of population and size of its economy, Nigeria is overcoming a history of military dictatorship and corruption with GDP growth averaging 7.5 percent per annum so far this decade. Nigeria has a very youthful (median age 17.9 years), fast-growing population, extensive natural resources, the largest African stock market outside of South Africa, and a large domestic market.

Population	GDP per Capita	Market Cap.	Corruption	Income Inequality
174.5 mill.	$2,700 p.a.	$39.3 bill.	139/174	47/136 (2003)

With the return of civilian rule in 1999, Nigeria has experienced three relatively peaceful elections while the economy has expanded substantially and begun to reduce its dependence on oil and gas. With 70 percent of the workforce still employed in agriculture, a 50 percent urbanization rate, and 55 percent mobile telephone penetration, it stands to benefit from the move from rural areas to cities and the increased productivity that results from such a massive shift. While its exports of US$98 billion in 2012 were dominated by energy, its stock market capitalization is now over US$40 billion despite including few oil and gas companies. A number of its companies are listed as Global Depositary Receipts (GDRs) on the London Stock Exchange.

The unrest in the Niger delta by local inhabitants over the unfair distribution of Nigeria's oil wealth continues to lead to supply disruptions and the rise of Islamic militancy, especially in the Muslim northern states, is another political issue causing observers concern. Other negatives include Nigeria's high corruption and income inequality.

However, it has made remarkable progress in growing its domestic economy to offset its reliance on commodities and should continue to be the leading economy in sub-Saharan Africa outside of South Africa.

Bangladesh

Bangladesh is one of the ten most populous nations on Earth with a youthful and fast-growing population, a developed stock market and a large domestic market. Although its political class continues to squabble, it is a functioning democracy and has become a major low-cost manufacturing base as some Emerging Markets such as China have become more expensive.

Population	GDP per Capita	Market Cap.	Corruption	Income Inequality
163.6 mill.	$2,000 p.a.	$23.6 bill.	120/174	98/136 (2005)

Bangladesh has managed to grow its GDP by 6 percent per annum for most of the last decade despite poor political leadership and natural disasters such as typhoons and flooding. Its low urbanization rate of 28 percent and 52 percent mobile telephone penetration mean it should benefit substantially from the move of people from rural to urban living, helping reinforce its strong position as a low-cost manufacturer by providing ample supplies of labor. Its exports of US$26 billion can be expected to grow rapidly over the next few years.

The legacy of Bangladesh's independence struggle in 1971 is reflected in bad relations between political leaders. The collapse of a garment factory in 2013 which killed over 1,000 workers illustrates the weakness of Bangladesh's government controls. Its lack of natural resources has also left it exposed to commodity fluctuations, although recent developments in the oil and gas sector may alleviate some of these issues.

On the more positive side, perceptions of corruption have lessened substantially, with Bangladesh moving up to 120th out of 174 countries in 2012. Bangladesh continues to grow steadily despite its problems, and is well positioned to become one of the major global exporters of consumer goods this decade, supplemented by its large domestic market.

Peru

The Peruvian economy has been dominated by minerals exports for most of the last century and it ranks as one of the largest copper and precious metals producers both in Latin America and globally. With a youthful (median age 26.7 years) population of 30 million, a reasonable domestic market, extensive natural resources, and much improved political leadership in recent years, Peru is included in the MSCI Emerging Markets Index and a number of its companies have American Depositary Receipts(ADRs) listed on the New York Stock Exchange. However, it is also considered a crossover market, meaning that it is on the cusp between Emerging and Frontier Markets and is one of the five Emerging Markets included in the MSCI Frontier Emerging Markets Index, along with Colombia, Egypt, Morocco, and the Philippines.

Population	GDP per Capita	Market Cap.	Corruption	Income Inequality
29.8 mill.	$10,700 p.a.	$153.4 bill.	118/174	27/136 (2012)

Peru's GDP has grown at over 6 percent per annum in recent years. Although its urbanization rate is relatively high at 77 percent, like most Latin American countries, it has the ability to add value to its natural resources, which comprised most of its exports of US$47 billion in 2012. That should enable it to maintain its rapid growth.

With a mobile telephone penetration rate of 109 percent and a relatively well-educated population, the possibility of service industries becoming more important exists.

The legacy of Peru's struggles with the Shining Path guerillas in the 1970s and 1980s and ex-President Fujimori's security policies are a lingering issue. However, both of his successors as President, ex-Marxist Alan Garcia and ex-military Humala Tasso, have followed pro-growth policies since his departure in 2006. Local unrest at exploitation of Peru's mineral reserves has led to delays, but its corruption perceptions score is the third best in South America, after Brazil and Chile.

Peru should continue to experience rapid growth over the next few years and be among the best-performing Frontier Markets.

Kenya

Kenya is the leading economy in East Africa with a large population, a vibrant and functioning democracy, natural resources, and a well-developed stock market. While unrest in neighboring countries poses an issue for Kenya, as demonstrated by the terrorist attack on a shopping center in Nairobi in 2013, its economy appears likely to continue growing rapidly over the next decade.

Population	GDP per Capita	Market Cap.	Corruption	Income Inequality
44 mill.	$1,800 p.a.	$10.2 bill.	139/174	49/136 (2008)

Kenya's rapidly growing very youthful population with median age at 18.9 years is still largely based in rural areas with urbanization at a very low 22 percent. Despite that rate, mobile telephone penetration is 64 percent and Kenya has been among the leaders in using mobile technology for Internet banking and money transfers. That makes it reasonable to expect substantial GDP growth as people move from the countryside to cities and productivity increases.

Kenya had a disputed election in 2008 but a more peaceful one in 2012 and political governance has somewhat improved. Its involvement in African peace-keeping forces in neighboring Somalia, Rwanda, and the Democratic Republic of the Congo has brought security issues for the country, while Islamic militancy has led to terrorist attacks such as the American embassy bombings in 1998.

Despite these concerns and the negative effects they had on its important tourism trade, Kenya looks set to continue growing GDP around 5 percent per annum for the rest of the decade and will be one of the leading Frontier Markets in Africa, and it appears able to increase its exports from their present level of $6 billion.

Romania

Romania is the second largest East European country after Ukraine in terms of population and size of its economy, and it becomes a full member of the European Union in 2014. Its reasonably sized domestic market, well-developed stock market, natural resources, and well-educated population mean that it is the best positioned of the former Soviet satellites to display decent GDP growth over the next few years.

Population	GDP per Capita	Market Cap.	Corruption	Income Inequality
21.8 mill.	$12,800 p.a.	$9.6 bill.	66/174	97/136 (2011)

Despite its flat population growth and high median age of 39.4 years, it still has almost one-third of its workforce employed in agriculture and a moderate urbanization rate of 55 percent, giving it the opportunity to experience substantial improvements in productivity with an acceleration of migration from the country to the cities. With a well-educated population and mobile telephone penetration of 109 percent, it should benefit from its full membership in the EU with a low cost base for services and outsourcing to complement its auto manufacturing and energy sectors. Those sectors produced most of its US$68 billion in exports in 2012.

Notwithstanding protests over elections since the overthrow of the Ceaucescu regime in 1989, Romania's democracy has been robust enough to gain its entry to the EU. Disputes with Hungary over border issues and disruption to trade due to the Balkans conflicts have diminished in the last decade. The major issue for Romania and other Eastern European states remains their unattractive demographics, with a stagnant population and high median age.

Romania is the most attractive of the Eastern European frontier economies due to its size, well-developed stock market, high proportion of the workforce in agriculture, and moderate urbanization, as well as acceptable corruption perceptions and income inequality scores. It should experience reasonable GDP growth over the next few years and graduate to Emerging Market status, helped by full membership in the EU.

Sri Lanka

Sri Lanka is emerging from a 20-year civil war with the rebellious Tamil minority and beginning to benefit from stronger GDP growth and a more productive use of its finances and resources than military expenditures. With a reasonably sized population, these natural resources, a well-developed stock market, and the end of the civil war, Sri Lanka has the potential to become one of the stronger performing Frontier Markets in the next few years.

Population	GDP per Capita	Market Cap.	Corruption	Income Inequality
21.7 mill.	$6,100 p.a.	$16.9 bill.	79/174	24/136 (2010)

Sri Lanka has the lowest urbanization rate of any of the Frontier Markets included in the indices, with only 14 percent of the population living in cities and towns. Combined with 32 percent of its workforce in agriculture, it has the potential for substantial increases in productivity and a rapidly growing domestic market with the acceleration of the movement from countryside to cities. With 84 percent mobile telephone penetration and a well-educated, largely English-speaking workforce, services and out-sourcing could be major growth industries, as well as tourism, given improvement in the security situation.

It still has a legacy of the civil war and there are still concerns over the government's human rights record. Relations with its major neighbor India, which has extensive Tamil minorities itself, need to be monitored. Its lack of energy reserves is also a concern, given its trade deficit, with its US$11 billion in exports being much exceeded by its US$19 billion in imports in 2012.

While Sri Lanka is smaller than some other frontier economies, its recovery from a lengthy civil war, relatively high income, and low level of urbanization should combine to make it one of the faster growing economies over the next decade. That could lead to an upgrade to Emerging Market status.

Chapter 19

The Ten Most Promising Developed-Nations Companies

In This Chapter

▶ Researching big Frontier Market players

▶ Discovering industries worth investing in

Many investors choose to gain access to Frontier and Emerging Markets by purchasing global multinational companies domiciled in the United States, Europe, or Japan.

This may represent a less risky way to gain exposure to these markets. We certainly understand why investors choose this route — they're buying familiar companies listed on recognized exchanges with high standards of reporting and accounting. One point to consider is that, regardless of the fact that Frontier and Emerging Markets often account for 30 percent or more of these companies' revenues and earnings, their stock prices are most influenced by what's happening in the stock market in the country in which they are domiciled.

In this chapter, we give you a list of ten of the most promising developed-nation companies that derive a meaningful share of their revenues and earnings from Frontier and Emerging Markets.

Note: In the interest of full disclosure, at the time of publication, either of the authors may own shares in one or more of these companies.

Unilever (NYSE:UL; LSE:ULVR)

Unilever is the third-largest global consumer products company with 57 percent of its revenues in 2012 coming from Emerging and Frontier Markets. It makes ice-cream, packaged food, personal care, and cleaning products. Its best known brands include Dove soap, Hellmann's Mayonnaise, Knorr soup, Lipton's Tea, Vaseline body lotion, and Persil laundry detergent. You've probably used a

Unilever product in the last month; the company calculates that it sells 190 billion packs of its products annually and that its products are used more than 2 billion times a day.

With operations in 100 countries and sales in 190, Unilever employs more than 171,000 people and had sales of EU51.3 billion (US$66.7 billion) in 2012, up 10.5 percent (6.9 percent after taking into account the effect of acquisitions and foreign exchange). New Chief Executive Officer Paul Polman, formerly with Nestle and Procter & Gamble, bought Radox and Alberto Culver for US$5 billion in 2010 to increase exposure to the fast-growing personal care area, while selling off smaller brands in the slower-growth food area like Findus Frozen Food in Italy in 2010 for US$1 billion, and Bertolli, P.F. Chang's, and Skippy Peanut Butter in the United States in 2012–2013 for $987 million.

Despite rising 50 percent over the last five years to November 2013 against a 20 percent increase for the UK FTSE100 Index, Unilever sells at a P/E ratio of 17 times 2012 earnings and a dividend yield of 3.2 percent. While no longer cheap, its ability to grow its revenues by mid-to-high single digits over the next few years makes its valuation reasonable. It accomplishes this by acquiring such Emerging and Frontier Markets businesses as Russian beauty and skincare company LLC Concern Kalina, with sales of US$420 million. It bought this company for 82 percent for US$715 million in 2011.

SABMiller (LSE:SAB; OTC:SABMRY)

SABMiller PLC is the second-largest global brewer, with 76 percent of its revenues in the year up March 2012 coming from Emerging and Frontier Markets. It has more than 200 beer brands and 70,000 employees in more than 75 countries. It owns such global brands as Pilsner Urquell (Czech Republic), Peroni Nastro Azzurro (Italy), Miller Genuine Draft (United States), and Grolsch (the Netherlands). Its portfolio of brands also includes such leading local brands as Aguila (Colombia), Castle (South Africa), Miller Lite (U.S.), Snow (China), Victoria Bitter (Australia), and Tyskie (Poland). SABMiller also has a growing soft drinks business and is one of the world's largest Coca-Cola bottlers.

SABMiller was formed from the merger of South African Breweries (SAB) and Miller Brewing in 2003 and has taken over well-known brands such as Peroni, Tyskie, and Grolsch in the last decade. It also paid US$10.2 billion to acquire Fosters, the largest Australian brewer in 2011. In 2006, it acquired control of Bavaria Brewery (Colombia), the leading beer company in Colombia, Peru, Ecuador, Honduras, El Salvador, and Panama, and in 2013 it bought Kingsway Breweries in China for US$864 million. That complemented its existing Snow joint venture, the No.1 brewery in China, which makes the best-selling beer in the world. It also has a joint venture with Coors in the United States, MillerCoors, making it the No.2 brewery in the U.S., and with Andolu Efes of Turkey, covering 16 European countries, including Russia and the Ukraine as well as Turkey.

Over the five years to March 2012, SABMiller's revenues have grown 32 percent to US$31.4 billion, and earnings before interest, tax, and amortization have grown 36 percent to $5.6 billion ($2.14 per share).

Its share price has risen by over 100 percent over the last five years up to November 2013 against a 20 percent increase for the FTSE100. While it is not cheap, given its mid-to-high single-digit increase in revenues expected over the next few years, it is reasonably valued at 18 times 2013's earnings and 1.6 percent dividend yield.

Mead Johnson Nutrition (NYSE:MJN)

Mead Johnson Nutrition is one of the largest global manufacturers of infant formula, making such well-known brands as Enfamil, Sustagen, and Enfagrow and over two-thirds of its revenues came from Asia and Latin America in 2012. Spun off from its parent drug company Bristol Myers Squibb in 2009, it has delivered strong revenue growth as the middle class in developing markets increase their use of infant formula.

Consumption of infant formula per live birth was only 7 kilograms per annum in Emerging and Frontier Markets in 2011, compared to 47 kg. p.a. in the U.S. and 36 kg p.a. in Europe.

Mead Johnson is the number one infant formula maker in China, the world's largest infant nutrition market, worth $8 billion in 2011. Flat sales in 2012 resulted from overstocking, price increases, and accusations by the Chinese government of price fixing against formula makers such as Mead Johnson, Abbott Labs, and Danone in 2013. The companies have strongly denied the charges and the outlook for further long-term growth remains strong. Mead Johnson is also number one in Mexico, Argentina, Thailand, Peru, Ecuador, and Colombia, number two in the Philippines and Malaysia, and number three in Vietnam in infant formula, and number one in Brazil in nutritional supplements.

Revenues grew 7 percent to US$39 billion in 2012 after accounting for foreign exchange movements, and earnings before interest and tax rose 10 percent over the previous year to US$1.15 billion. Although its share price has doubled since its spin-off, the issues in China have meant that it declined slightly in 2013, leaving it on a still-expensive 22 times 2012's earnings and a 1.5 percent dividend yield.

With its ability to produce high single-digit to low double-digit revenue and earnings growth for the next decade, this appears a reasonable valuation for a fast-growing company in markets that still enjoy high birth rates and are increasing their use of infant formula.

Standard Chartered Bank (LSE:STAN; HK:2888)

Standard Chartered Bank plc is a long-established London-headquartered global commercial and investment bank with over 90 percent of its profits coming from Africa, Asia, and the Middle East. Rated A+ by Standard & Poor's (S&P) and A2 by Moody's, it has 1,700 branches and employs more than 85,000 people in 71 countries. Formed by the 1996 merger of Standard Bank of South Africa (founded in 1862) and Chartered Bank (founded in 1858) in Shanghai, Mumbai, and Kolkota, it is one of the three note-issuing banks in Hong Kong. Its stability seems assured since it has the government of Singapore's investment company, Temasek, as its largest shareholder with 11.5 percent.

Takeovers in the last few years have made it the largest foreign bank in India and South Korea, and among the ten largest banks in Pakistan, Indonesia, Taiwan, and Thailand. Operating income grew 50 percent to US$17.6 billion in 2012, while pre-tax profit was down slightly at $6.5 billion due to fines of US$667 million by American federal and state authorities for misreporting transactions for Iranian clients. The transactions had breached sanctions. Nonetheless, with approximately 40 percent of its assets from consumers and 60 percent from businesses, and 24 different countries making profits of more than US$100 million a year, the bank is exceptionally well diversified.

Over the last five years, Standard Chartered has only performed in line with the FTSE100 Index, up 20 percent, and as a result, sells for a very reasonable P/E ratio of 13.5 times 2012's earnings and a 2.8 percent dividend yield.

Diageo (NYSE:DEO; LSE:DGE)

Diageo is the largest global spirits company and derived 45 percent of its revenues from Emerging and Frontier Markets in the year up to June 2012. Formed from the merger of brewer and Scotch whisky producer Guinness with conglomerate Grand Metropolitan in 1997, its major brands include Johnnie Walker and J&B scotch, Seagram's VO and Crown Royal Canadian whiskies, Smirnoff vodka, Captain Morgan's rum, Gordon's and Tanqueray gin, Bailey's Irish Cream, Guinness Irish stout, and Harp Lager. It also owns a 34 percent stake in French wine and spirits group Moet-Hennessy Louis Vuitton. It made a net profit of $4.2 billion on sales of $24.8 billion in the year to June 30, 2013.

A study by HIS Global Insight estimated that consumption of alcoholic beverages in Emerging and Frontier Markets totaled US$8.5 trillion in 2012 and will more than double to $20.5 trillion by 2022. One-third of that will be in China, another quarter in the three remaining BRIC countries of Brazil, Russia, and India, and 13 percent in Mexico, Indonesia, and Turkey. Given this strong growth, Diageo has acquired emerging and frontier spirits groups such as United Spirits and the leading Turkish spirits maker Mey Icki for US$2.1 billion in 2011. In addition, it bought the second largest Ethiopian beer maker, Meta Abo Brewer, for US$225 million in 2012 and in Brazil bought the Ypioca Group, one of the leading cachaça makers there for US$480 million. Cachaça is the leading spirits category in Brazil.

At the end of November 2013, Diageo was selling for 18 times 2012–2013's earnings and had a 2.4 percent dividend yield. With organic sales growth of 6 percent to 8 percent p.a. after foreign exchange movements are removed and earnings growth of 7 percent to 9 percent p.a., the valuation seems reasonable for a defensive way to play rising middle-class incomes in Emerging and Frontier Markets.

Yum! Brands (NYSE:YUM)

Yum! Brands owns the KFC, Pizza Hut, and Taco Bell fast food chains and ranks as one of the largest global fast food chains with over 37,000 outlets in 2012. Approximately 75 percent of its US$12 billion in sales were outside of the U.S., with 44 percent in China alone. KFC operated 4,000 restaurants in more than 800 cities in China last year while Pizza Hut had 700 outlets and 140 home delivery units there. Yum! Brands India had 220 KFCs, 170 Pizza Huts, and over 100 home delivery units. It also acquired the 425-outlet Little Sheep dine-in Chinese restaurants in 2011.

In 2012, Yum was hit by a health scare in China over excessive levels of antibiotics in its chicken supplies, which led to an 8 percent decline in same store sales in the fourth quarter for KFC and over 20 percent decline in 2013. KFC was not fined by the authorities, and has strengthened its supply-chain management, while opening 895 new stores in China in 2012 and over 700 in 2013. While earnings per share are forecast to be flat in 2013, this has left the company on a forecast P/E ratio of 24 times and a dividend yield of 2.1 percent. Although the fall in KFC's sales in China has caused a break in

Yum's sequence of 11 years of earnings-per-share growth above 13 percent, growth in China should resume if it successfully addresses health concerns. Yum is expensive but provides a concentrated exposure to rising consumer incomes in Emerging and Frontier Markets.

Vodafone (NYSE:VOD; LSE:VOD)

Vodafone is one the world's largest mobile telephone operators, with 72 percent of its revenues derived from Emerging and Frontier Markets after the sale of its 45 percent stake in Verizon Wireless in 2013 for $130 billion. Of that, 38 percent comes from India, 14 percent from Africa, and 10 percent each from Egypt and Eastern Europe. The remainder comes from the United Kingdom (5 percent), Germany (8 percent), and southern Europe (12 percent).

The sale price of its minority stake in the largest U.S. mobile telephone operator was considered satisfactory and will result in a distribution of US$84 billion to shareholders after the US$5 billion in expected capital gains tax. This will leave Vodafone with US$10 billion to invest in upgrading its networks, as well as with enough cash to make further Emerging and Frontier Markets acquisitions such as its transforming takeover of Hutchison's Wind mobile phone operations in India five years ago.

With revenues of US$71 billion in the year to March 31, 2013, and net profit of US$11 billion before exceptional expenses, Vodafone is selling for a very reasonable P/E ratio of 11.5 times and a dividend yield before special payments of 4.5 percent. It is the global mobile telephone operator with the highest exposure to Emerging and Frontier Markets. That may increase if it uses some of its deal proceeds to buy more operators in those markets.

Sherritt Corporation (TSX:S)

Sherritt is one of the world's largest producers of lateritic nickel ore and cobalt from its 50 percent-owned Moa joint venture in Cuba, where it also operates electricity plants that provide 10 percent of the country's electricity and oil fields producing 20,000 barrels a day. It has recently bought the Ambatovy nickel mine and refinery operation in Madagascar, which is forecast to be the largest nickel mine in the world when it reaches full production.

Its 50-year involvement with Cuba has meant that its senior management is banned from visiting the United States and it's not allowed to list its securities on American exchanges. For that reason, it trades on the Toronto TSX Exchange. With 21 percent of its assets in Cuba and 31 percent in its 40 percent joint venture in Madagascar, Sherritt is also the largest producer of thermal coal for power plants in Canada and mines coal for export as well as producing phosphate fertilizer.

With the price of nickel and cobalt falling by one-third in the two years to 2013 due to the slowdown in Chinese demand, Sherritt's revenues and earnings have also declined. However, cash flow remains positive and the company remains rated BB by S&P, as the Ambatovy joint venture is non-recourse to the shareholders until output reaches 70 percent of capacity. That is not forecast to occur until early 2014.

Sherritt is selling at forecast P/E ratio of 7 times 2014's earnings and a 5 percent dividend yield. It is a cheap way to access growth in Cuba's economy and a turnaround in the nickel and cobalt price as demand revives from Emerging Markets.

British American Tobacco International (AMEX:BTI; LSE:BATS)

British American Tobacco is the most international of the major tobacco companies and its major brands of Dunhill, Kent, Lucky Strike, and Pall Mall are used worldwide. In 2012, 33 percent of its volume came from Eastern Europe (including Russia), 27 percent from Asia Pacific, 20 percent from the Americas including Latin America, and only 18.5 percent from the declining markets of Western Europe.

Sales of cigarettes and tobaccos for BAT continue to decline by around 3 percent per annum. However, price increases and upgrading to more expensive brands perceived to be "classier" by smokers in Emerging and Frontier Markets has meant that BAT and its rivals have been seeing 3 percent revenue growth in constant currency terms over the last few years. With revenues of US$24 billion and net earnings of US$8.9 billion in 2012, BAT was selling on a reasonable P/E of 15 times and a dividend yield of 4 percent. The company is in a declining industry, but as long as cigarettes remain an affordable pleasure for the inhabitants of the Emerging and Frontier Markets, the growth in these markets and price increases in developed markets will continue to make tobacco companies very profitable.

PZ Cussons (LSE:PZC)

PZ Cussons is a consumer products company with over 60 percent of its revenues from operations in Africa, especially Nigeria and Ghana, and Asia, particularly in Indonesia.

It makes Imperial Leather soap and is vertically integrated as it refines the palm oil to manufacture soaps and personal care products. It also produces edible oils and spreads as well as infant nutrition products and washing detergents and consumer electrical products with its Chinese partner Haier.

Its sales have grown in the high single digits to $1.4 billion in the year to May 2013, and with its net profits of $115 million, it was selling at a P/E ratio of 22.5 times and a dividend yield of 2 percent. With its new palm oil refinery and efficiencies made in its supply chain, Cussons is a good play on rising consumer incomes in Frontier and Emerging Markets.

Chapter 20

The Ten Riskiest Frontier Markets

In This Chapter

▶ Researching the riskiest Frontier Market countries

▶ Understanding why you shouldn't invest in some countries

*Y*ou can justifiably believe that all Frontier Markets have at least some risk if you define risk as volatility. However, as we have noted elsewhere, adding Frontier Markets to an existing portfolio reduces its volatility as they are not correlated with either developed or Emerging Markets.

Individual Frontier Markets themselves are quite volatile. However, as we have also noted, volatility should not be confused with risk in the sense of permanently losing your initial capital. In the end, that is the *real* risk of investing in the less-developed markets that have low standards of corporate governance and political culture.

The following list contains the ten countries where we believe you have the greatest risk of suffering a permanent loss of capital in the absence of a significant change in circumstances within the next few years. We do not go into as much detail as with those countries we feel are the most promising Frontier Markets, because we think you should be very cautious about investing in these markets.

Argentina

Argentina's position at the top of the list of risky markets shouldn't come as a surprise if you've read any of the discussions about it in other chapters of the book. Its decline from one of the wealthiest countries in the world on a per-capita basis a century ago to being downgraded from Emerging to Frontier Market status in 2009 is a sad story of wasted advantages, including natural resources, a well-educated population, and decent infrastructure. Argentina is a great example of the importance of the political culture of a nation determining its fate.

Responsible for several notable bankruptcies in the 19th century, Argentina continued its tradition of taking foreign investors' money and then reneging on its obligations or nationalizing the assets that foreign capital had built in the second half of the 20th century. That culminated in the then-biggest ever international default of US$83 billion in 2001–2002. Add to that the hyperinflation and military dictatorship in the 1970s and an unsuccessful foreign war in the Falklands in 1982, and Argentina's ruling elite has proven again and again that it will take the easy path of blaming foreigners and exploiting its own citizens rather than follow sensible economic policies. Note, however, that while some individual Argentinean ADRs may be worth buying as short-term trades, investors should steer clear until we see a clear change of attitude by the country's government.

Ukraine

A country with natural resources and a well-educated population, Ukraine has, like many members of the Former Soviet Union (FSU), been handicapped by the legacy of its Soviet-era politics. While its geographic situation right next to Russia, making it the major gateway for any invader, was always likely to make it difficult for Ukraine to steer an independent path, Russia's determination to prevent Ukraine from joining western organizations such as the European Union and the North American Treaty Organization has led to severe economic consequences, including gas supply problems. The most recent series of protests in December 2013 against President Yanukovich's decision to not sign a trade agreement with the European Union, instead choosing to become a closer partner of Vladimir Putin's Russia, illustrates the difficulties Ukraine faces in reforming its system.

With politics deadlocked by the struggle between pro- and anti-Russian parties, necessary reforms in energy pricing and denationalization of inefficient state-owned industries have been postponed, leaving the economy relatively unproductive and losing competitiveness. Considering also its declining birth rate and high median age, its longer-term future appears unattractive and its stock market remains underdeveloped.

Iran

With its youthful, relatively well-educated and large population (79.8 million), extensive oil and gas reserves, and well-developed stock market, Iran should rank at the top of any list of promising Frontier Markets. Indeed Goldman Sachs made it one of its Next 11 markets most likely to succeed the BRICs (the Emerging Market acronym referring to Brazil, Russia, India, and China). However, all of these positive factors cannot offset a regime that sees itself as the leader of the Islamic Revolution against the forces of the United States, alias the Great Satan.

For more than 35 years, Iran has supported groups and regimes that have been generally anti-Western and more specifically anti-American. These groups and regimes include opponents of conservative Arab regimes such as Saudi Arabia, the Gulf Emirates, and Egypt under the Mubarak regime. Its attempt to create a nuclear capability in the last decade has led to sanctions against the regime from the U.S., Canada, and the European Union. Despite the tentative agreement between Iran and the western powers to suspend some sanctions in late 2013 for a 6-month period, unless attempts to end or suspend the nuclear program prove permanently successful, Iran will remain closed to foreign investment. Even if such an attempt succeeds, the Islamic regime remains hostile to capitalism and western influences such as freedom of speech and assembly.

Venezuela

Like Argentina, Venezuela is another South American economy included among developed countries in the first half of the last century and now downgraded to frontier status as the result of consistently misguided policies. This process culminated in the election of the late Hugo Chavez in 1999, who epitomized the populist tendencies of many Latin American leaders in the 20th century with his Bolivarian Revolution policies of price controls, nationalization, and anti-American rhetoric between 1999 and his death in 2013. Even before his arrival, despite its extensive natural resources and relatively well-educated population, it had not been a well-governed country.

Its very large reserves of oil have been as much a curse as a blessing, permitting governments to bribe the population with cheap energy and provide foreign currency to pursue policies of redistribution. With loyalty to the regime prized above competence, Venezuela's infrastructure has gradually been eroding, with the result that despite being a major oil exporter, it now needs to import refined products, due to its aging refineries and the absence of trained staff to run them. While individual Venezuelan ADRs may be worth trading on a short-term basis, the country does not appear to be an attractive investment destination until there is a change in regime.

Serbia

Despite its strategic geographic position at the center of Balkan trade routes and a well-educated population, Serbia, the rump state of the former Yugoslavia, remains an unattractive investment given the legacy of its failed conflicts with other former members of Yugoslavia — Croatia, Bosnia, and Kosovo — between 1991 and 1998. The post-breakup civil war led to bombing strikes by the North Atlantic Treaty Organization on Belgrade, the Serbian capital. It also led to ongoing court cases at the International Court of Justice in The Hague for wartime atrocities. International sanctions caused longer lasting damage and were finally removed in 2001. However, they had led to constraints on international investment and access to funds from multilateral institutions like the World Bank and the International Monetary Fund.

While conditions have improved since the easing of sanctions and some multinational companies are examining major investments, Serbia's stock market remains underdeveloped and the attitude of its leadership towards capitalism and pro-growth policies appears uncertain. That can be especially troubling since many of these individuals have a Communist background.

Azerbaijan

Despite its extensive energy resources and infrastructure projects such as the Baku Tbilisi Ceyhan (BTC) oil pipeline, which provides an export route to shipping Azerbaijan's oil as an alternative to shipping only via Russia, this member of the FSU displays many of the less-attractive features of resource-dominated Frontier Markets. Like Venezuela, Azerbaijan has extensive energy exports to provide hard currency inflows which allow the regime to bribe its population with cheap energy. This also allows a relatively high standard of living while enabling the leadership and its allies to accumulate wealth.

When combined with an ethnic conflict with neighboring Armenia over the primarily Armenian region of Nagorno-Karabakh within its boundaries, the overall case for investment is not attractive and until there is a change of regime, Azerbaijan seems likely to remain regarded as a risky destination. That contrasts with the other FSU economy with extensive energy reserves in the Caspian Sea. Kazakhstan demonstrates that political leadership can make a major difference even when the underlying economies are similar.

Lebanon

Formerly regarded as the Switzerland of the Middle East, Lebanon had ranked as the region's tourism and banking center with a complicated but stable government structure that balanced the interests of Christian and Muslim sects and national minorities. The Israeli-Palestinian conflict in the early 1980s destroyed this balance and led to civil war and the creation of independent *statelets* within Lebanon.

It currently remains a divided state, despite its well-educated and relatively wealthy population, the rebuilding of the capital Beirut after some stability was restored under leadership of its neighbor Syria in the last decade, and the apparent success of the more moderate groups in the Lebanese elections in 2010.

The descent of its neighbor Syria into civil war removed the control it had exercised to maintain stability in Lebanon, which now has an uncertain outlook. The safe haven financial flows that might have flowed to Lebanon in earlier years now go to the United Arab Emirates and Qatar and the possibility of a Mideast conflict involving Lebanon remains high.

The Democratic Republic of the Congo (DRC)

The government of the former Belgian Congo, perhaps the worst ruled of the former colonial states in Africa, has continued its track record of exploiting the population and natural resources for its own benefit. With the fall in 1997 of President Mobutu Sese Seko's regime, which had ruled the Congo (renamed Zaire as part of his attempt to de-colonialize the country) for 35 years, his replacements have struggled to maintain central control over the vast country. Mobutu had run the country as his personal fiefdom and his rule was characterized as a *kleptocracy,* or robber state. He and his family are estimated to have stolen between US$4 billion and $15 billion during his regime.

Since his overthrow and death, the country has suffered from rebellions in its eastern provinces, some them inspired by refugees from the ethnic conflicts in neighboring Rwanda. It is estimated that over 5 million inhabitants out of a population of 75 million have died since the civil wars began in 1998, although the government of President Joseph Kabila has regained control of most of the country since 2009. In the meantime, the DRC's extensive natural resources, particularly copper and other minerals, remain underdeveloped. Foreign investors (such as Canada's First Quantum Mining) that

296 Part V: The Part of Tens

had developed mines saw them expropriated in 2010 in favor of other groups rumored to have political connections. The DRC remains an unattractive destination for foreign investors at present.

Zimbabwe

Once the breadbasket of Southern Africa and a major exporter of grain and tobacco, the policies of President Robert Mugabe have reduced Zimbabwe to poverty in the last 20 years. His expropriation of commercial properties owned by white farm owners in the late 1990s led to a 45 percent fall in output, starvation, and 80 percent unemployment. Meanwhile, the government's printing of money to fund its deficits and involvement in the civil war in the DRC led to hyperinflation in 2007–2008 and the replacement of the local currency by the South African rand and US dollar.

While the economy has stabilized and the opposition parties led by Morgan Tsangvirai were allowed to control some ministries after an indecisive election in 2009, Zimbabwe remains among the poorest frontier economies with a real gross domestic product per capita of only $500 per annum. Ironically, its stock market is one of the largest in Africa outside of South Africa as stocks were the only asset class that retained their real value during the period of hyperinflation. Until there is a change in regime, an unlikely turn of event given the reelection in 2013 of 89-year-old Mugabe, Zimbabwe remains unattractive despite its many natural resources and well-developed stock market.

Libya

Libya's economy suffered during and after the civil war that led to the overthrow and death of long-ruling dictator Muammar Qaddafi in 2011. Exports of its principal natural resource, light crude oil, have been substantially reduced by damage to its infrastructure and the takeover of some oil fields by rebel groups. The government's control of the country remains tenuous, as demonstrated in 2012 by the successful attack on the American consulate in Tripoli and in 2013 by the kidnapping and release of the Prime Minister.

While its geographic location — close to its major export markets in Europe and possession of substantial reserves of good quality oil and gas — make Libya a potentially attractive destination for investment, the absence of established institutions and tribal conflicts mean that the risks of investing there are too high to justify even a small investment.

Chapter 21

Ten Mistakes to Avoid When Investing in Frontier Markets

*I*n any endeavor — whether a new job or new investments, the rules are usually clear about what you *should* do. However, the sand traps — the things you *should not do* — are often much less clear. Consider the very meaning of the word *frontier*. It refers to untapped opportunities that no one has completely mapped, but that hold the attraction of new discoveries and of new riches for those brave enough to venture across the boundaries.

We're still figuring out what's involved and proceeding carefully. After all, Frontier Markets really only started becoming available to retail investors in 2008 with the launch of the Templeton Frontier Markets Fund.

In other chapters of this book, we suggest some of the dos of frontier investing. In this chapter, we suggest the don'ts. These mistakes can mean opportunity cost at best or at worst, real cost.

We didn't carry out a scientific survey to arrive at this list of mistakes. Between us, we've spent over five decades working with fund managers, advisors, and investors and so have repeatedly observed these mistakes at close range.

One secret to effective investing in any category is the quality of information on which you base your decision. Doing your own research with materials from reputable publishers and obtaining good advice from a trusted financial advisor will help you avoid most of the mistakes listed in this chapter. Frontier Market investing is still new and we're still figuring out what works in this investment category so we start by looking at some core mistakes that could cost you money in any investment category at any time.

Having Insufficient Liquidity

Insufficient liquidity means not having sufficient wiggle room in your portfolio to allow for emergencies. How many individuals do you know who cashed in all or part of an asset that had become depressed during the Financial Crisis of 2009-2009 — not so much because they wanted to be rid of it, but because they needed money and couldn't wait for it to recover? Have you found yourself in that position? Have you ever had to cash in an asset that you would have left intact otherwise? You can avoid this unhappy state of financial affairs by ensuring that your asset allocation contains enough cash and near-cash holdings to allow for any reasonable emergency.

To avoid having to liquidate an asset such as a mutual fund prematurely, calculate how much cash you would need to cover all possible developments, including job loss, medical problems not covered by insurance, and family emergencies. Include the amount you need for ongoing living expenses and then add 10 percent to that figure for life's unforeseen surprises. And after 2008–2009, we certainly know that we are going to face some unforeseen surprises. Keep that amount in cash or near-cash instruments such as bank certificates and fixed income investments. From there, set up your asset allocation, which will include a proportion of frontier investments.

You can avoid this mistake by building up your asset allocation plan with a knowledgeable financial advisor. An asset allocation plan is always important and you can finish the job by sticking to it!

Messing Up Your Asset Allocation

Sometimes an individual has an online trading account that he or she may "forget" to mention to the otherwise trusted financial advisor. Meanwhile, the well-meaning advisor has carefully constructed an asset allocation plan that takes into account the individual's needs, obligations, investment horizon, known assets, risk tolerance, and other considerations. However, when the individual has a sizeable online trading account unknown to the advisor, it throws the asset allocation out of whack. Advisors anecdotally suggest that these accounts tend to hold more risky investments that they would not normally likely include in the client's investment portfolio. This means that the client may have more money actually at risk than would be justified, more than the advisor comprehends and more than actually appears to be the case.

You can avoid this situation by telling your financial advisor *everything*. If you are not comfortable with that, you may need to look for another advisor. Then come to an agreement with your advisor about the difference between how the advisor structures your investments and how you structure your online account.

In a typical scenario, the advisor might handle long-term value investments while you do the more risky trading in your online portfolio.

Tell your financial advisor everything and do regular reviews which include the mandates of each portion of your wealth. As well as keeping the asset allocation intact, this strategy reminds both parties of the function of each portion of wealth.

For example, the mandate of the Frontier Markets component should be long-term growth but it would not be short-term liquidity. The mandate of fixed income assets could be short-term liquidity but it would not be long-term growth. The mandate of your online trading account could be momentum investing.

Overestimating Risk Tolerance

You may be especially prone to this mistake when markets are doing well. During 2007 when stock markets were rising, we periodically heard the phrase "a rising tide lifts all boats," meaning that many stocks — both solid and not-so-solid — rose in share value. With that kind of market it was easy to take risks on growth stocks.

Then we had the Financial Crisis and many investors learned they could not deal quite as well with risk as they had believed.

Estimate how much of your portfolio you can honestly afford to have at risk. In most cases, this would not exceed 15 percent of nonregistered assets. As with most other financial planning strategies this varies with the individual. Ask yourself honestly about your own threshold.

Confusing Growth in a Country's GDP with Its Stock Market Performance

A common error often made by investors in rapidly growing economies such as Emerging and Frontier Markets occurs when an investor confuses a rise in gross domestic product (GDP) growth with stock performance. Just because a country grows rapidly, this does not mean that this growth will be reflected in the performance of stocks.

Often, companies listed on the stock market in developing countries are not from those sectors that are experiencing rapid growth, or the government may own the companies in that sector. Alternatively, even if the government privatizes some of these companies, it may control the prices that they are allowed to charge, or how rapidly they can lay off workers for reasons of social policy. This is an anomaly that has happened with Chinese investments, (although we note that China is an Emerging Market, not a Frontier Market). Chinese GDP has grown at over 7 percent per annum for the last decade, yet the Shanghai Stock Index is no higher than it was in 2005.

Letting Your Emotions Control Your Decisions

A sudden drop in share prices can lead to a costly decision to sell the shares. How many people do you know who sold shares during the panic of 2008, only to find that those shares recovered over time? We know that it is most profitable to buy low and sell high but panic can lead to selling low. Frontier Market investments are particularly vulnerable to this phenomenon, as they are very volatile, partially because they are not very liquid at present.

To avoid selling at the wrong time, do your research, speak to a qualified financial advisor, and as with other areas of life, never make a decision in the heat of the moment. You can counter this mistake by looking past what has recently happened and focusing on what you and your advisor believe is going to happen.

Any investment in Frontier Markets needs a horizon of at least five years, and, although we recognize this is difficult, you should, to the best of your ability, ignore what is happening on a day-to-day basis and leave your Frontier Market fund alone to grow undisturbed.

Being Susceptible to Home Bias

Being susceptible to home bias means restricting your investments to familiar names on your home turf. This provides comforting reassurance but forecloses the opportunities provided by Frontier Markets. Perhaps lack of familiarity breeds contempt — the opposite of the old maxim which suggested exactly the opposite result with familiarity. For example, most investors are not familiar with the opportunities in African stock markets but at the time of writing, a number of equities in these markets have provided handsome returns. How familiar are you with the high returns of some African markets during 2012? Do some research and speak to your advisor before dismissing Africa as a suitable investment for your portfolio.

Investing in Frontier Markets can be like any other form of venturing into the unknown — try a small amount first and then increase it when you build your confidence.

Confusing Volatility with Risk

Most investment research analysis defines volatility as the propensity of an investment to post sharply fluctuating values over time. This is known as the standard deviation of returns. This definition was primarily chosen because it's easy to measure, but says nothing about what most investors would define as risk, which is the potential for permanent loss of an initial investment outlay. We would define risk as the likelihood that an investment will sharply fall in value without chance of recovery.

Given the volatility inherent in most Frontier Markets and the likelihood that this volatility will continue, you and your advisor need to ensure that you clearly understand the difference between volatility and risk and that you are comfortable with the outlook for this asset class. Understanding this difference allows you to be more relaxed about the volatility that occurs in Frontier Markets. Investing through an actively managed Global Frontier Markets Fund helps reduce volatility, because Frontier Markets are not correlated with each other. Some will move in the opposite direction to others, reducing the overall volatility of the fund.

Tarring an Entire Region with the Same Brush

Not all countries in a particular region suffer from the same pressures and problems at the same time. As we write this book, several countries in the Middle East are in tumult and it would be easy to decide to avoid any equities or funds that have MENA (Middle East and North Africa) holdings. That rush to judgement overlooks several realities. The Middle East is no more a single homogenous region — whether politically or for investment decisions — than the whole of Europe is a single homogenous region.

Notwithstanding the tragedies occurring in Syria at the time of writing, the United Arab Emirates and Qatar maintain their status as safe havens in the region. Longer term, if the Saudi Arabia authorities proceed with a plan to open the Tadawul, as the Saudi exchange is known, to foreign investors and if the owners of large family businesses in Saudi Arabia monetize some of their holdings, the stock market in Saudi Arabia will expand several times over.

Avoid generalizing about any country and any region whether in Frontier Markets or any other markets. During the recent European crisis, it would have been a costly mistake to generalize about the entire region, as some economies, such as Germany and the United Kingdom, continued to perform while the southern tier countries of the Euro-zone, such as Greece, Portugal, and Spain, suffered recessions.

Keeping Clear on the Purpose and Function of Your Frontier Investments

Understanding your investment portfolio goes beyond checking the dollar figures. It includes understanding the investment function of each asset. Some assets, such as cash and near-cash investments, provide a hedge against your ongoing cash needs and sudden emergencies. Some growth assets such as domestic equity funds give you a stake in the country's economy.

However, the function of Frontier equity funds is to provide long-term growth with a minimum five-year horizon, while reducing the volatility of your total portfolio, as they are not correlated with either developed or emerging equity markets. That doesn't necessarily mean you won't see serious growth in less than five years, but it does mean that we urge you to use your frontier investments as a long-term proposition.

Selecting the Right Destination but Wrong Venue

This mistake includes putting all your Frontier dollars into one country, a mistake exacerbated by the political volatility of some Frontier countries. You can avoid this costly error by investing in an actively managed Global Frontier Markets Fund in which the manager can over-weight those countries doing well and under-weight those experiencing political or economic problems.

You may have noticed that we frequently suggest both that you do your own research and that you consult your financial advisor. Frontier Market investing is still new and a coherent approach to it offers the chance to invest in some of the fastest-growing economies in the world. But be sure you have a strong, knowledgeable guide to separate the risk from the volatility and to diversify your portfolio safely.

If you ever decide to travel to one of these countries for a holiday, you would most likely do a fair amount of research before your trip and in many cases you would explore the country with a tour guide. This combination would likely give you a greater comfort level in strange surroundings and ensure that you do not make any mistakes resulting from inexperience. We suggest applying the same principle when you invest in Frontier Markets.

When venturing into unknown investment territory, do your research and get a good advisor. Then choose an actively managed Global Frontier Markets Fund with a good track record, allowing the experienced fund manager to make the investment decisions on your behalf. This is not the time to go it alone.

Appendix

A Quick Survey of Some Emerging and Frontier Market Countries

● ●

*I*n the following tables, we list key statistical information for many Frontier Market countries. For comparison, you'll also find a few Emerging Market and Exotic Frontier Market countries as well.

	Angola	*Argentina*	*Bangladesh*
Population (mil)	18.6	42.6	163.6
Age % 0-14	44	25	33
Age % 15-64	52	64	62
Age % 65+	4	11	5
Median Age	17.7	31	23.9
Pop Growth %	2.8	1	1.6
GDP 2012 (PPP) — $bil	126.2	746.9	305.5
GDP Growth % 2012	6.8	2.6	6.1
GDP Growth % 2011	3.9	8.9	6.5
GDP per Capita 2012	$6,800	$18,200	$2,000
GDP per Capita 2011	$6,000	$17,900	$1,900
Unemployment % 2012	NA	7.2	5
Government	Democracy	Democracy	Democracy

	Botswana	*Brazil*	*Bulgaria*
Population (mil)	2.1	201.1	7
Age % 0-14	33	24	14
Age % 15-64	63	69	67
Age % 65+	4	7	19
Median Age	22.7	30.3	42.3
Pop Growth %	1.3	0.8	-0.8
GDP 2012 (PPP) — $bil	32.7	2,360	103.7
GDP Growth % 2012	7.7	1.3	1
GDP Growth % 2011	5.1	2.7	1.7
GDP per Capita 2012	$16,800	$12,000	$14,200
GDP per Capita 2011	$16,400	$12,000	$14,000
Unemployment % 2012	17.8	6.2	9.9
Government	Democracy	Democracy	Democracy

	Colombia	*Croatia*	*Ecuador*
Population (mil)	45.7	4.5	15.4
Age % 0-14	26	15	29
Age % 15-64	67	68	64
Age % 65+	7	17	7
Median Age	28.6	40.8	26.3
Pop Growth %	1.1	-0.1	1.4
GDP 2012 (PPP) — $bil	500	79.1	134.7
GDP Growth % 2012	4.3	-1.8	4
GDP Growth % 2011	5.9	0	7.8
GDP per Capita 2012	$10,700	$18,100	$8,800
GDP per Capita 2011	$10,400	$18,300	$8,600
Unemployment % 2012	10.3	20.4	4.1
Government	Democracy	Democracy	Democracy

	Egypt	*Ghana*	*India*
Population (mil)	85.3	25.2	1220.8
Age % 0-14	32	39	29
Age % 15-64	63	57	65
Age % 65+	5	4	6
Median Age	24.8	20.7	26.7
Pop Growth %	1.9	2.2	1.3
GDP 2012 (PPP) — $bil	537.9	83.2	4,784
GDP Growth % 2012	2	8.2	6.5
GDP Growth % 2011	1.8	14.4	6.8
GDP per Capita 2012	$6,600	$3,300	$3,900
GDP per Capita 2011	$6,600	$3,200	$3,700
Unemployment % 2012	12.5	11	10
Government	Democracy	Democracy	Democracy

	Kazkhstan	*Kenya*	*Kuwait*
Population (mil)	17.7	44	2.7
Age % 0-14	25	42	27
Age % 15-64	68	55	71
Age % 65+	7	3	2
Median Age	29.5	18.9	28.8
Pop Growth %	1.2	2.3	1.8
GDP 2012 (PPP) — $bil	231.3	76.1	165.9
GDP Growth % 2012	5	5.1	6.3
GDP Growth % 2011	7.5	4.4	8.2
GDP per Capita 2012	$13,900	$1,800	$43,800
GDP per Capita 2011	$13,200	$1,800	$42,400
Unemployment % 2012	5.2	40	2.2
Government	Autocracy	Democracy	Monarchy

	Lebanon	*Lithuania*	*Namibia*
Population (mil)	4.1	3.5	2.2
Age % 0-14	22	14	33
Age % 15-64	69	69	63
Age % 65+	9	17	4
Median Age	30.9	40.8	22.4
Pop Growth %	-0.04	-0.3	0.8
GDP 2012 (PPP) — $bil	63.7	64.8	16.9
GDP Growth % 2012	2	3.5	4.6
GDP Growth % 2011	1.5	5.9	4.9
GDP per Capita 2012	$15,900	$20,100	$7,800
GDP per Capita 2011	$15,800	$19,400	$7,600
Unemployment % 2012	NA	13.2	51.2
Government	Democracy	Democracy	Democracy

	Nigeria	*Pakistan*	*Peru*
Population (mil)	174.5	193.2	29.8
Age % 0-14	44	34	28
Age % 15-64	53	62	65
Age % 65+	3	4	7
Median Age	17.9	22.2	26.7
Pop Growth %	2.5	1.5	1
GDP 2012 (PPP) — $bil	450.5	514.8	325.4
GDP Growth % 2012	7.1	3.7	6
GDP Growth % 2011	7.4	3	6.9
GDP per Capita 2012	$2,700	$2,900	$10,700
GDP per Capita 2011	$2,600	$2,800	$10,400
Unemployment % 2012	23.9	5	7.7
Government	Democracy	Democracy	Democracy

	Qatar	*Romania*	*Russia*
Population (mil)	2	21.8	142.5
Age % 0-14	13	15	16
Age % 15-64	86	70	71
Age % 65+	1	15	13
Median Age	32.4	39.4	38.8
Pop Growth %	4.2	-0.3	-0.02
GDP 2012 (PPP) — $bil	189	274.1	2,504
GDP Growth % 2012	6.3	0.9	3.4
GDP Growth % 2011	14.1	2.2	4.3
GDP per Capita 2012	$102,800	$12,800	$17,700
GDP per Capita 2011	$88,300	$12,700	$17,000
Unemployment % 2012	0.5	6.5	5.7
Government	Monarchy	Democracy	Democracy

	Serbia	*Slovakia*	*Slovenia*
Population (mil)	7.2	5.5	1.99
Age % 0-14	15	16	13
Age % 15-64	68	71	69
Age % 65+	17	13	18
Median Age	41.7	38.4	43.1
Pop Growth %	-0.5	0.1	-0.2
GDP 2012 (PPP) — $bil	78.4	132.4	58.1
GDP Growth % 2012	-2	2.6	-2
GDP Growth % 2011	1.6	3.3	0.6
GDP per Capita 2012	$10,500	$24,300	$28,600
GDP per Capita 2011	$10,600	$23,700	$28,800
Unemployment % 2012	22.4	12.8	11.9
Government	Democracy	Democracy	Democracy

	South Africa	*Sri Lanka*	*Tanzania*
Population (mil)	48.6	21.7	48.3
Age % 0-14	28	25	45
Age % 15-64	66	67	51
Age % 65+	6	8	4
Median Age	25.5	31.4	17.3
Pop Growth %	-0.5	0.9	2.8
GDP 2012 (PPP) — $bil	578.6	125.3	73.5
GDP Growth % 2012	2.6	6	6.5
GDP Growth % 2011	3.1	8.3	6.4
GDP per Capita 2012	$11,300	$6,100	$1,700
GDP per Capita 2011	$11,100	$5,800	$1,600
Unemployment % 2012	22.7	4.5	NA
Government	Democracy	Democracy	Democracy

	Tunisia	*UAE*	*Ukraine*
Population (mil)	10.8	5.5	44.5
Age % 0-14	23	21	14
Age % 15-64	69	78	70
Age % 65+	8	1	16
Median Age	31	30.3	40.3
Pop Growth %	0.9	2.9	-0.6
GDP 2012 (PPP) — $bil	104.4	271.2	335.4
GDP Growth % 2012	2.7	4	0.2
GDP Growth % 2011	-1.8	5.2	5.2
GDP per Capita 2012	$9,700	$49,000	$7,600
GDP per Capita 2011	$9,500	$48,500	$7,300
Unemployment % 2012	18.8	2.4	7.4
Government	Democracy	Monarchy	Democracy

	Venezuela	*Vietnam*	*Zimbabwe*
Population (mil)	28.5	92.5	13.2
Age % 0-14	29	25	39
Age % 15-64	65	69	57
Age % 65+	6	6	4
Median Age	26.6	29	19.5
Pop Growth %	1.4	1	4.4
GDP 2012 (PPP) — $bil	402.1	320.1	6.9
GDP Growth % 2012	5.7	5	5
GDP Growth % 2011	4.2	5.9	9.4
GDP per Capita 2012	$13,200	$3,500	$500
GDP per Capita 2011	$12,800	$3,400	$500
Unemployment % 2012	8	4.5	95
Government	Democracy	Communist	Democracy

Index

Notes

Notes

Notes

Notes

Notes

Notes

Authors' Acknowledgments

I would like to thank my wonderful family, including our three always stimulating children, for helping me with this book. As my youngest daughter said, "Daddy, do you have to be a dummy to write a *For Dummies* book? But I don't think you're so dumb." I'd also like to thank all of the fund managers, analysts, and journalists who manage money, analyze companies, or cover stories in the Frontier Markets whose input helped us complete this book.

—Gavin Graham, March 2014

I would like to thank the *For Dummies* editors for their unstinting support of this book and their understanding of the editor-author relationship. No one ever suggested that it was an easy relationship, but it works when the central core is a shared vision of the goal of the text, and we enjoyed and valued that advantage.

I would also like to extend special thanks to Steve Spector, JD MLS, for his comprehensive research, and appreciation of the intricacies of Emerging and Frontier Markets investing.

—Al Emid, March 2014

About the Authors

Gavin Graham has over 30 years experience in investment, particularly in asset management, having started his investing career in the City of London in 1979, where he spent eight years working for major UK institutions before moving to Hong Kong in 1988. In his eight years based there, he managed money for several leading Asian investment houses, including running the original Tiger Fund and the largest UK-listed closed-end Asian investment fund for Thornton Management, finishing as Senior Investment Officer responsible for over $1 billion in assets at Citigroup Asset Management (Asia). He then was a co-founder and investment manager at a specialist Asian fund management company based in San Francisco from 1996 to 1999. Gavin's extensive Emerging Markets experience gained during a period of rapid growth in the leading Asian economies makes him well qualified to provide insight and analysis to investors and companies.

Most recently, he spent over a decade in Toronto as Chief Investment Officer for a leading Canadian mutual fund company, Guardian Group of Funds, where he was responsible for over C$6 billion in assets. He also became Director of Investments in 2008 at its parent company Bank of Montreal, where he supervised over C$30 billion in mutual funds. He became well known as an investment commentator on Canadian television and in the press, as well as a contributor to several of Canada's leading investment newsletters. Recently he has written *Investing in Frontier Markets* with coauthor Al Emid, published by Wiley in 2013. He hosts *Emerging and Frontier Markets Investing with Gavin Graham* on the VoiceAmerica Business network.

Apple & Mac

iPad For Dummies,
5th Edition
978-1-118-49823-1

iPhone 5 For Dummies,
6th Edition
978-1-118-35201-4

MacBook For Dummies,
4th Edition
978-1-118-20920-2

OS X Mountain Lion
For Dummies
978-1-118-39418-2

Blogging & Social Media

Facebook For Dummies,
4th Edition
978-1-118-09562-1

Mom Blogging
For Dummies
978-1-118-03843-7

Pinterest For Dummies
978-1-118-32800-2

WordPress For Dummies,
5th Edition
978-1-118-38318-6

Business

Commodities For Dummies,
2nd Edition
978-1-118-01687-9

Investing For Dummies,
6th Edition
978-0-470-90545-6

Personal Finance
For Dummies,
7th Edition
978-1-118-11785-9

QuickBooks 2013
For Dummies
978-1-118-35641-8

Small Business Marketing Kit
For Dummies,
3rd Edition
978-1-118-31183-7

Careers

Job Interviews
For Dummies,
4th Edition
978-1-118-11290-8

Job Searching with
Social Media
For Dummies
978-0-470-93072-4

Personal Branding
For Dummies
978-1-118-11792-7

Resumes For Dummies,
6th Edition
978-0-470-87361-8

Success as a Mediator
For Dummies
978-1-118-07862-4

Diet & Nutrition

Belly Fat Diet For Dummies
978-1-118-34585-6

Eating Clean For Dummies
978-1-118-00013-7

Nutrition For Dummies,
5th Edition
978-0-470-93231-5

Digital Photography

Digital Photography
For Dummies,
7th Edition
978-1-118-09203-3

Digital SLR Cameras &
Photography For Dummies,
4th Edition
978-1-118-14489-3

Photoshop Elements 11
For Dummies
978-1-118-40821-6

Gardening

Herb Gardening
For Dummies,
2nd Edition
978-0-470-61778-6

Vegetable Gardening
For Dummies,
2nd Edition
978-0-470-49870-5

Health

Anti-Inflammation Diet
For Dummies
978-1-118-02381-5

Diabetes For Dummies,
3rd Edition
978-0-470-27086-8

Living Paleo For Dummies
978-1-118-29405-5

Hobbies

Beekeeping
For Dummies
978-0-470-43065-1

eBay For Dummies,
7th Edition
978-1-118-09806-6

Raising Chickens
For Dummies
978-0-470-46544-8

Wine For Dummies,
5th Edition
978-1-118-28872-6

Writing Young Adult Fiction
For Dummies
978-0-470-94954-2

Language &
Foreign Language

500 Spanish Verbs
For Dummies
978-1-118-02382-2

English Grammar
For Dummies,
2nd Edition
978-0-470-54664-2

French All-in One
For Dummies
978-1-118-22815-9

German Essentials
For Dummies
978-1-118-18422-6

Italian For Dummies
2nd Edition
978-1-118-00465-4

e Available in print and e-book formats.

Available wherever books are sold. For more information or to order direct: U.S. customers visit www.Dummies.com or call 1-877-762-2974. U.K. customers visit www.Wileyeurope.com or call (0) 1243 843291. Canadian customers visit www.Wiley.ca or call 1-800-567-4797.

Connect with us online at www.facebook.com/fordummies or @fordummies

Math & Science

Algebra I For Dummies,
2nd Edition
978-0-470-55964-2

Anatomy and Physiology
For Dummies,
2nd Edition
978-0-470-92326-9

Astronomy For Dummies,
3rd Edition
978-1-118-37697-3

Biology For Dummies,
2nd Edition
978-0-470-59875-7

Chemistry For Dummies,
2nd Edition
978-1-1180-0730-3

Pre-Algebra Essentials
For Dummies
978-0-470-61838-7

Microsoft Office

Excel 2013 For Dummies
978-1-118-51012-4

Office 2013 All-in-One
For Dummies
978-1-118-51636-2

PowerPoint 2013
For Dummies
978-1-118-50253-2

Word 2013 For Dummies
978-1-118-49123-2

Music

Blues Harmonica
For Dummies
978-1-118-25269-7

Guitar For Dummies,
3rd Edition
978-1-118-11554-1

iPod & iTunes
For Dummies,
10th Edition
978-1-118-50864-0

Programming

Android Application
Development For
Dummies, 2nd Edition
978-1-118-38710-8

iOS 6 Application
Development For Dummies
978-1-118-50880-0

Java For Dummies,
5th Edition
978-0-470-37173-2

Religion & Inspiration

The Bible For Dummies
978-0-7645-5296-0

Buddhism For Dummies,
2nd Edition
978-1-118-02379-2

Catholicism For Dummies,
2nd Edition
978-1-118-07778-8

Self-Help & Relationships

Bipolar Disorder
For Dummies,
2nd Edition
978-1-118-33882-7

Meditation For Dummies,
3rd Edition
978-1-118-29144-3

Seniors

Computers For Seniors
For Dummies,
3rd Edition
978-1-118-11553-4

iPad For Seniors
For Dummies,
5th Edition
978-1-118-49708-1

Social Security
For Dummies
978-1-118-20573-0

Smartphones & Tablets

Android Phones
For Dummies
978-1-118-16952-0

Kindle Fire HD
For Dummies
978-1-118-42223-6

NOOK HD For Dummies,
Portable Edition
978-1-118-39498-4

Surface For Dummies
978-1-118-49634-3

Test Prep

ACT For Dummies,
5th Edition
978-1-118-01259-8

ASVAB For Dummies,
3rd Edition
978-0-470-63760-9

GRE For Dummies,
7th Edition
978-0-470-88921-3

Officer Candidate Tests,
For Dummies
978-0-470-59876-4

Physician's Assistant Exam
For Dummies
978-1-118-11556-5

Series 7 Exam
For Dummies
978-0-470-09932-2

Windows 8

Windows 8 For Dummies
978-1-118-13461-0

Windows 8 For Dummies,
Book + DVD Bundle
978-1-118-27167-4

Windows 8 All-in-One
For Dummies
978-1-118-11920-4

Available in print and e-book formats.

Available wherever books are sold. For more information or to order direct: U.S. customers visit www.Dummies.com or call 1-877-762-2974.
U.K. customers visit www.Wileyeurope.com or call (0) 1243 843291. Canadian customers visit www.Wiley.ca or call 1-800-567-4797.
Connect with us online at www.facebook.com/fordummies or @fordummies

Take Dummies with you everywhere you go!

Whether you're excited about e-books, want more from the web, must have your mobile apps, or swept up in social media, Dummies makes everything easier .

Dummies products make life easier!

- DIY
- Consumer Electronics
- Crafts

- Software
- Cookware
- Hobbies

- Videos
- Music
- Games
- and More!

For more information, go to **Dummies.com®** and search the store by category.

For Dummies is a registered trademark of John Wiley & Sons, Inc.

FOR

DUMMIES

A Wiley Brand